Fiscal Disobedience

 FORMATION *Series*

Series Editor
PAUL RABINOW

A LIST OF TITLES
IN THE SERIES APPEARS
AT THE BACK OF
THE BOOK

Fiscal Disobedience

AN ANTHROPOLOGY
OF ECONOMIC
REGULATION IN
CENTRAL AFRICA

Janet Roitman

PRINCETON UNIVERSITY PRESS

PRINCETON AND OXFORD

Library of Congress Cataloging-in-Publication Data

Roitman, Janet L. (Janet Lee)
Fiscal disobedience : an anthropology of economic regulation in Central Africa / Janet Roitman.
p. cm. — (In-formation series)
Includes bibliographical references and index.
ISBN 0-691-11869-8 (cloth)—ISBN 0-691-11870-1 (pbk.)
1. Taxation—Cameroon.   2. Tax evasion—Cameroon.   3. Wealth—Social aspects—Cameroon.
4. Wealth—Social aspects—Chad Basin Region.   5. Cameroon—Economic policy.   6. Economic
anthropology—Cameroon.   7. Economic anthropology—Chad Basin Region.   8. Cameroon—
Politics and government.   9. Chad Basin Region—Politics and government.   I. Title.

HJ3069.R64 2005
330.96711—dc22   2003069017

British Library Cataloging-in-Publication Data is available

This book has been composed in Minion and Futura

Printed on acid-free paper. ∞

pup.princeton.edu

Printed in the United States of America

10   9   8   7   6   5   4   3   2   1

For Gérard

Desire knows nothing of exchange, *it knows only theft and gift.*

—GILLES DELEUZE AND FÉLIX GUATTARI, *Anti-Oedipus*

Contents

Acknowledgments

Tʜɪs ʙᴏᴏᴋ is the result of several phases of research, which benefited from the support and insights of many people and institutions. It began as a Ph.D. dissertation in the Department of Political Science at the University of Pennsylvania. Thomas Callaghy supervised my graduate studies as well as the dissertation. I thank him for his unfailing support of my work and his advice in matters both intellectual and practical. Sandra Barnes was a constant source of guidance and encouragement, for which I am appreciative. Ann Norton read the entire dissertation manuscript with great care. Arjun Appadurai accompanied this work through its myriad stages, from start to finish; I thank him for his consistency and his inspiration.

A preliminary trip to northern Cameroon and a stay at the Fondation nationale des sciences politiques in Paris, France, was made possible by the Social Science Research Council International Predissertation Fellowship. Subsequently, an extended period of field research from October 1992 to December 1993 and a year's tenure at Columbia University was supported by the Social Science Research Council–MacArthur Foundation Program on Peace and Security. A large part of the writing of the dissertation was enabled by two consecutive Graduate School of Arts and Sciences Dissertation Fellowships provided by the University of Pennsylvania. An extended return visit to Chad from January to November 1997 and a year in residence at the University of California–Berkeley was undertaken under the aegis of the Ciriacy-Wantrup Fellowship at Berkeley. Finally, I was able to return to the Chad Basin for a year from September 2001 to September 2002 and to complete the final stages of this book under the auspices of the John D. and Catherine T. MacArthur Foundation Research and Writing Grant, Program on Global Security and Sustainability. I thank these institutions for their generous funding and patient assistance with my work, which often took place under difficult circumstances.

In Cameroon, my affiliation with the Department of Sociology at the University of Cameroon in Yaounde was made possible by Jacqueline Ekambi, whose help and hospitality are appreciated. Likewise, I am grateful to Jean-Marc Ela, Sidonie Zoa, Célestin and Yvette Monga, and Jeanette Chambonnière, all of whom opened their homes to me and taught me much about Cameroon and living ambiguity.

In northern Cameroon, my debts are outstanding. Clearly, all those who assisted me could never be accounted for. Particular gratitude goes to Hamidou Bouba for accompanying me in my research and for his friendship. Likewise, I learned an enormous amount and was greatly assisted by Professor Saïbo Issa of the University of Ngaoundere, who I thank for his audacity and for conducting certain conversations that are reprinted herein. I thank the Abatcha family, Oumarou Abdoulaye aka Assaba, Hamadou Adji, Abdoulaye Aguibey, Thierno Mouctar Bah, the late Boubakari, Abdou Daouda, the late Monseigneur Jacques de Bernon, Alhadji Baba Djara, Philippe Douryang, Brian Fulton, Bouba Hamadou, Hassana of RPM, the late Issa Yérima, the late Abdou Inoua, Rosalie Mahop, Margueritte and Antoinette Maïgoura, François Mbaïdodjim, Alhadji Oumarou Mal-Haman, Amadou Haman Ndjidda, Alphonse Ndowiya, the late Vianney Ombe Ndzana, Alhadji Mamoudou Oumarou, Alhadji Adamou Ahmadou Sadjo, Adri van den Berg, Diny van Est, Jose van Santen, Soubiane, Yves Tabart, Dominique Terri, Samuel Yonga, Maître Yacouba Zoua, and the community of Mbankara. Those working in Maroua at the Centre de Service d'Elevage, the Commune Urbaine, the Délégation Provinciale and Direction des Prix, des Poids et Mesures of the Ministère du Développement Industriel et Commercial, and the Préfecture were all helpful with information and documentation, as were those attending to the Cameroonian National Archives in Yaounde. The Institut de recherche pour le développement (IRD, ex-ORSTOM) antenna in Maroua offered me essential support; my thanks go to Christian Seignobos, Henry Tourneux, and especially to Olivier Iyebi-Mandjek. In N'djamena, Chad, many collaborators prefer to remain unnamed. Mahamat Guedi, Peter Harding, Tam Lambert, Major Roland Lane, Ahmed Mahamdi, Mouktar Djibril Mahamat, Ali Abbas Seitchy, Samir Zoghby, and the people at the Centre de formation pour le développement assisted me, as did the advice of Claude Arditi and Javier Herrera.

At other stages and in various ways Richard Banégas, Bill Batt, Mabel Berenson, Carol Breckenridge, Lee Cassanelli, Jean Comaroff, John Comaroff, Mamadou Diouf, Julia Elyachar, Nancy Farriss, Mariane Ferme, Brian Ford, Mitzi Goheen, Jane Guyer, Clifford Hill, Pat Horn, Lucas D'Isanto, Mark Kesselman, Janet MacGaffey, Dominique Malaquais, Roland Marchal, Aihwa Ong, Ann McClintock, Jack Nagel, Rob Nixon, Tobias Rees, Antoine Socpa,

Robert Vitalis, Jean-Pierre Warnier, Michael Watts, and Roger de Weck all contributed to this project. Paul Rabinow challenged me to ask questions of this work that helped me to see it in many different lights and yet also as a very specific mode of intellectual engagement. He also read and critiqued an early draft of a crude manuscript in difficult circumstances, for which I am grateful. I owe special tribute to Jean-François Bayart, whose combined Parisian-Cameroonian sensibilities have been constant provocation and who saw me to Paris, as well as to Peter Geschiere, who has read myriad outlines, proposals, and drafts of this work, and even made the trip to Maroua.

Ruth Marshall-Fratani and Béatrice Hibou accompanied me through many formative moments. I thank Adam Ashforth for being my very best counselor, critic, and friend. And in countless ways, Achille Mbembe has inspired and contributed to this work; I can only hope that it speaks to his passion for ideas.

One full chapter and some sections of this book have been published previously. Somewhat revised herein, chapter 4 originally appeared as "Unsanctioned Wealth; or, the Productivity of Debt in Northern Cameroon," *Public Culture* 15 (2003): 211–237 (reprinted with the permission of Duke University Press). Sections of chapter 2 are reprinted by permission from *Anthropology in the Margins of the State*, edited by Veena Das and Deborah Poole (copyright 2004 by the School of American Research, Santa Fe). A short and preliminary version of chapter 7 first appeared as "Le Pouvoir n'est pas souverain: Nouvelles autorités régulatrices et transformations des États dans le Bassin du Lac Tchad," in *La Privatisation des états*, edited by Béatrice Hibou (copyright 1999 by Éditions Karthala, Paris). The English translation of that text is to appear as "Power Is Not Sovereign: New Forms of Regulatory Authority in the Chad Basin," in *Privatising the State* (London: Hurst Publishers). A shorter version of this text was published in English as "New Sovereigns? Regulatory Authority in the Chad Basin," in *Intervention and Transnationalism in Africa: Global-Local Networks of Power*, edited by Thomas Callaghy, Ron Kassimir, and Robert Latham (copyright 2001; reprinted with the permission of Cambridge University Press). Sections of chapter 7 were also incorporated into an article published in "La Garnison-entrepôt: Une manière de gouverner dans le bassin du lac Tchad," *Critique internationale* 19 (2003): 93–115 (copyright Presses des Sciences-po), and in "Modes of Governing: The Garrison-Entrepot," in *Global Anthropology: Technology, Governmentality, Ethics*, edited by Aihwa Ong and Stephen Collier (copyright 2004 by Blackwell Publishers). The French translation of this book will be published as *Incivisme fiscal: Une anthropologie de la régulation économique dans le bassin du Lac Tchad* by Éditions Karthala, Paris, in 2004. I thank the editors of these various publications for their assistance. I also thank Mary Murrell of Princeton University Press for her support, and Kathleen Cioffi and Susan Ecklund for their hard work.

Finally, I would like to thank Harry and Leonore Roitman, Noël and Yvette Roso, Marjorie and John Oxaal, Steven and Julie Roitman, Susan Roitman and Alan Silverberg, Karen Roitman and Harry Vail, Jonathan and Marisa Roitman, and David and Toni Roitman for their abiding humor and respite. My deep gratitude goes to Gérard Roso; without his care, this project never would have been achieved. Along the way, Eva Isabel Roso and Rebecca Leonore Roso came into the world.

Fiscal Disobedience

Chapter One   *Introduction: An Anthropology of Regulation and Fiscal Relations*

Iɴ ʜɪs 1993 televised campaign speech, John Fru Ndi, presidential candidate and head of the main opposition party, the Social Democratic Front (SDF), referred to the ambitions the people of Cameroon harbor for their children. He spoke of the environment and the economy: "The land is rich, we are hardworking. So why can we no longer afford to send our children to school?" Cameroon has some of "the best engineers, doctors, teachers . . . and *bayam-sellam* in the world." A pidgin term, from "buy and sell 'em," the bayam-sellam are mostly peddlers, itinerant traders, and small-scale merchants generally associated with the opposition to the Rassemblement Démocratique du Peuple Camerounais (RDPC), the reigning party led by President Paul Biya. In his address, Fru Ndi urged the people to vote for "change" as opposed to continuity, insisting that thirty years of "terror" has "destroyed the imagination and energies" of Cameroonians. Just after Fru Ndi's speech, a campaign advertisement run by the incumbent, Paul Biya, also made reference to "the ruined economy." Cameroon had been "brought to its knees," declared Biya. This, he said, was a result of "vandalism" and "banditry" committed and inspired by the opposition, insinuating that the bayam-sellam, who largely follow the opposition, participated in their own economic demise. Against images of street violence, mass demonstrations, charred cars, and smoke-filled streets, Biya asked, "Is this change?" This footage was ostensibly taken during the mass strikes and demonstrations of the opposition-led "dead cities," or Opération Villes Mortes, campaign. But it is not clear whether the smoke-filled atmosphere was caused by burning cars and tires left in the wake of demonstrators or rather by tear gas sprayed on the latter by the police and army. A Mr. Gassagay then appeared on screen to withdraw his candidacy. As leader of the Front National du Progrès (FNP), "for youth," he explained that he was stepping aside "in the name of peace." He was choosing "peace over wealth."[1]

This choice between peace and wealth seems to be archetypal insofar as it partakes in the perennial history of social mobilization for redistribution. And yet despite its generality and durability, the specificity of such an option is, of course, found in local histories; its terms are not universal. This book is an attempt to appreciate the terms of that history and thus to understand the nature of present-day conflict and change in a particular part of the world. Today, references to "wealth" and "peace" structure debates in Cameroon, and in the Chad Basin more generally. To a great extent, these debates can be described as controversy over historical understandings of, on the one hand, *the appropriate or legitimate foundations of wealth* and, on the other hand, *the forces that transgress or destabilize representations and idioms of sociability and unity.*

At a very basic level, then, this book is about the work of historical inscription of truths about wealth creation and sociability. This involves, in part, continuity of practices, of modes of representation, and of narrative acts. However, while often efficient, the process of historical inscription takes place in a heterogeneous field. The possibility for variable and conflicting appropriations of concepts and practices is thus part of what defines a power situation and makes the exercise of power a ceaseless endeavor, being reactualized in myriad situations and against all other possible ways of rendering particular ideas and judgments conceivable. Furthermore, such situations often occasion moments of rupture or intense disagreement about appropriate and valid behavior insofar as they entail the redefinition and refiguring of key concepts that regulate social relations. In that sense, although this is a story about historical inscription and its effects on a particular community of people, it is also an account of the creases and fractures that can be discerned by tracing the various sources of political vocabularies and conceptual domains from which economic notions have arisen.[2] History implies contingency, and the very fact of heterogeneity means that concepts about the economy, or of the economy, are shot

---

[1] It was rumored that this party (FNP) was created by the party in power (RDPC) to compete for the young voters who were drawn to the opposition (SDF). In his withdrawal, Gassagay transferred his support to the ruling RDPC. These presentations were made on Saturday, October 11, 1993, the night prior to the presidential elections, on CRTV, Cameroon.

[2] I am taking my cue here from Foucault's work (1979b, 1989, 1991) on the political genealogies of economic categories (e.g., "welfare" or "interests") and practices (e.g., statistics) in his writing on how, in the eighteenth century, population became the "terrain par excellence of government" and political economy emerged as a new form of power. Original accounts of the emergence and institutionalization of political categories that become essential regulatory mechanisms have also been put forth by Meuret 1988; Miller and Rose 1990; Daly 1991. Their work has greatly inspired my own.

through with multiple histories.[3] While ever present, the latter are most evident to us in times of conflict, when the terms of logical practice are interrogated and the intelligibility of the exercise of power is not necessarily taken for granted.

This point becomes clear when one considers, for example, how economic concepts and institutions, such as tax and price, are political technologies that serve to constitute "that which is to be governed" or, in this case, a field of regulatory intervention based on a set of presuppositions about the nature of economic life and economic objects. Such political technologies are mechanisms that render aspects of social life both intelligible and governable. They are thus not simply instrumental methods for obtaining or assuring power; they are, rather, the very material form of power itself.[4]

Claims to Wealth: Incivisme Fiscal

My fixation on the problem of regulatory authority arose, quite frankly, because the topic was thrown up to me by the people among whom I lived. From 1992 to 2002, I lived, during various extended periods, in the northern part of Cameroon and in N'Djamena, Chad.[5] This part of Cameroon tapers into a slight triangle, pointing up to Lake Chad and thinning out between the economic weight of its westerly neighbor, Nigeria, and the explosive power of its incessantly warring eastern neighbor, Chad. The northern region of

[3] I make a distinction between discourses *of* the economy, which are productive and are constitutive of the very field of "economy," and discourses *on* the economic, which refer to that field. Economic truth is produced in the very inscription of the boundaries of "the economic," as Foucault argued in his demonstration of the historical—and hence contingent—construction of the limits of "the disciplines," or the domain of "economics" per se, from the other social sciences. It is also a matter of inscribing that truth in the material world. See chapter 6 ("Échanger") in Foucault 1966; and see Tribe 1978; Hacking 1983; Tomlinson 1983.

[4] This perspective is greatly influenced by Foucault's writing on liberalism as a modern form of political intervention, or what he called the arts of political rationality. It is important to signal the limits of the relationship between the context of my work and Foucault's interest in liberalism as an ethos of government entailing a particular and historically contingent approach to the problem of government. Evidently, liberalism and neoliberalism are historical arrangements that have emerged and evolved in very specific historical circumstances, which have not obtained in the same manner and with similar results in the Chad Basin. Nonetheless, Foucault's approach to the conditions of possibility for the emergence of specific forms of political reason, especially his *methods* for understanding the limits and objectives of government, have been inspiration to my own approach. Cf. Foucault 1989: 99–120. And refer most notably to Rose and Miller 1992; Barry, Osborne, and Rose 1996.

[5] Maroua, northern Cameroon: July 1992 to August 1992, October 1992 to December 1993, and October 2001 to June 2002. N'djamena, Chad: January 1997 to November 1997. The term "northern Cameroon" is a formulation from the early days of French colonization. While this was not an official administrative cadre at that time, the term came to refer to an

Cameroon is the home of the late Ahmadou Ahidjo, who presided over the country through the one-party state, the Union Nationale Camerounaise (UNC), from 1958 to 1982. Ahidjo rose to power in the wake of almost a decade of armed struggle for decolonization, which makes Cameroon somewhat of an exception on the African continent (cf. Um Nyobe 1984, 1989; Mbembe 1989, 1996). The nationalist movement failed in its endeavor, leading to the installation of personalities who had been long-standing or were newly formed clients of the French government, many of whom came from the northern part of the country. During this time, the fairly arid savanna region of the north, which depended largely on groundnut and cotton production, benefited greatly from financial advantages accorded to northerners, such as nonguaranteed bank credits and contracts for public works projects. Ahidjo retired from the presidency in 1982, leaving his place to Paul Biya through a constitutional succession. In 1984, tensions between the northern-based old guard, still led by Ahidjo, who had retained the presidency of the UNC even after his retirement from state power, and the newly installed regime led by Biya resulted in a coup d'état. The attempted putsch failed, and Biya consolidated power by ousting northern political figures and by forming, in 1985, the RDPC, which replaced the UNC as the only legal political party in the country (see Bayart 1979, 1986). The RDPC has retained its hold on power up until today, despite recent modifications in the political landscape.

One of the most significant of these changes occurred in 1990, when independent political parties were legalized in Cameroon. This was a response to pressures from international donors, whose interventions increased during the late 1980s with the dramatic downturn in the once very prosperous economy, and the emergence of a national movement demanding political reforms.[6] While the legalization of opposition parties was accompanied by plans for multiparty elections and increased freedoms for an independent press, the Biya administration refused to respond to certain demands of the opposition. The call for a national conference to devise a new electoral code

---

administrative entity in 1961. In 1976, the Northern Province covered 35 percent of the national territory and included about 29 percent of its population. In 1983, the Northern Province was partitioned, forming the three provinces of Adamawa, the North, and the Extreme North. Today, the Extreme North Province includes an estimated 2,838,000 people, and the town of Maroua, where I lived, is inhabited by an estimated 396,000 people (Seignobos and Iyebi-Mandjek 2000: 61; and see Paba Salé 1980). Most of the conversations and interviews referred to herein were conducted in either French or Fulfulde (Fulani), or a mix of the two. Some interviews near or in Chad were conducted in Arabic or Kanuri. Hamidou Bouba, Saibou Issa, and I undertook translations to French. All translations from French to English of conversations, dialogues, or published materials are my own.

[6] Pressure from donor institutions followed the signing of a stabilization agreement with the International Monetary Fund in 1988, the rescheduling of debt with the Paris Club in March 1989, and agreement on a World Bank Structural Adjustment Loan in May 1989. The

and revise the constitution in keeping with political reforms was most notably ignored. Nevertheless, Cameroonians pushed for change in their spring of 1991 (see Champaud 1991; Noble 1991; *Africa Confidential* 1991a, 1991b; Monga 1993; Kom 1993; Roitman 1996). In the face of the regime's intransigence, the declaration of a state of emergency that put seven of ten provinces under military administration in May 1991, and in the context of extreme conditions of austerity, the National Coordination of Opposition Parties and Associations organized the Opération Villes Mortes campaign. On May 26, 1990, a pro-democracy rally was organized by the leader of the SDF, John Fru Ndi, in response to the legalization of multiparty politics and concomitant delays in the authorization of this same party. Similar demonstrations followed in other towns and cities. On the whole, Opération Villes Mortes entailed a strategy of civil disobedience, which involved a prolonged general strike, work boycotts, the refusal to pay taxes, and the use of clandestine services to deny taxation.

The Biya regime dubbed the movement *incivisme fiscal*, thus indicating that participation in the pro-democracy movement and refutation of certain instances of state power represented "uncivil" fiscal practice, being beyond the pale of civic behavior. The regime thus countered the movement by posing the question of who is a legitimate citizen. In the face of that rather extensive interpretation of the campaign, the opposition remained explicit about its aim: to undermine the fiscal base of the regime, which was said to utilize public monies in ways that did not benefit the populace. This interpretive battle is both the point of departure and the structuring theme of this book. As I observed the unfolding of this struggle between the state and its citizens, it became more and more clear to me that the pertinent question was not the outright rejection of regulatory authority or fiscal authority. Instead, I seemed to be witnessing disagreement over the *intelligibility of its exercise.* In an effort to understand the terms of that disagreement, I chose to study the ways in which tax, price, and even ideas about licit wealth and licit modes of appropriation have emerged and transformed historically in northern Cameroon, taken as part of the historical region of the Chad Basin.[7] Instead of assuming the nature of "tax" or "price," and hence simply analyzing contemporary resistance to taxation and fiscal authority, I attempted to clarify the ways in which certain forms of economic extraction have become normalized as part of fiscal relations. I asked certain questions: How has the right

---

histories of Cameroonian prosperity (until 1985–86) and subsequent indebtedness are recounted in *Marchés tropicaux et méditerranéens* 1976, 1988; EDIAFRIC 1984; World Bank 1989a, 1989b; *Nord-Sud Export* 1989, 1990, 1991; van de Walle 1993.

[7] While "the Chad Basin" is a fairly vague geographic concept, I use it here to refer to the area comprising northern Nigeria, northern Cameroon, Chad, and the Central African Republic. This is a working definition based on my research preoccupations.

to a part of people's wealth become an acceptable idea? How have specific forms of wealth been construed as legitimate targets of regulation? How have particular economic concepts, such as tax and price, emerged in a discursive field that engenders certain forms of power situations, including debt? How has the right to extract wealth via violent means (e.g., seizure) come to be deemed acceptable practice at certain moments in time, while it is rejected at others? Through these questions, I sought to understand not only how these historical institutions (tax, fiscal relations, the fiscal regime of truth) induce certain kinds of behavior (giving over tax once a year) but also how they establish the very limits of what is considered legitimate or reasonable practice.

The Concepts and Targets of Regulation

This problem of legitimacy can only be addressed if the economy is apprehended as a political terrain. Because conflict over regulation and redistribution means taking issue with the very rules that organize and govern economic life, such strife can only be understood by examining the very conventions that give rise to the concepts and objects of an economy. In Cameroon today, debates over the nature and legitimacy of certain economic relationships (e.g., fiscal), categories (e.g., the informal sector), or events (e.g., incivisme fiscal) all involve interpretive battles over political vocabularies or notions of propriety, equity, justice, and social order. These controversies structure the plot of this text. In that sense, this book is about the material effects of representations. It aims to explore the relations between representational forms and social practice, or how economic truths and "true" economic practices—being *dans le vrai*—are produced in and through a discursive field of concepts and objects. This is a matter of studying, as Paul Rabinow puts it (1986: 240), a "regime of truth as an effective component in the constitution of social practices."[8] It illustrates how historically specific discursive domains that establish social order, the natural state of society, the free individual, or the peaceful community inform manners of conceptualizing the economy. Nevertheless, this attempt to trace the historical constitution of economic categories and economic practices is not an effort to show how "culture" informs the objectification of the economy. Even though the pitfalls of culturalist explanations of social life have been spelled out ad infinitum (Marcus and Fischer 1986; Clifford and Marcus 1986; Clifford 1988; Appadurai 1986; Bayart 1996), economic practice and economic rationalities are still often depicted as being

---

[8] See especially Rabinow 1986: 238 for an elucidation of Foucault's reference to being "dans le vrai," or "in the true," an ultimate reference to Georges Canguilhem, and refer to the appendix to Foucault 1976: 215–37; 1980: 131–33.

induced by culture, or as being influenced by particular "cultural backgrounds" or symbolic repertoires. And culturalist readings of economic life have been given new vigor with the emergence of debates about "globalization" and the new wars over values (as is evidenced in Huntington 1997; Bourguinat 1998; Méda 1999; for a critique, see Roitman 2000). This approach is of course problematic, since it slights the heterogeneous practices and regimes of signification that constitute the worlds of any individual or community. As we know, reference to a person's or to a community's "culture" is in many ways nonsensical, since all persons and communities take part in synthetic and seemingly contradictory symbolic practices (religious, ritual, linguistic) and manners of affiliation.

To avoid the hazards of such reductionist explanations, I pay specific attention to the point that practices and concepts (economic or otherwise) have histories. By looking at the institutionalization of certain concepts and practices—for instance, the institutionalization of "tax" and "price" in Cameroon—we can glimpse the various ways in which specific economic concepts and metaphors have been assumed and performed by local actors. And by studying the institutionalization of these concepts or historical institutions, we see how their practices involve various modalities, or how they are both assumed and yet also disputed as forms of knowledge, which carry political and socioeconomic consequences for those involved. Instead of presenting representations and metaphors of the economy as an underlying generative system that induces behavior and leads to certain forms of organization, I show how, despite their efficacy, they tend to instability due to their fundamental ambivalence as institutions or political techniques. I thus try to respond to a difficult question: How does one delineate the emergent?[9] An answer depends upon rupture as much as continuity. It presupposes another question: In what domains are metaphors and representations *not* evident or *not* embedded over time?

In many ways, this work is a contribution to a history of the present, or an effort to demonstrate how a specific situation has become logically possible. Not an attempt to "explain" the present, this work seeks to discern a contemporary problem (see Rabinow 2003).[10] Specifically, it hones in on the manners in which people in the Chad Basin problematize their own relationships to economic regulatory authority, fiscal relations, and the concepts of economic regulation. In that sense, this book strives to delineate the contemporary limits of reason with respect to economic regulatory

---

[9] Put to me by Paul Rabinow during the seminar "The Production of Modernities" at the University of California, Berkeley, October 16, 1996.

[10] Not concerned with the "meaning" of contemporary events, this work nonetheless does not have the ambition to delineate contemporary problem spaces, an enterprise that is of another epistemological order (see Rabinow 2003 for elaboration).

authority in the Chad Basin. Instead of turning about the bottomless problem of the ontological status of particular practices or concepts—such as tax, price, wealth, debt, work, citizen, subject—it seems more worthwhile to look into the matter of their effects, or what they are producing in the world today. It is an inquiry into the productive nature of specific events. Such an endeavor asks, as I do, what is new (or not new) about regulatory authority, fiscal relations, and fiscal practice? What is new about recently articulated claims to wealth? And what is new about manners of representing peace? Answering these questions means taking note of the effects of power, or the ways in which the exigencies of discursive formations, conceptual frameworks, and specific rationalities are taken up by subjects who are "caught up in a power situation of which they themselves are the bearers" (Foucault 1979a: 201; cf. Foucault 1990 [1978]). It is about how human beings become subjects of particular kinds of knowledge, and how they become subjects to themselves. This is not merely a matter of domination over subjects, or the ways that individuals are structured by forms of knowledge and technologies. It is an inquiry into the ways in which techniques of the self are part of the very process of domination. It is clearly about what transpires when power is exercised over people, but power is not its ultimate object of inquiry. As Foucault said so plainly, "It is not power, but the subject, which is the general theme of my research" (1982: 209).

To circumscribe that problem, I take incivisme fiscal to be an event.[11] In other words, as a moment of struggle, it is a productive event in which the concepts, metaphoric relationships, and suppositions that serve to theorize and hence delineate the most appropriate means and ends of power are challenged, reviewed, and reconfigured. Although a moment of political conflict, it cannot be reduced to the mere jockeying of social groups for control over material resources. Disagreement over the intelligibility of regulatory power and fiscal relations goes to the heart of the problem of power by questioning the modes of classification and standards of evaluation that give order to hierarchies of value and establish the logics of practice.

This means that Cameroonians evaluate the allegedly impending choice between peace and wealth against the register of various claims to truth about the economy, economic relations, and regulatory authority. These claims make up a heterogeneous field, the state now being one among many contenders for unconditional authority over fiscal relations. And while sources of truth about the economy are always and everywhere heterogeneous and emergent—that is, economic knowledge about and of the

---

[11] On the construction of narrative and the event, cf., for example, White 1987; Trouillot 1995. For a brilliant interpretation of the productive nature of an event—the failure of the French Second Republic and the emergence of "society" and "the social" as preeminent political references—see Donzelot 1994.

economy is always organized against other, contending orderings—the discontinuity of regulatory authority has been exacerbated by the effects of economic collapse, national economic and political reforms, and the evident inefficacy of the predominant narrative of "economic development." Cameroonians perceive a lapse in the material potential for, and guarantee of, social mobility, which implies skepticism about representations of that possibility and that assurance.[12] This involves uncertainty about continuity, immutability, inevitability, and the natural quality of sources of wealth and prosperity and the putative progress of "development."[13] One might say, then, that the attenuation of social obligation inherent in certain forms of exchange and the concurrent suspension of confidence in the efficacy of state regulation and social mechanisms of redistribution indicate that certain historical understandings of the nature of wealth and wealth generation are no longer taken for granted. This is part of what I outline in the following chapters. This particular story is about the Chad Basin, but it reflects the more general point that "crisis" on the African continent is not simply a failure in an overarching structure of explanation or metanarrative (cf. Ferguson 1999). It is also, or perhaps more so, the destabilization and transformation of modalities for the self-regulation of society.

Contrary to appearances, the nationwide Villes Mortes campaign was not an amorphous uprising for some kind of dramatic "change." Nor was it the tide of "society" rising against the wall of "the state" (to refer to the classic Clastres 1989). Instead, citizens took issue with the nature of their economic relationships to the state; they questioned the legitimacy of regulatory authority, the logical bases for fiscal interventions, and the very concept of wealth as a public versus a private good. Furthermore, their modes of questioning and their forms of resistance were not unlimited. The contours of dissent were delineated by the very conceptual limits of the theories and practices that have defined the histories of regulation, fiscal practice, and the fiscal subject in the region. The chapters that follow pay specific attention to the histories of those theories and practices in order to surmise the

---

[12] I am implying that representations of economic organization and its implied teleology are as significant as the actual effects of material redistribution, since, regardless of real social and economic mobility, the understanding that life according to the logic implied in such organization will bring rewards is part of the efficacy of such representations. This point is developed in Mbembe and Roitman 1995.

[13] Some see this as a general crisis in the metanarrative of economic development as modernization. For one example, cf. Ferguson 1999. However, the interpretive power of abstract universalism and linear causality has been in question for several decades. And the crisis in the universalist pretensions of the narrative defining capitalist development as unambiguous linear progression and the privileged signifier of modernity has been the topic of commentary on the nature of post-Fordist forms of production and exchange (Offe 1985; Lash and Urry 1987; Jameson 1984; Harvey 1989). Despite these treatises, the desire for certainty about economic development as modernization is alive and well on the African continent, as Ferguson notes.

contemporary effects of historical modes and sites of regulation. In particular, I outline the possibilities for enunciation today by tracing out the various ways in which targets of regulation have been circumscribed through and in power relations over the nineteenth and twentieth centuries.

In consequence, this book is fashioned through a series of moves that bring to the fore crucial moments in which particular targets of regulation have been circumscribed as such. In each case, I explore how political rationalities associated with specific forms of power (e.g., the nineteenth-century Muslim jihad, French colonization) have given rise to a logic of economic governance that, while institutionalized over time, has had to constantly reinvent itself in its effort to domesticate potential targets of economic regulation. This includes the institutionalization of what I refer to as the "tax-price" complex, which founded French colonial power, as well as the circumscription of "the slave" during the nineteenth century Muslim jihad and of "the floating population" (*la population flottante*) during French colonization as particular forms of wealth and targets of regulation. These moments inspired—and were inspired by—intense conflict and debate over legitimate modes of alienation and appropriation, such as seizure and taxing. They also involved debate and struggle over the nature of wealth and property, such as spoils captured in conquest and the French franc. And they posed questions about the limits of productive versus unproductive space, as represented by the frontier or "the bush." The particular manner by which "tax-price," "the slave," and the population flottante were institutionalized as economic categories and targets of regulatory authority has had specific effects on representations of wealth and legitimate modes of seizure and appropriation, as well as resistance to such acts.

To take the case of tax-price—and to simplify for the time being—the materialization of French colonial power occurred, most obviously, through the institutionalization of *l'impôt*, or the head tax. The latter presupposed the insertion of French currency into circuits of exchange as well as its imposition as a primary referent of value. This meant that the colonized were to evaluate goods and exchanges in terms of certain equivalents based on the metropolitan measure of wealth. Hence the institutionalization of the impôt during colonization necessitated the establishment, at the same time, of a particular notion of price so that Cameroonians would become consumers of the French monetary sign, as opposed to other signs of value that circulated and underpinned various social hierarchies in the region. This particular notion of price was instituted at the same time as the colonial head tax, such that price figured as a necessary complement of tax and was objectified at this time as part of the discursive field of economic regulation. Tax-price became a political technology that exemplified the materialization of colonial power in its fiscal form. Through it, Cameroonians became both consumers of colonial currency and sources of European monetary wealth, or the fiscal subjects of French colonial empire. This meant that they assumed the idea of the French colonial administration's right to a part of their wealth, as well as the notion that certain things represented "private" wealth, and that they could be translated into "public" wealth. This act of translation took place through the tax-price precept, or the targeting of price as an object of regulation to ensure tax. For instance, the colonial authorities were critical of local accounting techniques, such as rounding up and bargaining, because they settled on "wrong" prices. In hopes of assuring "true" prices, the French authorities applied pricing policy, or price controls, which set forth the idea of consumer protection. In the application of this policy, local people took up a particular political rationale, and they did so seemingly *for themselves*, since pricing policy was formulated as consumer protection. The fiscal subject thus emerged as the consumer-taxpayer.

Obviously, during colonization, the tax-price complex was not inscribed on a blank slate. Like the French franc, it was subsumed by, and articulated with, extant and contending modes of evaluation and competing monetary signs in the region. These included the signs of wealth and value associated with past conquests, such as seizure and tribute, which were critical to the slave states and jihad; the institutional remnants of prior European colonial powers (e.g., the German mark, the British sterling); and regional networks of exchange and redistribution that were inherent to the larger political economy of the Chad Basin. Because of this, and as the refractory history of the institutionalization of tax-price reveals, the boundaries of value presupposed by the French colonial regime of value were constantly undermined and altered. The very integrity of colonial regulation was uncertain, since the French governed the economy defined by the newly instated borders of present-day Cameroon in the name of what was then deemed not only the penultimate paradigm of social order but also the most serious potential source of disorder: national unity within colonial empire. Colonial power governed the economy in the name of national integrity even while—or surely because—that very integrity was by no means assured (as indicated by Joseph 1977; Bayart 1979; Mbembe 1996). Thus the constant work of regulation—and even its raison d'être—has been to circumscribe and govern the social elements that have historically summarized sources of instability with respect to price, subversion with respect to tax, and transgression with respect to national identity. During the colonial period, that social element was pegged by the authorities as the "intermediaries," or the population flottante, which emerged with tax-price as a specific category and a primary target of regulation.

The events of the 1990s revealed the recursive nature of this constant work of domesticating supposedly destabilizing social forces. During the

11

Opération Villes Mortes campaign, or what was castigated as incivisme fiscal, the basis of the state's claim to a part of people's wealth was brought into question. Through this event, the idea of the state's right to a part of citizens' wealth was challenged. However, rather than an outright rejection of the principle of the fiscal relationship, people made claims to the guarantee of access to wealth, or the means to pay tax. In doing so, they raised the question of the very foundations of wealth in the Chad Basin today. The postcolonial regime's response to that problem has been consistent with the political rationale of consumer protection—even in spite of recent economic liberalization programs, which eradicated official price controls. Certain practices, such as price bargaining, and certain economic agents, such as the intermediaries and itinerant traders, have thus remained targets of disciplinary authority, since they are deemed contrary to consumer protection and a particular vision of what constitutes "reasonable profits" or economic justice. But, to a large extent, local people no longer judge the state's regulation of this behavior and these economic agents according to the logic of consumer protection. Historically located as the sources of price instability and tax evasion, the intermediaries and the peripatetic— or the population flottante—are increasingly perceived as critical agents in the process of wealth creation. Furthermore, their recourse to rounding up, bargaining, and negotiation is not necessarily perceived as economically problematic—the source of inflation; illogical and premodern; anticonsumer—since these practices are often viewed as the very means to account for social and economic differences, and hence promote certain forms of economic redistribution.

Debates that arose out of incivisme fiscal centered upon this question of how best to determine price, or the most just price. I argue that they also raised questions about relations of dependency and debt that are inherent to pricing mechanisms, or manners of establishing value. The debts, the social obligations, and especially the socioeconomic inequalities that are induced by particular manners of establishing "the just price" have come under scrutiny, being seen by some as normal practice and yet rejected by others as inappropriate. These divergent opinions reflect disagreement over present modes of redistribution and the means by which socioeconomic differences are inscribed through particular economic concepts and their attendant practices. To illustrate this point, I look at what people now refer to as "unsanctioned wealth," or wealth that is generated in exchanges that take place outside the confines of official regulatory relations. In elucidating the signification of that concept for people in northern Cameroon, I explore the ways in which wealth generation can be viewed as either normal and just (sanctioned wealth) or deviant and inequitable (unsanctioned wealth). Today, there is not much consensus about these distinctions in Cameroon and the Chad Basin, especially since international borders, the frontier, and the bush have become important sites of economic accumulation and socioeconomic mobility. Many of those who partake in economic activities based in these unregulated spaces subvert extant patterns of redistribution; they exercise claims to wealth through violent means, such as seizure and razzia, thus insisting upon the right to wealth through conquest and asserting that spoils are licit forms of wealth. They demonstrate that debt and social obligation are not necessarily insolvable situations.

This controversy over the nature of licit wealth reflects contemporary transformations regarding the frontiers of wealth creation and the very foundations of wealth. Since the nineteenth century, historical representations of the foundations of wealth have included the slave, the intermediaries, the population flottante, the civil servant, the citizen, and so forth. Rather than a linear succession, these categories are constitutive of the discursive field of regulatory objects, having emerged and receded at various moments in time. Indeed, their vacillations, which reverberate through the following pages, are indicative of the ways in which regulatory authority in this region has been an unstable mode of power—hence its constant efforts to govern the frontiers of wealth creation, which include the literal frontiers of the country as well as the conceptual frontiers of the economy. This last point is underscored herein at myriad points, all of which indicate how the foundations of wealth and the targets of regulation are inscribed in an ambivalent space. The latter is most often referred to as "the bush,"[14] but it is more generally indicative of various forces that have been historically located as those that transgress or destabilize sociability, the national economy, and national unity. These include, once again, the intermediaries as well as the heterogeneous and amorphous category of those who work the borders: the population flottante—or Fru Ndi's "bayam-sellam," Biya's "vandals and bandits," and Gassagay's "youth." But they also involve, for example, military personnel doubling as customs officials and armed road bandits working for highly organized gangs. These are, for the most part, underemployed, unemployed, and dispossessed people who have been claimed by various parties and for various reasons as the driving force behind the rise in unregulated economic activities. The representation of this category of people in terms of certain paradigms of social order is inherent to the ways they are represented as economic agents. They are theorized by local people either as the very source of subversion—and hence represent criminal, illegitimate economic activity; the transgression of national borders and national identity; and the demise of the nation-state—or, to the contrary, as economic empowerment and change, thus representing productive, rational economic behavior, national renewal, and even democratization. Ultimately,

[14] Referred to by locals as either "ladde" (Fulfulde) or "la brousse" (French).

13

these various representations interrogate the logics of redistribution and regulation, which are at the heart of contemporary debates in the Chad Basin today.

Dispossession and Wealth Creation: The Ambivalent Grounds of the Fiscal Subject

When reflecting on the ways in which redistribution works through regulation, I came to think about the very nature of wealth in the Chad Basin. As noted earlier, I have thus asked questions about how "things" are circumscribed as "wealth," representing a particular form of value, and how some forms of wealth have come to be defined as "licit" (slaves at one point, European currency at another). I ask how certain forms of wealth move in and out of "licit" and "illicit" status, such as "spoils" in former slaving economies and now in economic activities related to banditry and war. And I inquire as to how specific manners of appropriation and authority, or the right to a part of people's wealth defined in particular forms of value, have come to be accepted as valid in some moments while they are contested in others. This brings me to the problem of subjectivity: How is it that those subjected to fiscal interventions and regulatory authority become, to repeat, "caught up in a power situation of which they themselves are the bearers"? How are the exigencies of regulatory authority, and power situations more generally, taken up by its very subjects?

Because subjectivity is a fairly amorphous and extremely complex question, it is perhaps best taken in a somewhat limited way. For my purposes, this amounts to thinking about how the fiscal subject is delimited as a target of wealth and how that subject assumes this location as wealth and as a bearer of particular kinds of wealth, to which rights are conditional and contingent. In the context of the Chad Basin, this has forced me to grapple with the ways in which targets of wealth have been fixed both physically and conceptually in situations of constant physical mobility as well as social upheaval caused over the past decades by slaving, conquest, jihad, colonialism, war, poverty, and factional violence. Historically speaking, wealth has been a moving target in the region: cattle, slaves, nomads, dependents, and so forth. With the installation of tax-price as the primary means of regulation and redistribution during colonization, methods of fixing were transformed. And yet, even though the colonizers located the "head" (as in "the head tax" or "the head of the family") as both the primary source and the primary target of wealth, mobility remained an integral aspect of wealth creation, since local people undertook *la quête monétaire*, or the quest for currency to pay tax, which provoked movement. In that sense, circulation and displacement were reaffirmed as effective modes of wealth creation—as they have been over the centuries in this region of slaving and trading across the Sahara, where dominion has not always entailed presence. Thus those who have been forced to circulate incessantly for lack of resources are also those who have etched out the frontiers of wealth creation. They thus hold an ambivalent position in the history of regulation, being both expendable and essential to the reproduction and aggrandizement of national wealth and certain power relations. This is one of the subthemes of this book.

Today, the quest for currency continues and is surely exacerbated by newfound political and especially debt relations, such as those inherent to structural adjustment programs and even relations with nongovernmental organizations (see Elyachar 2001, forthcoming; Spivak 1999). Indeed, most people in the Chad Basin are living in a thick web of debt and liability spun out of local, regional, and international relationships. And yet here, at the edge of the desert in the midst of austerity and arrears, one finds a bastion of innovation and mobility. Amazingly, the contemporary drive for deregulation and privatization in an area marked by slaving, ongoing factional fighting, and recent regional warfare has not decimated the possibilities for livelihood. While the dissipation of the material basis of authoritarian rule has forced regimes of the region to undertake economic reforms defined by World Bank structural adjustment programs, these have only aggravated conditions of austerity (*Le Messager* 1993; Lottin 1994; Coussy and Vallin 1996). Nonetheless, having seen the postindependence economic boom dissipate in a matter of years, people not only survive but create economic futures. We find the odd pairing of dispossession and wealth creation, which was, for me, the constant paradox of life in the Chad Basin (as reflected upon in Roitman 1998b, forthcoming b; see also Comaroff and Comaroff 2000).

This paradox is partially produced by men and movement, or men in movement. When traveling through the dusty villages and arid cities of northern Cameroon and Chad, one meets up with a swirl of men—and especially young men—who are perpetually crossing borders, circulating between various national capitals, roaming the expanses of the bush, traversing mountain passes, switching deftly between myriad currencies, exchanging identity cards and birth certificates, and incessantly inventing ways of making money. These people partake in what are generally understood to be unregulated economic exchanges and financial relations. In the Chad Basin, they work alongside *les coupeurs de route* (those who cut off the roads).[15] These are groups of organized road bandits that have become a regional phenomenon linked to transnational flows. Composed of all nationals

---

[15] This phenomenon became most intense in the 1990s, being labeled a "war" by the press: Soudan 1996; Dorce 1996; *N'djamena Hebdo* 1997; Pideu 1995.

of the Chad Basin—Nigerians, Cameroonians, Chadians, Sudanese, and citizens of the Central African Republic and Niger—they are connected into regional and international markets in small arms and money counterfeiting. Most important, they establish and participate in a network of economic exchanges and employment relations that found a significant mode of accumulation in the region. Generally interpreted as existing beyond the state or even antistate, their tactics of mobility and misdemeanor are essential to the reconstitution of state power today. As part of the genealogy of that indeterminate and ever-elusive category, the population flottante, those who are on the frontiers of wealth creation in this time of indebtedness and austerity have become new targets of state regulation.

No doubt, these phenomena are rather indicative of the futures of state power, considering that, as in many parts of the world, unregulated markets constitute the contemporary frontiers of wealth creation.[16] In the Chad Basin, the most lucrative of these are based on regional and international networks of trade and finance. While these have historical precedents in the trans-Saharan and east-west Sahelian economies, their resurgence in recent times is in part due to the effective incorporation and novel use of resources derived from international markets. As elsewhere on the continent, the demise of certain markets (e.g., export crop commodities)—allegedly the foremost cause of the marginalization of African economies from the world economy (Callaghy and Ravenhill 1993; Castells 1998: 70–165; Bach 1998)—and the proliferation of certain resources for trade and accumulation (e.g., drugs, small arms) have resulted in a drive for new forms of economic integration (Bayart, Ellis, and Hibou 1997: esp. 18–22). These include high-risk and hence lucrative ventures such as the trade in small arms flowing through Sudan, Libya, Chad, Cameroon, Nigeria, Niger, and Algeria; provisioning of ongoing conflicts in Niger, Chad, the Central African Republic, and Sudan, which involves transiting petrol, hardware, electronics, grain, cement, detergent, and (mostly stolen) cars and four-wheel-drive trucks; the ivory trade centered around Lake Chad and the Central African Republic; the transfer of drugs between the Pakistani crescent, Nigeria, and Western Europe; counterfeiting operations in Cameroon and Nigeria; and large-scale, highly organized highway banditry.[17]

Today, the transgression of physical frontiers (e.g., national borders) and conceptual boundaries (e.g., spoils becoming licit wealth) is critical to

---

[16] Or what are often quite misleadingly summarized as the "informal economy" (for a critique, see Roitman 1990). On the productive and generative capacities of unregulated markets, see, among others, Bayart 1994.

[17] On Kalashnikovs, see *Jeune Afrique* 1992. On the continental drug economy, see Observatoire Géopolitique des Drogues 1995. On petrol smuggling, cf. Herrera 1998. On highway banditry, see Pideu 1995; Soudan 1996; Dorce 1996; *N'Djamena Hebdo* 1997. More generally, see Bennafla 1996, 2001; Grégoire 1998.

productive activity and the production of new forms of knowledge about the possibility of such activity.[18] In the Chad Basin, the transgression of national economies and political regimes is a border and bush phenomenon. The political frontier and the economy of the bush are defined by new concepts of wealth (e.g., spoils) and manners of appropriating wealth (e.g., rights-in-seizure). But these are not marginal: these concepts and practices are assumed by those who work the bush and border *as well as* those tending to the state bureaucracy and the national economy. States of dispersion are thus essential to wealth creation and the continuity of state power as much as immobility and permanence, the alleged bases for predictability in economic affairs and the rational-legal bureaucracy.

This point is especially underscored herein through this review of various, historical modes of governing in the region, which indicates how certain forms of political mediation, such as alliance and tribute, have been inherent to the exercise of power over people and wealth, as opposed to territory. During the nineteenth century, for instance, the exercise of rights over wealth issuing from conquest was not necessarily dependent upon the control of territory; certain rights inhered in states of movement and migration, making the right to spoils licit wealth. Today we witness debates over seizure as an appropriate mode of appropriation and over the nature of wealth that is attained through seizure. As in the past, these debates turn about particular questions: What do movement, migration, and flight signify? What is the status of wealth produced through conquest and raiding? What is the status of the limit zones—the borders and the bush—where such wealth is produced? And what is the status of those who regulate these zones and those who secure livelihood within them? This might be thought of as a pluralizing moment,[19] when the possibilities for reinterpretations of given relationships give rise to novel or modified ones, in this case engendering supplementary definitions of licit wealth and legitimate manners of appropriation. And with that expansion in the field of "the economic," so also "the fiscal subject" has come to mean new things. This is part of the story that follows: how the citizen's relationship to the state is being transformed by certain, increasingly prevalent practices of wealth creation (seizure), manners of signifying licit wealth (spoils), and the exercise of power over such wealth (regulatory authority). But in order to tell that story, we have to first consider the forms of power that give rise to and act upon the fiscal subject.

---

[18] The general point about transgression and creativity has been made by Bakhtine 1990; Simmel 1990; Deleuze and Guattari 1987; Appadurai 1986a; Stallybrass and White 1989. See also Balibar 2001, 2003, on the notion of the national border and the European border, used in the sense of both a literal and a figurative frontier, or a mediation.

[19] This is reminiscent of my previous comments on rupture, although it is inspired by W. Connolly's notes (1996: esp. 153–54) on the "possibilities of pluralization in the present," though I do not take up his concern with identities per se.

The Pluralization of Regulatory Authority

Today the Chad Basin can be described as a region of competing sources of regulatory authority and welfare, or redistribution. On the basis of both official and especially unregulated commercial and financial activities, sub- and transnational regimes of accumulation have come to dominate the Nigerian, Cameroonian, Nigerien, Chadian, and Central African Republic borders. Effective authority over these exchanges and the surpluses that result from them is exercised by an amalgam of personalities associated with the state bureaucracy, the merchant elite, the military, and nonstate militia groups. They form what I have referred to as a military-commercial nexus that has become the basis of livelihood for many people in the region (Roitman 1998a, 1998b, forthcoming a). They manage to regulate local populations and regional exchanges through the exercise of the power to define access to material resources and wealth, to tax the profits of economic relationships, and to establish preeminent authority over certain sectors of economic activity. Quite simply, by controlling access to possibilities for accumulation, they determine the right to work and wealth.

Most often, those who have managed to direct the financing, labor recruitment, and material organization required by these regional networks of trade are able to do so precisely because of their participation in military-commercial relationships that allow them to exercise authority over regional economic activities, essential resources, and local populations. In Chad, one example of these military-commercial figures is what locals refer to as *les douaniers-combattants*: literally, "customs officials–soldiers" or, more prosaically, "fighting customs officials." They comprise leaders of factions or rebel groups, such as the Mouvement pour le Développement around Lake Chad, and military personnel who find rents on fraudulent commerce more attractive than their official and most often unpaid salaries. These figures of authority compete with instances of national regulatory authority insofar as they have become the final arbiters of enrichment and employment. Through levies and duties imposed on local populations, they establish autonomous fiscal bases. In many respects, they have become the guarantors of economic security and access to wealth for local people in spite of their association with violence.

As one might imagine, emergent figures of authority associated with sub- and transnational regimes of accumulation pose problems for state regulatory authority, since their effective command over certain economic activities, regional or international resources, and local populations puts them in competition with the latter. Nevertheless, while this situation seems oppositional, it does not necessarily imply the demise of the nation-state in the face of nonnational forms of accumulation and power, as is sometimes presumed (as in Held 1995; Zartman 1995; Strange 1996; Badie 1999). As I show herein, the relationships between the two realms are highly ambiguous; they are often reciprocal and complicitous as much as they are competitive and antagonistic. That is, while antagonisms are manifest when it comes to the state's official regulatory authority over these regional economies, complicity is evident insofar as the state is dependent upon these regional economies for rents and the means of redistribution.

Generally interpreted as beyond the state or even antistate, unregulated economic activities are often quite misleadingly summarized as "the informal economy." While these economic activities are typical to allegedly marginal spaces, such as international borders or poor neighborhoods, the adjective "informal" is quite inappropriate. As this book makes clear, often such endeavors require and establish highly organized modalities for financing and labor recruitment, and are based on distinct hierarchies of authority relations. Furthermore, the only way in which one can indeed demarcate these activities from the official economy and official state administration is with respect to a particular shared characteristic: that is, circumventing state economic regulation. But this is a matter of a distinction between official and nonofficial, as opposed to formal versus informal. This might seem to be a semantic matter, but it is significant for two reasons. First, quite sloppily, the adjective "informal" has become a catch-all term to describe many economic pursuits and logics that are part and parcel of capitalist relations in both "the West" and "the rest." Some seemingly informal economic realms are in fact inherently linked to international financial networks (Elyachar 2001, 2002), as well as private strategies for capital accumulation (Hibou 1997, 1999b). Second, the informal economy is often signaled as a residual category; it refers to the physical margins (borders, ghettos), as well as the margins of economic life (smuggling, artisan activities), not to mention the margins of economic theory. Yet these realms and their associated activities are sometimes at the heart of productive economic life. They are one of the few means of accessing hard currency, scarce luxury goods, and state-of-the-art technology, as well as markets in small arms, minerals, gems, and drugs. More generally, they produce wealth in times of austerity and serve as essential mediations between the state and the global economy. As such, they are important resources for representatives of the national economy, providing new rents for the management of both internal and international conflicts and the redistributive logics of national politics. They are also a means of insertion in the world economy (Bayart 1994; Bayart, Ellis, and Hibou 1997; Marchal 1999). Therefore, although some practices associated with emergent regimes of accumulation and wealth might undermine forms of authority defined by the nation-state, they also contribute to its capacity to exercise power over wealth and people. Thus, while these economic activities can generally be signified as "unregulated," they cannot be described or understood as

19

marking out a realm distinct from either the official economy or official state administration.

Unregulated markets are at the heart of the postcolonial state's endeavor to fill its coffers and finance its constituents. When one considers the magnitude of the drug and small-arms trades, it seems fairly clear that these forms of productivity are by no means marginal; they offer distinct financial possibilities for currency-strapped and insolvent states. Likewise, although arguments persist for the "weak" nature of African states, their "failure," and their marginalization from the international political economy (Migdal 1988; Kaplan 1994; Zartman 1995; Reno 1995; Castells 1998), certain forms of productivity in the margins work against predictions about the demise of state power on the continent. The latter view maintains, somewhat tautologically, that state failure results from the state's incapacity to control national resources; incite industrial, commercial, and financial activity; and provide welfare to citizens. These failings are no doubt evident in many African states. However, my stay in the Chad Basin was not devoid of testimony to the strengths of certain African states, such as Cameroon, Nigeria, and Chad, all of which crushed, redirected, or surmounted rebellions and opposition movements through brute force as well as through savvy political maneuvering and co-optation, proving their respective capacities to monopolize the means of violence (armies, police) and to command at least central parts of the bureaucratic apparatus. Also, bankrupt state bureaucracies have been able to latch onto and even usurp rents associated with the regional exchanges just described. This has in some ways transformed the nature of the state bureaucracy, which now operates increasingly through private means (Hibou 1998, 1999a, 1999b), but it has not necessarily undermined the viability of the state apparatus.[20]

This process speaks to the paradox of the margin and is reflective of my own concern to think "the noncenter otherwise than as a loss of the center" (Derrida 1978: 292). Ultimately, while viewed by most as illegal, unregulated economic activities and violent methods of extraction are likewise described as legitimate; these alleged exceptional practices are elaborated as rational or reasonable behavior. To see them as such, one has to suspend particular judgments, the most obvious being the view that banditry and theft are illicit acts, and that unregulated commerce is a form of corruption. This presupposes, of course, a normative position that is often not relevant to those engaged in

---

[20] Some might argue that this is true for a regime or government, but not the state. That is, they understand the idea that the continuity of a regime might stem from appropriating the logics of wealth creation manifest in transnational networks, but insist that state sovereignty is at peril due to the lack of authority exercised over such networks themselves. But if these networks contribute to the very viability of state functions (extraction, enabling productive economic sectors, redistribution), they perpetuate the viability of the state as a political institution as much as a particular regime.

such practices. More important, it assumes distinctions between the public and private realms, and between rational and irrational behavior, which are neither universal nor generalized. That seems obvious. Often less apparent in commentary on banditry, theft, and unregulated commerce are the very distinctions between corruption, illegality, and illicit status made by those engaged in such practices. In reviewing them here, I am less interested in the fact that they are pronounced as statuses per se (as a *prise de position*), than in the ways in which they relate to one another as a relative ensemble. Those I spoke with in Cameroon and Chad distinguish quite explicitly between illegal activities and illicit practice. They also refer to a set of precepts relating to illegal status and comment upon the reasoning that leads one to engage in illegal practices—or, more distinctly, to maintain the status of illegality. More than viewing it as just an instrumentalist calculation, or a strategy to maximize economic gains or personal interests, they explain this exercise in maintaining illegality in terms of licit behavior, or what they see as the relationship between illegal and licit: being on the margins, but in the norm. In doing so, they respond to certain questions: In what ways do spoils taken in highway raids and contraband procured through smuggling operations constitute licit forms of wealth? In what ways are illegal activities rendered licit practice?

The connection they make between illegal and illicit, or the translation between the two, passes through the military-commercial bind and the nexus of the state. That is, these activities partake in prevailing modes of governing the economy in the Chad Basin. They are expressions of truths about state power, or the relationships through which one governs both populations and the economy. The practice of illegality is an ethics insofar as it is a practice of truth and, consequentially, a manner of self-understanding. In the Chad Basin today, it is likewise a manner of acknowledging truths about the economy and participating in practices of governing the economy.

This opinion runs contrary to many observations about the relationship between regional and especially transnational networks and the state, which presume that regimes of wealth and power such as those described herein are inimical to the propagation of national economics and especially state power. That is, beyond undermining a particular regime, they are said to be new sites of potential sovereignty and hence possible threats to the absolute and unique status of the nation-state. Without necessarily ushering in the demise of the nation-state form, networks of power that seem to parallel or compete with the nation-state—such as financial markets, agglomerations of nongovernmental organizations, or international legal regimes—are said to constitute domains of potential sovereign power (Walker and Mendlovitz 1990; Camilleri and Falk 1992; Brown 1995; Strange 1996; Rosenau 1997; and yet see Sassen 1995; Smith, Solinger, and Topik 1999). However, in the Chad Basin, regimes of wealth and power compete with the nation-state insofar as they undermine official regulatory authority. New manners of creating wealth and of articulating and exercising legitimate rights-in-wealth have been normalized through the military-commercial alliance described herein. This has given rise to new figures of regulatory authority in the region. These arrangements are part and parcel of the political logics of the state. As I have indicated, they contribute to the viability of state power through the production of rents and possibilities for redistribution. Even more important, the precepts underlying apparently novel relationships, activities, and modalities issue out of, or are consistent with, those practiced in the existing political economy or historical sociopolitical order. What we have is perhaps the dislocation of a political system according to novel economic arrangements, conceptual boundaries, and territorial distinctions: the state of exception—unregulated relations—being the very foundation of a new, fairly stable arrangement.[21] In that sense, while these regimes of power and wealth can be described as novel realms of thought and action—which is part of the story I tell—they are nonetheless inscribed in the same logical, or epistemological, order as that of the nation-state, which is part of the conclusion I draw.

Highlighting the distinction between state power and state regulatory authority serves to make sense of the supposed contradiction between the expansion of unregulated activities—such as fraud and contraband, which seem to indicate a loss of state control—on the one hand, and the continuity of state power in its military forms and its capacity for redistribution, on the other. Whereas state regulatory authority is in crisis on the continent, state power in Africa propagates itself even in conditions of war and bankruptcy.[22] Furthermore, by making this distinction, I have been able to explore more specifically the modalities by which state regulatory authority is contested, subverted, and even abetted. State regulatory authority is a principal source of strife in the region of the Chad Basin; in many ways, it represents the point at which the integrity of the nation-state is most unstable. Nonetheless, conflict over fiscal relations between the state and its citizens is less a matter of rejection of its application than disagreement over the intelligibility of its exercise. By taking the incivisme fiscal movement as an "event," or a productive moment in which the concepts and suppositions that serve to establish the most appropriate means and ends of power are challenged and rethought, I engage in an anthropology of regulatory authority, which ultimately describes the pluralization of figures of regulatory authority in the Chad Basin. This is an effort to understand contemporary disagreement over the intelligibility of regulatory power and fiscal relations and the ways in which that affects people's ongoing relationships with the state.

---

[21] A point inspired by Agamben 1997, 1998, to which I owe thanks to Luca D'Isanto.

[22] This seemingly impossible situation is in fact quite logical when one considers economies of war and the polities and social orders that arise therefrom. Cf. Tilly 1985; Marchal 1993, 1997; Bayart 1994.

Chapter Two   *Incivisme Fiscal*

An Event

In 1990, independent political parties were legalized in Cameroon. This was to be followed by multiparty elections and guarantees for an independent press. However, the opposition's demands for a "sovereign national conference"[1] to formulate a new election code and prepare revisions of the constitution in keeping with political reforms met with refusal from the Biya administration. The early 1990s were characterized by the tone of the regime's intransigence; the declaration of a state of emergency, which put seven of ten provinces under military administration in May 1991; and a context of extreme conditions of austerity.[2] These are the circumstances under which the National Coordination of Opposition Parties and Associations organized the Opération Villes Mortes campaign, in which lawyers, journalists, and university students played a prominent role.[3] This campaign

---

[1] National conferences have been held in Benin, Congo, Togo, Mali, Niger, Zaire, and Chad. Their records in responding to demands made by opposition groups are varied and have not instigated the democratization of political institutions in terms of either the decentralization of power or the institutionalization of counters to executive authority. On the idea of the national conference, see Boulaga 1993.

[2] Living austerity and the "crisis" is something that cannot be communicated in statistical terms. Apart from the extreme degradation of infrastructure, essential services became exceedingly difficult to access during the early 1990s through today. Deaths from minor ailments or unattended wounds and illnesses have skyrocketed. An effort to convey the materiality of the crisis, and how it becomes a figure of rationality, can be found in Mbembe and Roitman 1995.

[3] Political actors from the Anglophone Northwest Province and the Southwest Province were especially active in this campaign.

was precipitated by a pro-democracy rally that was organized on May 26, 1990, by the leader of the Social Democratic Front (SDF), John Fru Ndi, in response to delays in the legalization of his party. Quickly thereafter this late-May rally, similar demonstrations followed in other towns and cities, giving rise to a national movement defined by a strategy of civil disobedience involving a protracted general strike, work boycotts, the refusal to pay taxes, and the use of clandestine services—such as motorcycles that served as "hidden" taxis—to deny taxation.

The strategy of the opposition in this campaign was fairly explicit: its aim was to undermine the fiscal base of the regime through particular forms of civil disobedience. Those who participated in the movement expressed their criticism of the regime's exactions and levies, which ultimately finance the ruling party and the political elite; its very methods of extraction, which are often heavy-handed; and the regime's failure to provide economic opportunities and economic security. Opération Villes Mortes was in some respects a success: for a time, it crippled the Cameroonian economy and thus achieved its goal of depriving the regime of its fiscal base. In 1991, it was estimated that it resulted in a 40 percent decrease in economic activity, which represented a loss of 4 billion francs CFA per day for the state, including the collection of taxes and fees (Diallo 1991: 18), or 15 percent of the previous year's revenues (van de Walle 1993: 381).

The regime dubbed Opération Villes Mortes and the general refusal to pay taxes "incivisme fiscal." This was an attempt to delimit participation in the pro-democracy movement and refutation of state power, or at least fiscal authority, as beyond the pale of authentic civic behavior. By fixing the terms of conflict in an oppositional discursive construction—society against the state, civil versus uncivil—the struggle would be emptied of its heterogeneous content. During the time I spent milling about the markets and streets of small towns and cities, I tried to sound out the myriad enunciations relating to so-called incivisme fiscal. These statements and rationales interrogated the conditions of possibility for regulatory interventions and the codification of regulatory norms. They inspired me to take incivisme fiscal as an event in two primary senses: first, as commentary on the ways in which resistance has been structured through the institutionalization of certain political rationalities and economic concepts, such as tax and price, and, second, as a productive moment in the contemporary history of Cameroon and the Chad Basin, or a moment in which the intelligibility of regulatory authority and fiscal relations has been questioned at specific points and in specific ways. That is, certain questions have been asked and others have not; certain questions have been construed as intelligible, while others have not; and certain claims have been articulated, while others have not. Such questions indicate how particular regulatory concepts and institutions have been normalized as political technologies, tracing out fracture lines that have been defined as constant sources of both the guarantee of power (cf. Poole forthcoming) and its fallibility. These cleavages highlight the ways in which the contemporary moment, and especially contemporary strife, gives rise to emergent discursive domains and manners of circumscribing what is deemed necessary for government, as well as the ungovernable.

Claims to the State and to the Market

The conditions of possibility for certain regulatory interventions involve circumscribing "problems," or sources of disorder that need to be constantly governed or domesticated. In Cameroon, one of those fields—a dubious terrain since its conception—is national unity, a notion that was brought into question by many Cameroonian citizens in the early 1990s, at the time of the Villes Mortes campaign and the organization of the political opposition. This moment of uncertainty involved doubts and questions about the very field of positive knowledge in which state interventions in citizens' lives have been conceptualized and enacted. Debate thus centered upon certain interrogations: What is the ultimate source of wealth? And, as a corollary, what do "rights" (*les droits*) refer to? During the early 1990s, in the heat of the Villes Mortes campaign, I put these questions, albeit in more specific forms, to merchants in the main marketplace in the town of Maroua (pop. 396,000). Their responses varied, depending upon whether wealth was thought to be primarily localized in, or generated by, the state or the market, or even something else. Thus it was not uncommon to confront seemingly contradictory calls both for increased state action with respect to the economy and for the elimination of hindrances to market exchange. As an example, one merchant, who echoed the feelings of many others, insisted on the role of the state as guarantor of the market, which he viewed as threatened by foreign influences. As he explained:

> *With the crisis, workplaces are closed; merchants hardly sell anymore. Companies are closed, and functionaries are two or three months without salaries. With these months without salaries, they have debt. We don't sell, and some merchants can't pay their licenses. Nigerians go door-to-door with merchandise, through the neighborhoods, along all the paths, they hawk their wares. They sell cheaper. They don't pay for licenses, no taxes; the administration does not take care of the problem. . . . Nigeria is killing Maroua. People don't want to consume Cameroonian products. Money is going out of the country. . . . The state must make order; it must cover me. . . . If the state has its profits, I'll have mine.[4]*

---

[4] "Nigerians" refers to those peddling wares from Nigeria regardless of national origin. Merchant, Maroua, northern Cameroon, April 28, 1993.

Young merchants who work at the market in Maroua. Credit: Janet Roitman, 1993.

Many merchants who see foreign economic operators and those who evade regulation, such as the ambulatory sellers, as problematic likewise condemn the state for its inaction. However, they hone in on the civil servants, who are no longer the principal source of capital and who contribute to capital flight by purchasing goods in neighboring markets in Nigeria. The merchants thus find themselves in the contradictory position of having to "work the bush" (meaning unregulated markets) *and* pay taxes, as an angry retailer declared: "There is no market; there is no money. The civil servants don't earn money like before. Firms are shut; people are bankrupt; companies have no work. The problem is capital flight. I pay taxes, and they go to the exterior; there is no more money in Cameroon. We're obliged to work the markets in the bush—and to pay licenses. The government is the source of these problems. I sell at a loss because things are cheaper in Nigeria."[5] Others located causality in "crisis" (*la crise*), an agent beyond both state and market. This is a claim that was articulated even by those belonging to the youngest generation, one of whom remarked as follows: "The future is not rosy. What I mean is, the future is not sure. People aren't sure about their future because we think that, first of all, that there is a generation that missed its coming out, that had the possibility to create industries—maybe

[5] Merchant, Maroua, northern Cameroon, April 21, 1993.

26

small industries—there aren't any. Today, we [the younger generation] are victims, that is to say we're paying the [inaudible]. Why? Because we arrived on the market—we found absolutely nothing; the crisis is there.[6]

During the so-called incivisme fiscal movement, the Biya regime sought to establish a homologous relationship between sources of political disorder and sources of economic disorder—between, for instance, "antinational" activity and the so-called informal economy, or what one of the merchants just quoted referred to as "markets in the bush." Consequently, the terms of debate about economic citizenship, or the nature of rights and responsibilities inherent in the fiscal relationship, were restricted, for the most part, to the question of security through the state versus security from the state. Basically this involved, as the Opération Villes Mortes movement itself articulated, rights to security either *through* the fiscal actions of the state or *from* the fiscal actions of the state. Hence, while paying taxes has been construed historically as requisite for, or even constitutive of, the status of a "citizen," in the present context the constitution of the "citizen" is construed less in terms of a founding economic transfer than in terms of the conditions that allow for that transfer. The merchants' remarks are exemplary of this general viewpoint insofar as they state that those conditions include security through state interventions and from foreign economic and political influences, as well as access to a market.

The refusal, during the 1990s, to pay *la patente*, or commercial licenses, underscores this point. As a form of tax, the patente enters into the general category of droits, which in French signifies, depending on the context, duties, fees, and taxes, as well as rights of entry and access, and entitlements. From my experience, those who pay taxes in northern Cameroon—including Europeans[7]—have generally referred to droits in terms of rights of access: one pays taxes so that one has the right to access certain markets, or the privileged relationships that ensure exchanges and commercial relationships. Tax is often signified as a "price" (*le prix*); it is the price to pay for the right of access. I will return to the historical inscription of this relationship between tax and price in the next chapter, with the aim of indicating the consequences of the representation of this relationship for contemporary practice and moments of resistance. For now, suffice it to say that today the tension between obligations and entitlements that forms the spinal column of "rights" has become quite taut. Thus the chief of one of the butcher's

---

[6] Merchant, Maroua, northern Cameroon, October 16, 1993.

[7] When trying to understand people's use of the term "price" when referring to what I would call "tax," I was surprised to discover that many European businessmen conflated price and tax, putting forth the same reasoning as that I received from Cameroonians: tax is a price because it is a right of entry or access. The Europeans were surprised at their own semantic slippage and agreed that this manner of apprehending tax was specific to their experience in Cameroon; they generally felt that they would not use "price" to signify tax in the European context. The conflation between tax and price is explored in chapter 3.

markets (*sarki pawa*) in Maroua insisted that one "pays for rights" and that the emergence of unregulated trade in cattle and the proliferation of neighborhood butchers who work in back streets, backyards, and the bush is a negation of rights of access in both economic and political terms: "Before, to be a butcher, you had to have the paper. . . . Now, they go get the paper— the license [*la patente*] . . . but they no longer slaughter under my eye. . . . If they have their papers, they have paid for certain rights. I explain that they must see me, they must respect the rules. Ten years ago, it wasn't like that. . . . They're not in agreement now; it's not democracy yet."[8] And yet merchants now contest the idea of paying for the right to trade, or the idea of paying for access to the market, by making claims to "the right to a market" (*le droit du marché*), or to the very conditions that would allow one to pay tax. This semantic slippage implies certain forms of protection and effective regulation, as many people made clear to me in conversations in the marketplace during the height of protests in 1992–93:

> *Everyone slaughters in back alleys. It's killing the butchers' market. I pay the license, taxes, and I buy cattle in the marketplace. . . . The others, they do as they please and they have no losses. We need [authorities in the cattle market] to seek out the clandestine.*[9]

> *I'm obliged to pay taxes, and I don't earn anything. If the state obliges me, I must do it. The administration must take its responsibilities in hand . . . they must eliminate the ambulatory sellers . . . [who] sell stolen sheep. Even the Nigerians who sell in the neighborhoods must stop slaughtering if they haven't paid for a license.*[10]

> *There is no market because of contraband. I buy merchandise in Douala [Cameroon], not in Nigeria. . . . Contraband is breaking us. There are a lot of taxes on us; la patente is too costly. The functionaries go to Banki [Nigeria] for everything, even for household items and food. Who are we going to sell to?*[11]

This call for simultaneous state protection and access to a market as prerequisites for the enactment of the fiscal bind reflects the lack of consensus regarding the significance of incivisme fiscal or Opération Villes Mortes. Although I will not quote them at length (see Roitman 1996), those I spoke to basically agreed on the need to deprive the regime of its fiscal base to force it to respond to certain demands. However, some insisted that this response should entail increased and effective regulation to combat the

---

[8] Sarki Pawa, Maroua, northern Cameroon, May 19, 1992.
[9] Maroua, northern Cameroon, May 23, 1992.
[10] Maroua, northern Cameroon, June 2, 1992.
[11] Maroua, northern Cameroon, May 21, 1992.

extension of unregulated trade, whereas others underscored the liberating effects of unregulated exchange and the desire to throw off the shackles of state regulation. So I was told, by one individual, "The state must function; they [merchants] have to pay their 'droits' [taxes and duties]. The problem is Nigeria; the border is permeable, the smugglers must be countered. They [Cameroonian merchants] can't sell their products, and they don't want to pay for a license. They're selling at a loss. They'd be willing to pay if the smugglers were stopped, if they could sell their own products. They refute the authorities in the market because they're threatened by Nigeria, and they hold the authorities responsible. Or it's because of democratization; it's democratization misunderstood [la démocracie mal comprise]—that's why they live this ambiguity."[12]

Others also couched the refusal to pay tax and the right to access a market in terms of democracy and democratization, misunderstood or not. As a municipal worker told me: "They burned the controllers' post and the police post in the marketplace. Now they say it's democracy, and it spills over and it's anarchy. Even when the police whistle they say they're free, it's democracy. It's an adjustment. . . . People don't want to pay [taxes], they say it's democracy."[13] This civil servant's reference to "adjustment" is astute. The economics of democratization, being part and parcel of structural adjustment reforms, have led to unintended consequences that have foiled the previsions of liberalization. In any case, for many of those I engaged with, democratization was reduced to the question of establishing freedom from tax or, more specifically, a means to negate exclusions heretofore established through regulation. While walking through the crowded marketplace after confrontations between crowds and the police, I was told:

[Before], the authorities could prevent certain people from selling [through licensing]. [Now] it's democracy; anyone can sell.[14]

The petrol trade is not clandestine anymore not only because the gendarmes and customs officials are all involved, but also because it has been democratized; anyone can do it, and everyone does.[15]

The police encircled the city and the market. People decided to stay at home. The police were asking for tax receipts; if you didn't have it, they put you in a truck. No one came to the market. There was great disorder. People burned tires; they prevented anyone from circulating, even the police. We haven't paid for a year now. We have entered into politics. Politics helped us refuse to

---

[12] Maroua, northern Cameroon, October 28, 1993.
[13] Administrator in the mayor's office, Maroua, northern Cameroon, March 27, 1992.
[14] Maroua, northern Cameroon, March 8, 1992.
[15] Maroua, northern Cameroon, May 13, 1992.

The Mobil station at Waza during the height of the Villes Mortes campaign. Credit: Janet Roitman, 1993.

Illegal petrol sold at the side of the road. Credit: Janet Roitman, 1993.

pay. It's democracy. If we pay taxes, it finances the RDPC. Forty-nine million remains to be paid. It's their problem; this government doesn't interest us. We used to be obligated; now it's democracy, we're no longer obligated. The [authorities] are afraid of the vandals; they'll come burn them alive in their houses and in their cars. The state doesn't have any means. It's the population that has the means; they can sell from their homes.[16]

People are willing to confront the authorities because they have petrol. They can burn things, and the gendarmes are afraid of being burned alive in their cars or in their houses. And all the people have petrol; it's everywhere because of the traffic with Nigeria; it's all over the streets and in every house. And the gendarmes can't do anything because they [themselves] are all involved in the traffic.[17]

The very willingness of the general public to confront the authorities in a concerted manner was consistently explained as a matter of access to, and control of, petrol: "We have *zoua-zoua; c'est le feu public*"—the public fire or the public's fire.[18] Calls for le droit du marché were thus both appeals for state protection of national markets and concomitant assertions of the freedom to engage in commerce regardless of means, which counters the gate-keeping functions of entitlements construed as rights of access. In this sense, one might argue that the "right" to wealth, which involves both entitlements and duties, was not constructed in the name of the "consumer," as it has been in Eastern Europe (Laclau and Mouffe 1987; Daly 1991). Nor was it put forth in the name of the "producer" or "worker," as for the *cheminots* (rail workers) in France during the 1990s. Instead, claims were made in terms of an idea of the "fiscal subject."

Enacting Claims to Wealth

Those who have been condemned by state authorities for incivisme fiscal and those who are best described as dismissed, dispossessed, downsized, and under- or unemployed have taken to the bush, highways, and borders, where they partake in unregulated and sometimes clandestine activities. From these spaces, they are making claims to the freedom to engage in commerce regardless of means, and even to the very right to wealth. These are the

[16] Maroua, northern Cameroon, May 21, 1992.

[17] Ibid.

[18] The appropriation of Nigerian petrol into the signifying regime of the Cameroonian political economy and oppositional politics was indicated by a shift in terminology from *le Federal*, in reference to the federal state of Nigeria, to *zoua-zoua*, a term that remains a mystery to me. Most Cameroonians claimed that it means "to burn," but this was not the consensus.

31

unassimilated, or those who have been construed as unassimilable. Many unemployed people, for instance, have some form of education yet find themselves obligated to scavenge for money. The economy of the bush and borders provides them with cash and has given them a means to counter what they feel is the state's monopoly over surpluses, or to exercise claims to wealth. Sometimes these claims have been realized through various forms of seizure, such as theft, raids on villages and markets, and especially road banditry. Alienation of property through violent means has been a common practice of past governments—including that of the slave-based precolonial states, such as Mandara; the nineteenth-century jihad and the resulting Sokoto Caliphate; and the German and then French colonial regimes. Through these various instances, seizure has been experienced historically as a right of state (Roitman 1998b). Today, however, this *force d'état* is no longer self-evident. To repeat the grievances of one merchant I spoke to: "Before, they came to the market to collect money—it was paid in installments, and we got a receipt. They came every Monday. Even if the government sent a crazy man, we did what they asked. Now, the people who come are not children; they are big. If you say you have nothing, they close your shop. . . . For five years now, they shut us down, chain our stores, and they leave. If they close your store and you stay in the market they say, 'Go steal.' "[19]

Many people, and especially demobilized soldiers and dispossessed youth, have inverted this power equation by seizing spoils themselves. In the end, seizure has become a widespread means of enrichment: financial regulators chain merchants' stores shut, haul the merchants off to prison, confiscate goods, and exact fines; customs officials and gendarmes skim off of trucks and travelers, usurping contraband and often going poaching themselves; and professional road bandits hijack cars and attack road convoys. But, beyond material gain, seizure, other violent modes of appropriation, and unregulated economic activities more generally are also seen in terms of mastery over the icons of the contemporary landscape. My conversations with the foot soldiers of the economy of the bush always returned to the idea that—in spite of strong nationalist and especially protectionist sentiments, some of which were voiced above earlier in this chapter—the expanding trade in unregulated goods is a source of economic freedom and empowerment. Often associated with the right to engage in commerce regardless of means, those who smuggle petrol on the Nigerian-Cameroonian border described their activities as part of "democratization," since "anyone can participate"; moreover, their supply keeps gas prices low, thus aiding the impoverished consumer. Yet this call for the right to accumulation and consumption was not merely an appeal for the "freedom of the market" against a predatory or parasitic state. More subtle than that

---

[19] Maroua, northern Cameroon, April 21, 1993.

crude contrast, it was in many ways an attempt to dismantle exclusionary references to "democracy" and *la vie moderne* (modern life).[20]

Until recently, the "nation-state," "economic development," and "democracy" have prevailed as the preeminent signifiers of "modern life." But this changed as impoverishment, indebtedness, and increased factional fighting and warfare have accompanied the rather disingenuous process of political and economic liberalization on the continent. Hence "austerity" has become a predominant emblem of postindustrial society (cf. Comaroff and Comaroff 2000; Ferguson 1999). And since international donors have made multiparty elections the condition of continued financing, "democracy" is no longer taken to be a sign of the affluent society. In many parts of Africa, it has led to the militarization of society, where large parts of many countries have come under military jurisdiction (Haitian-style democracy of the early 1990s) or even militarism, where violence is generalized as a political procedure.[21]

In this context, those who participate in the unregulated economy in the Chad Basin maintain, quite rightly, that they have not made significant gains from the trappings of "modern life," which include education, health care, employment in industrial and service sectors, and, of course, consumption. Yet their references to the "market" and "democracy" are capricious, being fashioned out of the proliferation of repertoires that now give sense to these regulatory concepts. These include the discourses of Christian independent church movements and Islamic missionary movements; the narrative of economic development or ideals of humanitarian aid associated with non-governmental organizations or the state bureaucracy; the visions of humanity or freedom put forth by human rights organizations, newly established political parties, community-based religious associations, and so forth.

---

[20] The people I knew in the Chad Basin referred to *la vie moderne* (modern life) as opposed to "modernity." I prefer to use their expression, since the term "modernity" issues out of a particular reading of Western history and philosophy, which is in many ways irrelevant to my interlocutors even though modernity, as a historical regulatory concept, does impact significantly upon their lives. Furthermore, while elaboration of the term is important, a formal definition would only serve the purpose of examining its teleology, which is not the aim herein. Michel Foucault (2001a: 1498–1507) thought of modernity not as an epoch but as an ethos of the present. For commentary, see Rabinow 2003. For interesting commentary on "modernity" as a regulative concept, see Spivak (1993), who insists on an important point about the nature of contemporary political claims: they are "tacitly recognized as coded within the legacy of imperialism: nationhood, constitutionality, democracy, socialism, even culturalism. In the historical framework of exploration, colonization, decolonization, what is being *effectively* reclaimed is a series of regulative political concepts, the supposedly authoritative narrative of the production of which was written elsewhere, in the social formations of Western Europe. They are thus being reclaimed, indeed claimed, as concept-metaphors for which no *historically* adequate referent may be advanced from postcolonial space" (48; also pp. 13–14). See also Hall, Held, and McGrew 1992.

[21] On militarization versus militarism as a mode of political action, refer to Mbembe 1990. On militarism and similar political claims, read Richards 1996, esp. chap. 7.

These various discursive fields lead to combinatory approaches to "modern life" and the problem of livelihood and economic security. These composite referents inform judgments about the sites and sources of wealth, desired forms of wealth, and legitimate modes of appropriating wealth. Thus we find an assemblage of apparent non sequiturs that string together associations between wealth, desire, and empowerment, as in the following explanation of the name chosen for the illegal "Boston City" street-side petrol selling post in Maroua: "Boston City is a big city in the United States. We chose this name in order to attract clients and so that they can locate us quickly. For us, Boston simply means petrol. We wrote Boston City simply to say to people that we sell gas. We chose a city in the United States because we want to fight against the economic crisis like Americans; we want to gather our courage to forge ahead."[22] Another young illegal petrol seller told me why he named his selling post "Hollywood": "To start with, Hollywood is one of the great cities of the United States, and I hope you're aware of the ambience that reigns there. A lively city at all hours, twenty-four hours a day; rich, pretty to live in. To me, Hollywood is money, cleanliness, wealth in general. Thanks to the resources I have from selling gas, I would like—Insh'allah [if God permits]—to make my entourage, my neighborhood, a Hollywood. . . . It's my dream, it's a point of reference."[23]

In the Chad Basin, as in many other parts of the world, the imaginings of wealth and "modern life" are mediated through both irreverent gangsta rap and the reverent mujahideen, often simultaneously. In this sense, young illegal petrol sellers, who procure their wares at the frontier garrison-entrepôts and from militia-led, cross-desert caravans, are reflections of the cosmopolitan subjects of late-twentieth-century cultural production. In this young man's terms—"Insh'allah"—Islam wills the realization of the capitalist dream or the riches of Hollywood; it is not construed as the antithesis of the West. The nickname of the young man who ran the Hollywood selling post is Alhadji Petel (Little Alhadji), a title that signifies success in Islam and in the local Muslim merchant society. Alhadji (El Hajj) is the title given to one who has made the pilgrimage to Mecca. In many parts of the Sahel, this is a sign of wealth and achievement and has come to signify a successful businessman whether or not the religious excursion has actually been undertaken (refer to Grégoire 1991, 1992).

No doubt, Islamic society is deemed by some as the very site of capital formation. As I was told by a merchant in the "Koweit City" selling post, "I sell every day, and the gas does not stop. Provisioning is permanent, and I earn considerable profits. Like Kuwait, where they say the oil wells never end, I think of my locality as a center of permanent provisioning. Kuwait

---

[22] Petrol seller, Maroua, northern Cameroon, October 1993.
[23] Ibid.

Petrol sellers at the illegal "Koweit City" point of sale, where the sign reads "Koweit City. Human Right" (Koweit City: Droit de l'homme). Credit: Janet Roitman, 1993.

City is wealth. I posted this sign high because I dream of becoming rich one day. . . . When you say 'gas' or 'petrol,' you make direct allusion to countries like the United States, the USSR, Saudi Arabia, and Kuwait. That's why I chose Kuwait as a model."[24] The billboard marking the busy intersection where provisioning is permanent reads: "*Koweit City. Droits de l'homme*" ("Kuwait City. Human Rights"), referencing the power of oil and the oft-admired stance of Saddam Hussein in the face of Western power in 1991, as well as the presumed association between profits and democracy ("oil" and "human rights"). But the correlation between the latter two is not evident in the Chad Basin.[25] Despite the instatement of multiparty politics in most countries in Africa, profits have flowed neither from the vote nor from the blossoming of human rights organizations.

[24] Ibid.

[25] This is a particularly apt moment to point that out, since oil around Lake Chad and in southern Chad is now the subject of much heated debate. At the time of the writing of this book, the World Bank was financing the construction of an oil pipeline from southern Chad, through the entire length of Cameroon, to the port of Kribi on the Cameroonian coast. This immense project was for some time stalled due to criticism from environmental and human

35

When I asked the illegal petrol vendor at the "Koweit City" post why he chose this place of war—which Kuwait was at the time—he responded that he was "not alluding to war, but only to becoming rich." Others, however, identified explicitly with embattled locales in the geopolitically defined world of Islam. Thus "Welcome to Baghdad" ushers clients into one garrison of gas: "I like this name because, before, Baghdad was a beautiful capital. Baghdad was destroyed during the Gulf War; that really bothers me. I would like this capital to be rebuilt quickly. The Americans are the cause of this destruction; they owe Saddam Hussein help. . . . If I ever have the means, I hope to go there one day."[26]

This comment is highly reminiscent of what people have to say (cf. Mbembe and Roitman 1995) about the once resplendent capital of Cameroon, Yaounde, which lies in the south, and about the the dilapidation, decay, and destruction that have scarred other northern towns as well. Indeed, the state of siege brought on by the administration's response to the Opération Villes Mortes campaign and the fact of being forced to sell petrol illegally at a sordid crossroads inspired the informal Association of Petrol Sellers to dub one spot "Sarajevo-Bosnia": "We chose this name because to be a petrol seller you must first be a strong and resistant guy, since you spend the whole day, and often the nights, selling. You don't rest. And if someone attacks us, we can respond en masse to the attack. We wanted to post that to show you that the petrol sellers aren't weak; they can fight like the people in Sarajevo."[27] "it's a site of war, and here, where I sell petrol, I see a lot of miracles. I say miracles because, day and night, I witness lots of accidents. . . . And late at night, the police come to take the taxi-motorcycles from the young people by force. Often they even rape the girls who pass by. For me, Sarajevo means disorder, trouble, noise. If they can take people's belongings by force, and if one ends up fighting incessantly in a place, don't you see that I'm right to choose a place of war like Sarajevo?"[28]

It is not insignificant that these young men's referents are the icons of urban violence and war, which are sometimes valorized in terms of empowerment in the periphery. The illegal petrol sellers' remarks register efforts to negotiate "modern life" in a time of austerity, but they also contest, with recourse to varying referents, present and increasingly problematic modes of redistribution and alienation. "War" has become a widespread paradigm for understanding the demise of specific metaphors and historical institutions that once regulated communities (e.g., economic development, national progress, social

---

rights groups, mostly represented by NGOs, but also associated with Chadian organizations and the armed opposition movement in southern Chad.

[26] Bouba, Maroua, northern Cameroon, October 1993.

[27] Petrol seller, Maroua, northern Cameroon, October 1993.

[28] Ibid.

welfare), the generalization of certain modes of appropriation (e.g., razzia, seizure, debt), and the rise of their associated figures of authority (e.g., militias, renegade customs officials, foreigners).

National Integrity: Peace or Wealth?

During the Villes Mortes campaign, southerners were the most frequent targets of attack in northern towns despite the fact that those living in the southwestern and western provinces had instigated and most effectively implemented this political strategy of the opposition. Regardless of political affiliation, southerners living in the North were apprehended as instances of state power, being mostly civil servants. In that sense, to many (mainly Muslim) northerners, they were representatives of the "southern" (read Christian) regime. Notwithstanding these representations, many northern-based merchants were in cahoots with the same civil servants' seditious strategies of accumulation or their deep involvement in unregulated commerce and financial activities, which those quoted earlier often vilified as a disruptive "foreign" influence. Therefore, while northern merchants decried the pervasive effects of "Nigeria," they were—and still are— at the heart of its ubiquity.

A meeting between high-level administrators and the merchants of Maroua, held in April 1993, was an attempt by the regime to bring insurgent traders and businessmen into the fold of "civic behavior," which involved the formation of a special commission to investigate tax evasion and regulation of the main marketplace. At this time, the local prefect took the opportunity to remind the merchants of the following:

> You are the ones who fostered the presence of Nigerians, Chadians—you benefit from their presence. The networks are very, very complicated. The Nigerians and Chadians rent stores from you . . . they're in the parallel and informal circuits that you have initiated. . . . The commission [on taxes and the marketplace] cannot work freely. . . . No one will reveal their profit margins. You say you have only four cartons of soap, and you're riding around in a Mercedes. We know that the command "Refuse!" [to pay tax] runs through the market. But you tell me that foreigners are the ones who tell the youth to attack the people from the Ministry of Finances. . . . Lots of activities take place in the form of traffic. Traffic was never the life of a country [faire vivre un pays]. And where that is the case—like in the Gambia— it was organized by the agents of the state itself. But if you have houses and cars . . . and the state has nothing, what can you do for Maroua? The roads must be tarred, public works are stopped; they must continue but there is no money. . . . If you don't pay taxes, the country will die. The country is on its

knees because its sons [fils du pays] don't pay their taxes. . . . It's no use to use a whip; it simply means that you are not free men.[29]

The prefect's statement sums up many of the questions raised by incivisme fiscal, or the Opération Villes Mortes movement. These include interrogations about the legitimate foundations of state wealth, the forms of wealth that are to be subject to state appropriations, the distinction between licit and illicit commerce, and the integrity of the contours of the nation-state. Ultimately, debate about these matters and their founding terms has occasioned cross-examinations of certain established truths, which are now challenged as possible fictions. The status of the "free citizen" is central to these debates: some argue that participation in the fiscal relationship is unfounded, since the state is not the basis of either security or wealth. Many merchants insist that they are not opposed to the fact of state regulation of their economic activities. They do, however, object to the state's manners of appropriation, as well as the presupposition that they are the ultimate sources of wealth, the foundations of the state treasury. Thus, just after the meeting, one shopkeeper explained to me: We are not against la patente; before we paid without force, without the police. They say that if you trade in the market you need a license, at 37,000 CFA. . . . The prefect says it's not a political problem. They want us to pay because the functionaries don't have money. If we pay the licenses, will that suffice to pay the functionaries? The prefect gave 120,000 CFA to 120 policemen to come massacre the market. If we don't pay, they close down our shops. Now merchandise doesn't turn over like before; after you buy your food, there is nothing left over."[30] An older man, who described himself as "the head of a family" (*baaba sare*) spoke, albeit in elusive manner, of his rights: "Before, they came to the market to collect money—it was paid in installments and we got a receipt. . . . I'm a baaba sare; I have a lot of children. There are a lot of people like me. I don't have great means, but I get by. When they say, 'Give me your license,' it's not good. They say, 'Get out, shut down'— that kills me. If I could just avoid that, everything would be okay. . . . Once I went to pay my license at the [government] office. I had money in my hand. They wanted to throw me outside. I gave it to those people; I told them, 'The government, it's us.' If they come calmly, it's okay."[31]

In this view, although the citizen is at the heart of government, and thus may be the foundation of the state treasury, state appropriations require certain conditions. Others constructed the idea of rights with specific reference to the rights of citizens and to local political parties, such as the northern-based

---

[29] High-level administrator, Departement du Diamare, northern Cameroon, in an address to the merchants of Maroua and their political representatives, Maroua, April 15, 1993.

[30] Merchant, Maroua, northern Cameroon, April 21, 1993. CFA, or Communauté financière africaine, is the currency used in former French African colonies.

[31] Ibid.

UNDP, that found aspects of their legitimacy in specific understandings of Islam:

From here [the North], it's forbidden to send cattle to Yaounde [South]. I went to see the people [in the administration] at Yaounde; I discussed the problem with them for two months. They don't want any cattle from here; they say it will ruin the market. They want animals from Ngaoundere—the people from there force the issue. But I'm going to continue with the problem after the elections. . . . It's a just cause because this is our country. They say it will spoil the market, but that's corruption. I have the right because it's my country; that's why I won't abandon the problem, I have the truth. Change comes from Allah. Multipartyism comes from the power of Allah, the party of truth.[32]

During the 1990s, both "national wealth" and the "nation-state" were at the heart of such comments. At the same time, and contrary to "economic crisis" or "legitimacy crisis" readings of such moments in many parts of Africa, the destabilizing effects of this recognition of the heterogeneous nature of these seemingly invariable national referents did not simply lead to a loss of sense and meaning in the world.[33] As a productive moment, incivisme fiscal and the process of questioning it entailed led to transformations in the discursive field in which "wealth" and "the national" are figured. Incivisme fiscal posited a fundamental debate, as can be gleaned from the earlier comments, about the rightful foundations of regulation and state wealth. The present regime has insisted that the dramatization of citizenship should take place primarily through the fiscal relationship, an assertion that presupposes, of course, a stable representation of national affiliation. National wealth rests upon national unity, which is construed as an objective reality. During the 1990s, the very idea of national unity was explicitly contested by various groups, including members of the opposition, some of whom have called for decentralization and federalism, and the secessionist movement in the Anglophone provinces. It was also implicitly challenged by ongoing conflicts between various communities—such as the Kotoko and the Choa communities in the North (Socpa 1999; Issa 1997)—as well as the intensification of unregulated

[32] Merchant, Mbankara, northern Cameroon, May 20, 1992. As an administrator remarked with respect to protection of the cattle market at Ngaoundere and failed efforts to export animals from the Extreme North Province to southern cities, "You start to wonder if you're even from the same country. It's a political problem." Administrator, Centre National de Formation Zootechnique et Vétérinaire, Maroua, northern Cameroon, March 20, 1992. The comment refers to protectionist practices that date back to the French colonial authorities' establishment of a special breeding zone at Ngaoundere; free movement of cattle was further restricted in 1962 by a barrier at Mbe. Today, the Service d'Élevage competes with customs officials for control of this traffic.

[33] As is implied by James Ferguson's (1999) recent and otherwise interesting reading of the situation in the Zambian copper belt. For critique of the "disenchantment" reading of contemporary economic phenomena, cf. Bayart 1994.

cross-border trade (Herrera 1995; Bennafla 2002) and its attendant forms of affiliation (Roitman 1998a). National unity has been localized in the national treasury as opposed to ethnic, racial, or religious authenticity, which has perhaps mitigated tendencies toward decentralization, fragmentation, adversity between nationals, and regionalization. In his address to the merchants of Maroua and their political representatives—and in a tone quite reminiscent of colonial wisdom—the prefect insisted, through circular reasoning, that "the Treasury is the unity of the country . . . the unity of the country depends on the coffers of the state."[34]

During the same meeting, the provincial administrators argued repeatedly and with much foreboding that establishing nationality and the subjectivity of the free citizen in the exchequer was to be counterposed to the "slide into ruins" (*la dérive*), where forces that are thought to transgress sociability and unity would engulf those that are said to represent "society." The mayor thus warned: "Our children, who are the province's true capital—they make up 60 percent of the population of the province—are not going to pardon us. . . . We are going to punish the children; they will inherit an improper situation. . . . The state is suffering now; now, we cannot seek provisions at the General Treasury. People wonder, 'Where did the money go?' Look at our neighboring countries; they know this problem. It's the same thing."[35] Another high-level administrator enjoined:

> *The mayoralty is dying . . . we are watching. . . . The SONEL [electric company] is cutting us off. It's shameful; the capital of the province is in obscurity; people will see, it will be noted; tourists and spies will come see. And the electric company always acts with its sister, the SNEC [water company]; water will be cut; it's the lifeblood of humanity, the life of cattle. . . . It's death, it's a tragedy. . . . Vandalism will increase. . . . The poor have nothing to lose, it's the rich who have something to lose. When people are laid off from the SODECOTON [cotton industry], the mayor's office, etcetera, are we going to continue to roll around in stout cars? People will only have recourse to millet and cotton. The Extreme North cannot survive on millet and cotton.[36]*

[34] Prefect, Ministère des Finances, Departement du Diamare, northern Cameroon, Maroua, April 15, 1993. These remarks were made with specific reference to the idea that tax receipts in the various provinces contribute to the central government's ability to pay civil servants everywhere in the country.

[35] Mayor, Commune Urbaine de Maroua, northern Cameroon, in an address to the merchants of Maroua and their political representatives, Maroua, April 15, 1993.

[36] High-level administrator, Departement du Diamare, northern Cameroon, in an address to the merchants of Maroua and their political representatives, Maroua, April 15, 1993. The noise of the civil servants is an oblique reference to discontent in the military, always a foreboding sign in Africa, as elsewhere.

A well-known merchant with strong connections to the party in power (the RDPC) alerted the other merchants to the possibilities of demise, with clear reference to the trope of the nation and its citizens: "We have to start thinking because if [this situation] arrives with force, they can even come into our homes and take what they want. You've seen what's happened in Zaire. . . . In Zaire, famine is starting to disturb [people], and then the civil servants start to make noise."[37]

The slide into ruins, or the space where untamed forces (youth, the poor, darkness, famine) overtake society, poses the problem of the "unassimilated" or "unassimilatable." Given that social mobility is now not only no longer assured but also potentially reversible, the contours of the category of "free men" have become permeable. Today, Cameroonians tend to underscore the contingent nature of the founding distinction between "free" and "unfree" and the forms of wealth this distinction consecrates. Appropriations that were once sanctioned when exercised over those outside the bounds of "freedom"—for instance, through enslavement or seizure of spoils—are now applied without distinction. These days, almost everyone, including the "free man," can expect to experience the alienation of wealth through violent means or seizure, be it by financial regulators, militias and gendarmes, or road bandits. It seems that everyone is seizing spoils.

In sum, and somewhat abstractly, the very hierarchy of social validity that is structured through redistribution is shifting. Thus efforts to ensure the continuity of the foundations of wealth—in the slave, the head of the family, the consumer, the civil servant, the salary, development aid, the national treasury—have intensified. This has brought the question of "national unity" to the fore. Historically, redistribution has occurred nationally through salary payments that have been ensured via external financing (Bayart 1979, 1989). These have underpinned the burgeoning civil service and parastatal sectors, providing the material means for national distribution and the construction of dependency relations through patronage networks and extended families. As everywhere, the salary system structures social stratification.[38] But, following in the traces of the colonial state, the Cameroonian postcolonial state is the nexus of the great majority of salaried activity. Therefore, since the salary creates relations of dependency and debt between *the state* and recipients (and their dependents), it is constitutive of, and reflects, a particular notion of citizenship. In Cameroon, salaries are

[37] Alhadji Amadou Ali, in an address to the merchants of Maroua and their political representatives, Maroua, northern Cameroon April 15, 1993.

[38] The centrality of salary payments in cycles of debt, redistribution, and reciprocity is examined in the case of the Ivory Coast by Mahieu 1989. For commentary on this same dynamic (and its crisis) in Europe, cf. Théret 1992.

most often construed as "privileges" as opposed to simple remuneration for productive activity. This is evident to anyone who has witnessed the pleadings of those who arrive, day after day, for months on end, at the barred windows of the public offices where salaries might (eventually) be distributed. This perception of the salary as a privilege and not a right is the combined result of the deployment of the salary as part of a disciplinary apparatus establishing relations of dependency and indebtedness between the state and its subjects, as well as historical understandings of the relationships that bind wealth, work, and the state (Mbembe and Roitman 1995).

Therefore, the materiality of the civil link between the state and its subjects is realized as much through taxes and welfare services as it is through wealth, *or even simply money*, produced in state infrastructures. In northern Cameroon, people often call credits obtained from the state "cash," distinct from credit established between private individuals. That is, state credit is signified as "cash," since, as it was explained to me, "you cannot see" the creditor, which makes it not easily detected as credit per se. Moreover, since independence, the fundamental sources of wealth for northerners, who have extremely limited recourse to employment in local industries (most of which are, in any case, parastatals), are the state, civil servants, and state-derived salaries. "People of the city" are "people of credit," unlike those in villages and rural areas who have had, until recently, little independent access to "cash," or state credits. Those with money are "the end-of-the-month people" (*les gens de la fin du mois*), the people of paychecks. Ultimately, as they say, "there is no market without the civil servants."[39] In a novel interpretive turn, public servants, and not private individuals, constitute the market in exchange. But as I was told over and over during the 1990s, "the crisis" means that, these days, "the market pays more than employment"; that is, the civil service is considered to be employment (or "work"), the market being juxtaposed, then, to "work."

These comments reflect conceptions of the market that arise out of the historical institutionalization of money, credit, the state bureaucracy, and so forth. They obviously diverge from the ideal type aspired to by economic reformers and, much more important, are indicative of uncertainty as to the sources of wealth creation today. The "market" pays more, but it is not "employment" per se. Being among the few sources of currency, salaries and state-based credit transfers have ensured the political rationality of tax collection. Consequently, relations of domination inherent to the extant system of redistribution and regulation have not been perceived as the antithesis of the "freedoms" of the market. Structural adjustment programs,

---

[39] *Il n'y a pas de marché sans les fonctionnaires* was on oft-repeated response to my questions about the "cause" of the economic crisis.

which have endeavored to undermine the rent-seeking and clientelist logics of this edifice by supposedly depoliticizing the market, are interpreted as a new source of instability, the cause of what people referred to as "negative competition" (*la concurrence négative*) and "reciprocal mistrust" (*la méfiance réciproque*). The real irony is that, with the recent enactment of price liberalization policies, locals now say that conflict and disturbances in the market have arisen due to the fact that "politics have entered into the market."[40] Now, civil servants are no longer the paramount source of transfers. The entry of politics into the market entails a new form of interventionism involving, among other things, the externalization of certain forms of regulatory authority. This is best described as the internationalization of decision making, with regulatory authority and representation of local interests being claimed by various external agents, such as the International Monetary Fund (IMF), the World Bank, the Paris Club, NGOs, and private corporations (Coussy 1994; Hibou 1999b, Sassen 1995, 1998). But those living in Cameroon and the Chad Basin more generally have also witnessed the regionalization of regulation, or what I prefer to call the pluralization of figures of regulatory authority. This is such that redistribution is being performed in domains not normally associated with state power (at least as represented as a centralizing political apparatus). This situation arises out of and engenders transformations in representations of the ultimate sources of wealth. What people call "the crisis" is, in that sense, partly a crisis in established truths about wealth, and especially about the nature of what constitutes "national" wealth and where that wealth lies.

This is most evident in the prefect's address to the merchants of Maroua:

> *Taxes are not political; they are the life of the city, the life of the municipality. The problem must be resolved by responsible men. Maroua remains at an impasse: the mayor's office does not function. The mayor cannot have the garbage collected, execute other budgetary projects, pay the people. . . . They are your brothers, who have families; they can't feed their children. . . . There are political changes now. People are calling for the decentralization of the provinces. That means that each province will manage its own money. But you have to produce money. I don't know how the Treasury at Yaounde will find money for the Extreme North. Some think that the state creates money. We try to explain that the state does not create money; it lives thanks to money produced by citizens.*[41]

According to the prefect, the productivity of the citizen, and not the civil servant or even the consumer, as was previously the case (see chapter 3), is

---

[40] This was repeated to me many times during my stay in Cameroon.

[41] Prefect, Département du Diamare, northern Cameroon, in an address to the merchants of Maroua and their political representatives, Maroua, April 15, 1993.

presented as the source of national wealth and, in turn, state power. He went on to insist on the idea that the very "freedom" of the citizen is contingent upon this transfer, a point that was constantly underscored by the regime at the time: "When these obligations are fulfilled, you will be free citizens. . . . In order to allow the state to tar the roads, build schools and hospitals, reimburse the whites . . . [it comes to] 46,000 CFA a year [per person]. At the end of the year, you will be a free citizen. That's not the case today in the diamare [department]."[42] Other representatives of the state reiterated the idea that the economic future and very survival of the region depended upon national unity. A representative of the mayor's office in Maroua claimed with respect to tax payment: "It's not a political problem; today, thank God, we all speak the same language. In Yaounde, they're demanding decentralization; what will we do to survive? Will we survive with cotton and a few groundnuts?"[43]

But a common language is not apparent. A complete monopoly over the interpretive domain is challenged now more than ever by competing vernaculars, which suggest alternative definitions of security, wealth, mobility, and protection. These, and the specter of large-scale violence and the *maquis* (the anticolonial guerrilla movement of the 1950s), haunt present-day understandings of what constitutes national (versus regional) wealth, the nature of citizenship as expressed through the fiscal relationship, and the problem of national unity. Claims to the right to regional sources of wealth were advanced alongside those to national wealth, and foreboding about the potential vindictive behavior of various, often regional, communities laced discussions about the antifiscal movement and democracy. During this time, references to the maquis abounded, evoking the fear and trauma associated with this violent moment, the specter of war, and recourse to "the bush," denoted as a political, as well as an economic, space.[44] In a play on such fears, one official remarked with regard to the northerners' refusal to pay taxes: "We're talking about the honor of the Department [*Diamare*],

---

[42] Ibid.

[43] High-level administrator, Commune Urbaine de Maroua, northern Cameroon, in an address to the merchants of Maroua and their political representatives, Maroua, April 15, 1993.

[44] Of all the territories colonized by the French, Cameroon provided the only instance of armed struggle for national self-determination. The assassination of the movement's leader, Ruben Um Nyobe, by the French precipitated the demise of the resistance movement. Despite long-standing censorship, the memory of Um Nyobe (especially his tragic death and improper burial) and the unfinished business of the nationalist movement were very much alive in Cameroon during the 1990s. Various aspects of these events have been recounted by Joseph 1997; Um Nyobe 1984, 1989; Mbembe 1986, 1989, 1996. This historical memory has deterred many Cameroonians from violent insubordination today (Mbembe and Roitman 1995: 350; and, with regard to the Anglophone secessionist movement, M. Goheen, personal communication, November 1995).

the [Northern] Province. The others [provinces] are going to learn; they're going to say, 'We paid, but we don't want our money to go there [Diamare] because they don't pay.' If one day someone from here becomes head of state, they are going to remember this. They'll go underground, into the bush [*le maquis*]; they'll say, 'They didn't pay [when our man was in power], now it's our turn."[45]

We should remember that the Biya regime has posited "peace" as opposed to wealth as prerequisite for change.[46] But many Cameroonians now regard wealth creation and accumulation as inherently linked to insubordination and even violent means of appropriation: witness the petrol sellers. They say that "democracy" means "anyone can sell." Petrol is *le feu public*. Like the watershed term *indépendance* that marked off the 1960s, during the 1990s *multipartisme*—whether or not associated with democratization—signified the potential to transgress seemingly stable boundaries. In the context of so-called incivisme fiscal, this has generally involved the articulation of claims to wealth regardless of means. Incivisme fiscal has meant questioning the nature of rights and has entailed claims to both integration into capitalist exchanges (the market) and modes of redistribution (the state), interrogations that cannot be abridged through oppositions between the state and society, or civil and uncivil practices.

Often, the latter are taken up uncritically by observers, who typically view the critique of state regulatory authority as a critique of the state itself.[47] From this point of view, the supposed state-society conflict is a crisis in legitimacy; and the African state is consequently depicted as a "failed" state. Such judgments arise out of binary thinking about power; that is, the incapacity to think ambivalence—the exercise of power can be detested and yet considered logical, normal or even justifiable—and simultaneity or contradiction as stable conditions. This manner of apprehending power precludes appreciation

[45] High-level administrator, Departement du Diamare, northern Cameroon, in an address to the merchants of Maroua and their political representatives, Maroua, April 15, 1993.

[46] "Democracy is threatened if peace is compromised." P. Biya, national televised address as the incumbent presidential candidate, CRTV, October 11, 1993. A Nigerian woman commented that the precedence put on "peace" implies living under the "calm" assured by a state of siege. This remark was made the day after the announcement of the hanging of nine Nigerians, including Ken Saro-Wiwa. Personal communication, November 10, 1995.

[47] Although this particular case has received limited commentary, similar social and political movements in Africa (and elsewhere) are typically interpreted in terms of the emergence of "civil society," thus replicating the state-society dichotomy. See, for example, Rothchild and Chazan 1988; Bratton 1989; World Bank 1989b; Carter Center of Emory University 1989; Hyden and Bratton 1992. For a critique, see Roitman 1990; Callaghy 1994; and especially Comaroff and Comaroff 1999. Such interpretations are often inspired by the work of Habermas (1989 [1962]) on the emergence of the "public sphere." For critical views of the latter, see Fraser 1991.

for the intimacy of domination[48] or, in a somewhat less enchanting turn of phrase, what Michel Foucault described as the process of subjectivization (*assujetissement*). This is the process by which subjects are "caught up in a power situation of which they are themselves the bearers," a seemingly powerless situation at the heart of the exercise of power. It involves the constitution of self-governing subjects, whose conduct of the self, or moral regulation, emerges out of the nonsubjective grounding of actions and pre-occupations in a positive body of knowledge.

This topic of the formation of self-governing individuals has been taken up in much social science writing that claims to elaborate "marginal histories," or marginalized forms of subjectivity, often signified by gender or ethnic markers, that emerge through disciplinary power. While it is true that Foucault's research on the institutionalization or normalization of particular bodies of knowledge and practice showed how marginal categories become defined as such—that is, as not the norm, as representing pathologies—such categories are not the objects of study per se (Foucault 1979a, 1990 [1978]). They are not assumed as empirical facts at the onset but rather emerge as historical artifacts. Ideally, such a method reveals how the organization of knowledge gives rise to certain rationalities and practices, which are considered normal in specific, historical situations. But it also demonstrates how the organization of forms of knowledge and rationality structures resistance, certain forms becoming possible while others are not.

Likewise, the widespread adoption of Foucault's elucidation of disciplinary techniques and the marginalization of certain categories of life has obscured, to some extent, his preoccupation with the effects of the language of political philosophy on conceptualizations of power, as well as the relational nature of power. It might now be worth salvaging his idea that the effects of power—and especially its materiality—*give rise to* the infrastructures of the state.[49] Here, "infrastructures" refers to points of the exercise of power that extend beyond the specific institutions of the state itself and yet are integral to state power (cf. Foucault 1979a: 219–224). The infrastructural powers of the state exceed the state as a unified and coherent entity, which does not mean that such forms of power are totalizing or unqualified, since, not being a structure, power is rather "the name that one attributes to a complex strategical situation in a particular society" (Foucault 1990 [1978]: 93).

[48] A wonderful expression coined by Mbembe 1992 in a reversal of the book title *La domination de l'intime*.

[49] This follows from the fact that subjectivization was elaborated by Foucault (1990 [1978], 1997) in part through a critique of the ever-present subject of the juridical sovereign in analyses and representations of power. Barry, Osborne, and Rose (1996) also argue that this aspect of Foucault's work has been slighted in the social sciences. These concerns will perhaps be addressed by the recent turn toward ethnographies of the state in both the United States and Europe (cf. Steinmetz 1999; Hibou 1999b; Das and Poole 2004).

States of power are constantly engendered at the multiple points of their exercise. Their effects are apprehended according to specific, historical codifications of the rationality of power (of which the state is one locus among others) such that power relations are modified, strengthened, and weakened *in their very exercise* (95, 97). Because techniques of power are inscribed in particular forms of rationality, they are not intelligible from an exterior vantage point or from a separate logical or cognitive position that "explains" them. Legitimacy and resistance do not issue from a critique formulated outside the bounds of power and the rationality of its exercise; they mark the points where the intelligibility of power situations is either legible and communicated or, to the contrary, illegible and incoherent (94 and 96; and see Barthes 1974; Hebdige 1979).

Being less hinged upon appraisals of state legitimacy, the myriad and heterogeneous questions raised by and in the Opération Villes Mortes campaign, or incivisme fiscal, involve judgments about the intelligibility of unprecedented socioeconomic relationships and the state's efforts to implicate itself in and produce new fields of power and economy. Just as the predominant representation of the hierarchy of social relations was obscured during colonization by the social mobility of freed slaves and access, especially for youth, to new sources of wealth associated with colonial markets and Western education, at independence colonial wealth was brought into a new hierarchy of power and became subject to alternative definitions of the appropriate uses of wealth (Azarya 1978; Bayart 1989; Mbembe 1996). Today, similar transformations are manifest insofar as certain social domains have become illegible to some due to the objectification of new forms of value and wealth. This latter process involves more than the establishment of monopolies over new forms of wealth, or even the mere forging of novel relationships that define networks of exchange and accumulation. It entails the normalization of particular definitions of licit wealth and manners of appropriating such wealth. In this sense, recent allusions to the maquis, or the retreat into the bush, are not only symptomatic of the fear of violence and the trauma of the unconsummated deaths of the nationalist movement that charge the winds wafting through cities, hamlets, and woods. They are also a manner of interpreting the encroachment of the bush over towns and what the Prefect referred to as "civilized" space, or the emergence of unprecedented power relations that challenge received wisdom about national unity and the integrity of national wealth. In order to better understand that process, it is useful to first trace out the historical transformation of forms of wealth and especially the determination of appropriate sources of wealth and targets of wealth for fiscal power, to which I now turn.

Chapter Three   *Tax-Price as a Technique*
of Government

I**N NORTHERN** Cameroon today, one speaks of tax (impôt) as a price. *C'est le conseil municipal qui fixe les prix*: "the municipal counsel fixes the prices,"[1] a municipal authority explained with respect to certain tax rates. Conversely, prices are referred to by the French verb *taxer*, which signifies both fixing a controlled price, or rate, and the fiscal act of taxing. *Il m'a trop taxé* means "he charged me too much"; *ils nous taxent trop* means "we pay too many taxes". And, generally speaking, a price is often expressed as a determination unto itself: one "buys" a price as opposed to a number or quantity of goods. That is, one does not buy three oranges, one buys "500-500"; instead of three kilograms, one asks for "1,500" (CFA). *Tu prends l'argent qui te convient*: "you take the money that suits you," not the quantity, they say, when describing purchasing decisions.

Is there a logic that might be summarized by the trio *impôt-taxer-prix* (tax–to tax–price)? If so, this concatenate movement might be said to follow from the concerted, simultaneous historical institutionalization of impôt and prix as an articulated whole. Impôt and prix combine—indeed, they are thoroughly mutually constituted—insofar as they form the means and the mode by which not money per se but French currency—or the monetary form of colonial extraction and domination—was institutionalized. The institutionalization of the head tax, or the impôt, during colonization necessitated the establishment of a particular concept of price. By assuming the latter as the normal and even most just way of determining equivalents and negotiating exchange, the colonized themselves imposed the sovereignty of the French monetary sign, which eventually, but not

[1] Representative of the mayor's office, Maroua, northern Cameroon, March 27, 1993.

48

entirely, exceeded alternative forms of monetary value and wealth in the region. Moreover, they became consumers of French money forms and hence procured the material means for tax payments to the French colonial administration. Although forced payment was the manner of appropriation at the onset of colonization, the injunction to pay tax ultimately took place without the whip, since the fiscal subject was produced out of the tax-price complex. The latter can thus be described as a technique of government, which rendered the objects of the economy governable with respect to a particular political rationality.[2]

Although my remarks provide implicit commentary on the generalized role of money as a mode of power, a compelling and immensely complex topic, I will not insist upon that theme, since it takes me somewhat beyond the scope of this book. In what follows, I would simply like to consider impôt-taxer-prix as a conceptual whole and an eminently historical artifact so as to highlight the effects of its historical objectification, for one, on the institution of the impôt itself (taxes, taxing, and fiscal power) and, second, on the problem of value, or modes of valuation. These themes are important to the extent that they presage, and partially respond to, the more imposing matters of historical techniques of government and the structuring of possible modes of resistance to regulatory authority.

The impôt is best summarized as the head tax. Its significance in northern Cameroonian history is fundamentally bound up in its relation to the principles of political organization that defined it as a primary technique of government.[3] In that sense, it is obviously the counterpart to prix, since, in order to implement and extract the impôt, colonial authorities had to first institute colonial currency as a means of payment in local economies. As a composite, tax-price (impôt-prix) was an essential technique of the organization of colonial space; the conversion of local economic wealth into, in this case, a European form for subsequent extraction; and the integration of local production and exchange into colonial monetary and financial circuits. This is not to say, of course, that currency did not exist and that pricing was not practiced prior to the colonial presence. The institutionalization of tax-price during colonization does not imply that local socioeconomic relations were concomitantly structured, and are to be apprehended, in terms of a cataclysmic "fall" into commerce. The self-limiting nature of the way

---

[2] Or the "means, mechanisms, and specific instruments which make possible forms of administration, power, and rule," such as systems of accounting and methods for organizing the workplace (Dean 1994: 187). See also Miller and Rose 1990; Rose and Miller 1992.

[3] Here I refer to l'impôt as a technique of government that nonetheless can also be described as a political technology, since, like price, it was part of a whole political-economic program for the institutionalization of fiscal relationships and fiscal practices (*fiscalité*). It was a technology that produced the materiality of the state, or the state effect. On these points, see Dean 1994: 187–89; see also Mitchell 1999.

I have formulated the questions I am asking about tax-price as a political technology works against, I hope, the idea of any necessary history, and certainly that which is associated with presuppositions about distinctions between monetary and nonmonetary economies, or barter and exchange. This is in keeping with the torrent of recent work that has contributed to the blurring and effacing of that distinction, not to mention the hurdling and sometimes toppling of the barricades separating the long-segregated realms of economic and cultural practice (Sahlins 1976; Bourdieu 1977, 1984; Chapman 1980; Hart 1982; Reddy 1984; Munn 1986; Appadurai 1986; Herrnstein-Smith 1988; Strathern 1988; Parry and Bloch 1989; Humphrey and Hugh-Jones 1992; Geschiere and Konings 1993; Bayart 1994). Without engaging fully in that debate (cf. Roitman 1995, 2000), suffice it to say that the quest for the determinants of the ontological status of money, or the attempt to discern what money "is," is not of concern here. The historical question of the objectification and "naturalization" of loci of standards and unity is, however. In that sense, what money signifies is a less pertinent question than how it signifies— or how it signified in this particular region of the Chad Basin.

Instituting French Colonial Currency: Manque d'argent, Mal d'argent

The valuation of goods and services in terms of French colonial currency was only effected to the extent that the imperative to produce and render the impôt was taken up by local people—that they became the bearers of its political rationale. As is well known, currencies existed prior to the arrival of European monetary forms, as did the practice of establishing equivalents relative to a particular standard of value (pricing). In northern Cameroon, local currencies included bars of iron and *gabbaks* (cloth bands). These objects served as currencies, as opposed to bartered items, to the extent that they were a means of exchange, a store of value, and a means of account (Polanyi, Arensberg, and Pearson 1957: 264–66; and see Rivallain 1986: 14–27, 50–56). Monetary forms that had regional currency or derived from international exchange included gold, glass beads, cowries from the Maldives, and Maria Theresa thalers coined in Austria and Spain. These also functioned as units of account, being set apart as standards of value with fixed rates (Johnson 1970; Fisher 1977: 284; Hogendorn and Johnson 1986; Rivallain 1986).[4] These objects often came to be *objets-monnaie* (money-objects), their

---

[4] The extensive literature on the other varied forms of currency in the region includes Kirk-Greene 1960; Mauny 1961; Gray and Birmingham 1970; Colvin 1971; Lovejoy 1978a, 1980, 1986. For interesting commentary on multiple-currency situations beyond the region, see Régis 1986; Guyer 1995: esp. 21–23; Ikejiuba 1995.

exchange values not necessarily taking precedence over their use values. Nevertheless, in situations where "several materials circulated simultaneously as money . . . only one or two of them could enter into all transactions and play the role of a unit of account. . . . These objects do not have to have distinctive signs. The choice of one over another is difficult to explain. . . . These money-objects are always integrated into other usages of everyday life: millet and salt for food, cloth for clothing, beads for adornment, reserve metals for instruments. . . . In commercial transactions, their presence is not requisite if one is dealing with other mutually exchangeable objects. But the price of these two latter objects is appreciated with respect to the monetary unit" (Rivallain 1986: 11).[5] Thus, in the sixteenth-century savanna and Sahel economies, a common monetary standard, based on the circulation of cowries and gold in tandem, is said to have permitted long-distance trade in a common monetary zone (Lovejoy 1985 [1971]: 669–70).[6] And the nineteenth-century Sokoto Caliphate, which spanned present-day northern Nigeria and northern Cameroon, has been described as "highly monetized, with a common currency based on cowries, gold, and silver coins" (Lovejoy 1978b: 348; see Lovejoy 1974).

Colonial currency, like many other imported currencies that entered these circuits, did not meet with much "monetary success" (*vogue monétaire*; Rivallain 1986: 68).[7] This is thought to have been the result of the inherent instabilities (e.g., inflation) associated with currencies that are not locally produced (e.g., cowries; Colvin 1971: 117; Guyer 1995; Law 1995: 53–73). The French franc did manage, nonetheless, to become the ultimate signifier of submission to colonial power—it was, as one colonial administrator put it, material proof: *la preuve matérielle*.[8] But the exigencies of domination were at first difficult to satisfy, since, at the outset, Cameroonians had no European currency to brandish, let alone relinquish. Therefore, initial appropriations were in kind and were often taken through force or seizure. The *tournées de répresssion* (repression rounds), or what local

[5] The point that the monetary unit figured in calculations of value regardless of its actual presence is quite interesting when considered in light of "nonpresentist" theories of power. This is simply a thought; it deserves, perhaps, more serious reflection.

[6] Gold was calculated according to the *mithqal* (4 to 5 grams), with a long-standing rate being 1,200 cowries to the mithqal (Lovejoy 1985 [1971]: 669). The cowrie-gold standard can be further researched in Johnson 1970.

[7] Rivallain (1986: 68) mentions the exception to this rule: Maria Theresa thalers, which were used extensively in Ethiopia from the nineteenth century on. Thalers were also used in northern Cameroon but were most typically hoarded, like cattle, by local emirs and used primarily for adornment by women. Today they are still imported for their quality as silver, being melted down for the fabrication of jewelry (Colvin 1971: 117; and see Law 1995).

[8] Mr. Lenoir, Chef de la Circonscription de Maroua, northern Cameroon, cited in Beauvilain 1989: 354. See also p. 347 for the diatribe on "cette idée de colonisation. Faire rentrer l'impôt [this idea of colonization. Bring in the tax]" pronounced by M. Leiris in 1932 (cf. Leiris 1981).

people called *tournées tornades* (tornado rounds), left hundreds of "victims of the head tax" and were often consummated by the taking of entire cattle herds, which were carted away, the hamlets being subsequently burned to the ground.[9] For the victims, these bursts of utterly destructive and consuming force, often attributed to nonhuman agency ("tornadoes"), surely had great resonance in historical memory: the imminent loss associated with the slaving-razzia experience was in some ways redramatized in the colonial relationship. Moreover, these "military operations" were qualified in terms of tribute (Beauvilain 1989: 360),[10] which was the former material effect of the slave states of the past.

Regardless of efforts to render Africans productive both in terms of agricultural labor and, even more, as sources of European monetary wealth, the actual, initial sources of wealth—or targets of power—were, as prior to the European presence, not simply productive labor (i.e., in the form of wages) but goods that the colonial authorities deemed conceptually equivalent ("private wealth") to the tax they were attempting to institute.[11] Thus entangled with the issue of inserting colonial currency into local circuits of exchange was the more elusive matter of instituting the idea of the colonial administration's right to a part of people's wealth and the one-to-one correspondence between the "head of the household" and the "household's wealth," something that was not self-evident, as the colonial archives show (see also Beauvilain 1989: 360), to the targets of fiscal power. What the French colonizers saw as *private* wealth—represented by the head of the family, certain material goods, and the head tax—was *likewise* construed as inherently *public*, being claimed by the French treasury as such. At the onset, the translation from private to public occurred through forced appropriation and seizure, but eventually the colonial authorities' command—"Here are our coins, please give them back to us"—took place through less repressive techniques.

The efficacy of this translation from private to public, or the institutionalization of the colonial right to wealth and the measure of the efficacy of colonial power (the impôt), was not simply neatly gauged in terms of the positivity of stocks of coinage. It was also appraised in terms of its negation,

[9] The archives are replete with such scenarios, as is local historical memory. The matter is well covered by Beauvilain 1989: 316–48.

[10] Beauvilain cites the colonial administrator, Capitaine Petit, Chef de la Circonscription de Maroua in 1920.

[11] Undeniably, this included people insofar as extraction took the form of forced labor. But, building roads aside, agricultural labor was initially not a significant locus of extraction. Later, when such labor was oriented toward the production of export crops and, ultimately, the insertion of local economies into—or extroversion toward—the European monetary sphere, the aim continued to be extraction of monetary value in the form of tax. This is gleaned from the archives, which are cited later. For commentary, cf. Azarya 1978: 81, 85.

its denial, or what the French authorities called *le refus d'argent* (the refusal of money) and *le refus d'impôt* (the refusal of tax). What, in 1924, was castigated by colonial authorities as the northern Cameroonians' "vivid repugnance for these monetary signs" (*vive répugnance pour ces signes monétaires*)[12] buoyed the adage "subjugate first" (*il faut soumettre d'abord*).[13] That sums up, in fact, the double-edged nature of the problem of inserting French currency into local circuits of exchange in order to intersect, reorient, and extrovert local logics of circulation and surplus creation. That is, the refus d'argent was a denial of both the currency form (the sovereign) and the logics of the transformation from private to public, or even the very conception of wealth as currency (versus cattle) or as French coins.

However, the colonizers first thought it was symptomatic of the environment: naturally, locals refused bills, which were subject to termites and fires. This led to the depreciation of French notes relative to the signs of previous and neighboring colonial powers, the German mark and the British shilling, respectively. The antidote to soft French money and the energies of the Cameroonian habitat was the solidity of coinage, which replaced certain paper notes in 1924.[14] Yet natural conditions were evidently not the only element that seemed inhospitable. What French colonial authorities lamented as the very rarity of money (*la rareté d'argent*) was also often cited as a fundamental problem: "The circulation of coins immediately raised the price of bills on the local market. The bill that was worth, three months ago, about 3 marks is now worth 4 marks 90 [50? illegible]. It seems that shortly the local people will finally accept paper money for its value. Under the condition, of course, that money continues to circulate *without becoming scarce*."[15]

What was the nature of that scarcity? Why would coinage rarefy despite its capacity to stun termites and the abounding resources of the French treasury? Strangely, the scarcity of the French sovereign seemed to be a product of abundance. That is, there being no lack of alternative sources and signs of value in the region, the preponderance of French coins—and regulatory authority—was being constantly drained. Although they cannot

---

[12] Arrêté promulguant au Cameroun le Décret du 20 janvier 1924, *Journal Officiel*, April 15, 1924, 183–84.

[13] Rapport Annuel 1919, Circonscription de Maroua, p. 7, Archives nationales de Yaounde (hereafter ANY) APA 12032.

[14] This involved paper notes of 2 francs, 1 franc, and 50 centimes value. Cf. Décret du 20 janvier 1924 autorisant le Commissaire de la République au Cameroun à faire frapper et à emettre des jetons métalliques de 2 francs, 1 francs et 50 centimes dans les territoires du Cameroun placés sous mandat de la France, referred to in Arrêté promulguant au Cameroun le Décret du 20 janvier 1924, *Journal Officiel*, April 15, 1924, 183–84.

[15] Rapport Annuel, Circonscription de Maroua, Situation de l'encaisse de l'agence spéciale au 30 Novembre 1921, n.p., emphasis in original, ANY/APA 12032.

all be reviewed here, cattle, for one, was a long-standing and trustworthy source of value for local communities (Dupire 1962; Stenning 1959; Dumas-Champion 1983; Vincent 1991). It was accumulated as wealth; essential to marriage payments, rites of initiation, and religious ceremonies; the basis of family genealogies and alliances; and a major item of exchange. Even French colonial administrators wished to ensure that every family had at least one cow or a pair of cattle in order to decrease "absolute poverty."[16] No doubt, though, possession of this supposed equivalent to "private wealth" would also increase people's ability to pay their taxes, which might involve giving over those very cattle. Ensuring that all household heads had a minimum number of cattle was also supposed to mean more francs for tax payments, since the ordinary tendency to convert currency into cattle supposedly would be averted.

The economic situation in 1934 reveals dashed hopes, however, regarding such a scenario:

> *The predominant fact is the lack of money. Transactions take place using currency only on the biggest markets, even though they, too, meet with great difficulties. It is not that there is less merchandise for sale, but the buyers are slack. The result is both decreased prices and lack of sale. The harvest was good last year, but the product hardly sells. The condition of cattle has ameliorated, but prices are ten times less than they were a few years ago. All of this does not help the collection of taxes, which remains very difficult despite the efforts of the chiefs, which I witnessed. The collection of taxes in cash is extremely diminished and almost all payments are made in kind, cattle, cloth, grains. Even though this procedure could facilitate flight, it makes [our] payment into the public treasury late since [their] payments in kind have to be converted into currency. To do that, the entire region must go to the market at Mindif, the others [markets] not permitting the disposal of products rendered for lack of money. I had the experience myself during my trip to Midschiwin, where I was able to collect almost 3,000 francs in taxes, only a third of which was in cash, the totality being almost entirely constituted of bands of gabbak which can only be disposed of at Mindif or Maroua. Cattle is given reluctantly, and only when other resources have been sapped.[17]*

The rarity of money is stated here as a problem of valuation with respect to certain kinds of material goods. Thesaurization—or the capitalization of savings—in captives, slaves, gabbaks, iron bars, metal hoes, and cattle is a

---

[16] Rapport Semestriel 1933, 1er semestre, Circonscription de Maroua, p. 18, ANY/APA 11834/L.

[17] M. Leger, Administrateur-Adjoint au Chef de Circonscription et Chef de Subdivision de Maroua, Rapport sur la tournée effectuée du 18 avril au 17 mai 1934, p. 7, ANY/APA 11855/B.

well-known strategy for assuring the stability of value (and thus clarifies the role, described earlier, of certain of these objects as referents in price setting).[18] What the colonizers soon dubbed "the affliction of money" (*le mal d'argent*) was attributed, despite the logics of thesaurization, to a lack of material goods that could be monetized. Meetings between colonial administrators and villagers are replete with instigations to "find things to sell": "We met with the inhabitants [of Marfaî] and encouraged them firmly to give over the totality of the taxes, emphasizing that they can get money by selling skins, foodstuffs, by making wax"[19] and "At Lara and Kilguim we came to an understanding about the variety of ways the natives have to pay their taxes: fabricating wax, selling skins, cotton, millet, cattle."[20] Cotton and groundnuts are singled out as definitive sources of money.[21] But the circularity of the problem of material goods (or, depending on perspective, the affliction of money) becomes apparent once locals are empowered to purchase: when the people of Mada and Podogo make considerable gains from groundnut production, they transform it into cattle.[22]

Concretizing wealth in cattle meant fewer francs in circulation within the contours of colonial Cameroon, since cattle were mostly obtained from outside French colonial frontiers. More important, though, it signified a certain register of value or referred to a whole regime of truth about wealth and well-being. Hence with respect to the imagined (and specifically French) category of "the peasantry," one administrator remarked: "The needs of this social category are not based on the amelioration of subsistence but rather on goods susceptible of attracting the consideration of others or, amongst certain pagans, which permit them to marry or marry their sons. For example, for the Fulani, the wealthiest and most respected peasant is not he who feeds himself well, but he who has the most cattle, clothes of the finest cloth, numerous servants."[23] It is not surprising that the French authorities were astonished to find a community that did not evaluate wealth and

---

[18] This is reviewed briefly by Beauvilain (1989: 415). The special case of cattle—being precarious with respect to value due to vulnerability to disease and drought while, at the same time, serving as a central item of exchange and accumulation to the point of being nicknamed the "piggybank" in northern Cameroon—is nonetheless part of the social logics and cultural histories of various local groups.

[19] M. Bartoli, Chef de la Circonscription de Maroua, Rapport de tournée du 12 au 23 septembre 1933, p. 1, ANY/APA 11834/B.

[20] M. Bartoli, Chef de la Circonscription de Maroua, Rapport de tournée du 4 au 13 décembre 1933, ANY/APA 11834/B.

[21] Cf., for example, M. Leger, Administrateur-Adjoint au Chef de Circonscription et Chef de Subdivision de Maroua, Rapport sur la tournée effectuée du 18 avril au 17 mai 1934, 30 mai 1934, ANY/APA 11855/B.

[22] B. Lembezat, Adjoint au Chef de la Région du Nord, Rapport de la tournée effectuée dans la Subdivision de Mora du 18 mars au 2 avril 1947, p. 72, ANY/APA 10418/A.

[23] Rapport Annuel, Région de Diamare, 1951, n.p., ANY/APA 11618.

respect in terms of a *regime alimentaire*, or food. But, more seriously, since the colonial idea of a tax on surplus wealth depended on accumulation of currency, it also depended on particular notions of "profit," which led to the colonial administration's complaint that, for northern Cameroonian merchants, "profit is what remains *after* the purchase of items of consumption or clothing for themselves and their family."[24] That is, seemingly superfluous purchases are made with money that is not represented as profit from work. Tax would have to come out of that postconsumption residue of wealth. The colonizers' reference to a lack of money (*manque d'argent*) seems, then, to be more likely a lack of tax (*manque d'impôt*), since some forms of consumption and investment were clearly still taking place, albeit on a different scale of value.

Objectifying "price" as an appropriate site of regulation obviously involved problematizing value beyond the question of supply and demand, since habits of valuation were also to be governed—again, a matter of eliminating, or rendering illogical or irrelevant, contending sources of value. One of those was discerned by a colonial administrator: "In this country, the price of all commodities is, absolutely and uniquely, a function of millet. When millet is abundant, everything sells cheaply and 'money is expensive,' as the indigenous expression goes. If the harvest is average? Prices are normal. And if the harvest is short, all prices increase beyond measure. The value of money drops at once, to the point where it is no longer used in transactions . . . the buyer pays with millet."[25] However, qualifying millet as an "absolute" or "unique" referent belies colonists' efforts to divert strategies of thesaurization; they evidently recognized that cattle, a preeminent form of wealth and a sign of distinction, also served as a historical benchmark of value,[26] as did gabbaks, metal bars, and so forth.

Generally speaking, prices (and taxes) were apprehended in terms of an ensemble of locally produced goods (millet, groundnuts, cotton, cattle).[27]

---

[24] Ibid., my emphasis.

[25] Rapport Annuel, Circonscription de Garoua, 1928, ANY/APA 10027, cited in Beauvilain 1989: 464.

[26] Its role with respect to prices is noted extensively. Cf., for example, Rapport Annuel, Région du Nord Cameroun, 1948, p. 69, ANY/APA 11618.

[27] This is argued and demonstrated most forcefully by Beauvilain (1989: 464–65). It is still the case today. One of the specificities of the value of money (and hence prices and taxes) in the region of northern Cameroon is that its determinants (e.g., millet) are especially subject to the temperaments of an unforgiving and dramatic climate. Because, in local practice, prices and l'impôt have been evaluated and expressed in terms of an ensemble of agricultural products, variations are "considerable, differing from one year to another, and even from one month to another, to the rhythm, for the African producer, of 'expensive money' to money 'that's worth nothing,' even though the economic relationship is the inverse" (Beauvilain 1989: 464; and refer to the tables on p. 465). Acute collapses in market prices are as often the

This is in keeping with historical modes of pricing, such as the gold-cowrie standard noted previously. Furthermore, it is reminiscent of the practice of "assortment" bargaining, which produces the effect of apparent price stability. According to this method, which was practiced by both European and African traders, the "price" attributed to any one kind of European import was unchanging while adjustments were made in the assortment of goods bought and sold (Curtin 1984: 59).[28] Initially, the total value for the export goods (expressed in local currency) was established by the parties involved. The move to bring local currency as the value referent in relation to European values was made by determining the assortment of goods received as payment. At this point, "supply and demand entered . . . bargaining about [the] assortment of goods taken in payment, *not* about price per unit" (Curtin 1984: 59, my emphasis, who refers to Johnson 1976; cf. Curtin 1975: 233–70). Hence historical modes of apprehending "price" were not incommensurate with a situation in which different types of currency all having the same denomination circulated simultaneously and were operational as parts of an articulated whole. This was the combinatory, kaleidoscopic field in which colonial authority attempted to instill the sign of the sovereign as the determining hue or standard referent.[29]

The French colonial administration also attributed the manque d'argent and the mal d'argent to commercial languor (*carence commerciale*),[30] a surprising thing to note in this historical hub of exchange, which derived its dynamic from long-distance trade and circulation. The eventual development of easily monetized goods, such as groundnuts, led to a significant increase in purchasing power in French francs. But it also contributed to a dramatic increase in the cost of living. Thus it was said that "commerce is in no way developed," and prices increase by 100 percent, accounting, then, for the "lack of bustle" among buyers.[31] But the increase in prices was the effect of yet another, alternative source of value for local operators: the ster-

---

result of the tax moment (*le moment d'impôt*), when the quest for coin commences, as an overabundance of millet.

[28] Through this method, European traders attempted to rid themselves of items with low European prices, while African traders sought to obtain articles with both high African and low European values. This method of pricing is well known for having created the impression of the existence of price controls or "marketless" trade in eighteenth-century West Africa. Thus the existence of a state monopoly over the slave trade was posited in Polanyi (with Rotstein) 1966. Misinterpretation of the practice and erroneous assertions about state monopoly are addressed in Manning 1982.

[29] See Avis de l'Institut d'émission de l'AEF et du Cameroun pour la mise en circulation des nouvelles coupures de 5, 10, 20 et 100 francs, 1957, ANY/2AC 7218.

[30] Rapport Annuel, Région du Nord-Cameroun, 1949, p. 110, ANY/APA 11721.

[31] Ibid.

ling zone. The prognosis of endemic commercial lassitude in the northern region of the country belies the following description, in 1942, of exchange and evasion:

> *The motives of this exodus are economic. Not only, as Mr. Granier has observed, is the arable land better in the British territory, but there are also some very big markets scattered along the whole length of the frontier, the principal ones being Ouro Boki, Kinda-Guirma and Sorao, where numerous transactions take place.*

> *This year, the great majority of the peanut production of Demsa [Cameroon] was sold on these [Nigerian] markets where the prices were much better than at Garoua [Cameroon] and where, moreover, the natives found a great quantity of merchandise in exchange for their products. Also, they are amongst themselves, and much more at ease than at Garoua, where they meet up with guards, goumiers, tirailleurs, customs officials, and other agents of the administration, indispensable as they are, but whom the natives, for various reasons, try at all costs to avoid.[32]*

The stagnation and "isolation" of northern Cameroon are the product, then, of intense activity across the border: "The inhabitants of the region of the North [of Cameroon] completely ignore the South [of Cameroon] and look increasingly toward Nigeria, where they can sell their cattle and buy imported manufactures."[33] As recognized by the colonial administration at the time, this transborder—or noncolonial—orientation was in part the consequence of the French monopoly over the purchase of export crop production and the wholesale of imports.[34] As stated, though, it was equally inspired by the presence of *goumiers* (a supplementary military formation recruited by the French in Morocco during the first half of the twentieth century) and *tirailleurs* (soldiers recruited in the French overseas territories to serve as infantry) in Cameroonian marketplaces. The borders and the bush remained spaces in which the repressive figures of regulatory authority had not yet cast their shadows. Here, one could conceivably refute claims to the supposedly inherent correlation between French currency and tax.

Doubtless, profitable producer prices, troves of cheap merchandise, and minimal harassment all motivated Cameroonians to do business in the bush. But reactive behavior to supply and demand, prices, or monetary exactions does not explain why, in the early 1920s, when the Société Centre

---

[32] Letter accompanying the Rapport de tournée du Chef de la Subdivision de Garoua, ANY/Vt 17/202/V, cited in Beauvilain 1989: 487–88.

[33] Rapport Annuel, Région du Nord Cameroun, 1945, p. 6, ANY/APA 11618.

[34] Cf. the letter accompanying the Rapport de tournée du Chef de la Subdivision de Garoua, ANY/Vt 17/202/V, cited in Beauvilain 1989: 487–8; and Rapport Annuel 1949, p. 96, on the role of R. W. King.

Afrique offered .50 francs for cotton, Cameroonian producers opted for the .25 francs paid out on the local markets. It seems they estimated the .50-franc payment in paper money to be of less value than the .25-franc payment in coin (Beauvilain 1989: 458). This decision was a response to the nature of the regional monetary regime in which they traded, as well as the ways in which the monies that constituted that regime were apprehended. For one, this was a context in which "variations in prices are due more to the decisions of buyers than to the evolution of the world market toward which the products are drained since—and this is the specificity of the north of Cameroon in the French colonial world—exterior exchanges are essentially oriented toward the sterling zone" (459).[35]

The many efforts to undermine the sterling zone as a definitive locus of exchange included the 1939–40 formal abolition of the local currency exchange market, which essentially involved the British sterling pound and French franc.[36] But the flight of French capital into northern Nigeria was vertiginous enough even subsequent to the interdiction that the authorities then deemed all passage to Nigeria by Europeans and Cameroonians without official authorization to carry a specified amount of French currency a criminal offense.[37] This traffic was in fact cited as a cause of the rise in certain local prices (e.g., cattle, which were exported to Nigeria), and it was said to have undermined the guarantee of stability ostensibly ensured by French monetary policy.[38]

Pretenses to monetary stability were impaired further by the import via Nigeria of French monies that were no longer official currency. Bills considered by the authorities as not having any legitimate value were thus reintroduced into circuits of exchange, provoking the suspension of confidence in the continuity of value similar to that incited by the sudden withdrawal from circulation of, for instance, the German mark and earlier

---

[35] Beauvilain (1989: 459–60) explores the economic reasons for this orientation, emphasizing the role of monopolies on export purchases. My understanding of this is much indebted to his expertly documented examples of the determinants of the value of French colonial currency in northern Cameroon, even though our preoccupations are of a different order. On the regime of accumulation defined by the regions of Cameroon and Nigeria, see also Roupsard 1987.

[36] The trade in currencies was officially abolished in the terms set forth by the decrees of September 19, 1939 (cf. *Journal Officiel Cameroun*, 1939, p. 917) and May 20, 1940 (cf. *Journal Officiel Cameroun*, 1940, p. 510); see also the confidential letter from the Gouverneur du Cameroun Français au Chef de la Région de Ngaoundere, 26 novembre 1945, ANY/2AC 6374.

[37] Refer to the confidential letter from the Gouverneur des Colonies to the Chef de la Région de l'Adamaoua, 13 juin 1945, ANY/2AC 6374; see also the letter concerning the problem of itinerant traders and cattle herders with respect to the export of French currency from the Chef de la Subdivision de Banyo to the Chef de la Région de l'Adamaoua, 1 août 1945, ANY/2AC 6374.

[38] Cf. letter from the Gouverneur du Cameroun Français au Chef de la Région de Ngaoundere, 26 novembre 1945, ANY/2AC 6374; letter from the Chef de la Région de l'Adamaoua to the Gouverneur du Cameroun Français, 10 janvier 1946, ANY/2AC/6374; and Beauvilain 1989: 460.

59

forms of French money (including bills supposedly dumped by the Vichy government, which some local traders called, in good satirical form, "billets de Gaulle").[39]

In the end, persistent declines in the relative value of the franc did not spur purchases in northern Cameroon itself, as might be expected. Therefore, the colonial administration's remonstrance about the lack of material goods was more precisely an objection to the fact that goods were not being monetized via the French franc—or that Cameroonians had not become consumers of the French sovereign.

Consumer Protection: The Enlightened Consumer, or Taxpayer

I have argued that tax-price was a technique of government that exemplified the materialization of colonial power in its fiscal form. One of its effects was to turn Cameroonians into consumers of French currency, an incontrovertible sign of colonial power. This presupposed the translation of a particular idea of private wealth (profits from work evaluated in French currency) into public wealth, which, in turn, was predicated on the granting of the French authorities' right to a part of people's riches. In that sense, this translation turned upon a definition of the private subject as a consumer of a particular kind of wealth in a regional political economy of heterogeneous value forms. The tax-price complex produced this private subject as consumer, which, in the end, was the political subjectivity of the taxpayer.

Given the existence of myriad coexisting signs of value, one of the specificities of northern Cameroon and the Chad Basin is the situation in which several forms of currency (e.g., gabbaks, cowries, cattle, thalers, marks, shillings, francs) circulate, and are referred to, simultaneously. This poses the seemingly novel matter of the value of different forms of one and the same money: various coins of different denomination, paper versus

[39] The French and British colonial authorities accused the Vichy government of "dumping" bills issued by the Banque de l'Afrique Occidentale, which circulated in abundance alongside shillings issued by the West African Currency Board. According to these officials, the Vichy government sought to depreciate currency issued by Afrique Française Libre (Free French Africa). Cf. Confidential Circulaire No. 283/CF from the Gouverneur du Cameroun Français to the Chefs de Régions de la Frontière Cameroun-Nigeria, 5 avril 1941, ANY/2AC 6376; Confidential Circulaire No. 379/CF from the Gouverneur du Cameroun Français to the Chef de la Région de l'Adamaoua, 10 mai 1941, ANY/2AC 6376; Confidential Circulaire No. 1379/CE from the Gouverneur du Cameroun Français, 11 mars 1942, ANY/2AC 6376; Confidential Circulaire No. 1580/CS, from the Gouverneur du Cameroun Français, 7 avril 1942, ANY/2AC 6374; Confidential Circulaire No. 815 bis from Chef de la Région de la Benoué to the Chef de la Région de l'Adamaoua, 15 octobre 1942.

coin. As noted earlier, the local people's initial "repugnance" for French currency was a condemnation of its bondage to taxes. It was also the expression of an affiliation for the sturdiness of silver marks over shabby paper francs (not to mention the former's brilliant contribution to adornment). But when the French authorities expelled the magnetic mark from circuits of exchange (through concerted collection), the value of, for instance, the 5-franc note did not find its just worth: "The face value of a 5 franc note was now only determined with respect to the 1 franc coin. Thus, in the third trimester of 1925, this bill was only worth 3 or 3.5 francs in coin. Here, again, the explanation is quite simple. It resides in the great success of metal coins, and in particular in that of the 1 franc piece which, having the same form and appearance as the new Nigerian shilling, circulates in this country on parity with the shilling even though the official exchange rate of the shilling is . . . 5 francs" (Beauvilain 1989: 457, summarizing colonial trimesterial reports).[40]

In 1926, according to archival sources quoted by Beauvilain, the 5-franc note was worth 2.5 francs with two 1-franc coins and one .5-franc coin *or* it was worth 3 francs in .5-franc coins. In 1937, a silver 5-franc coin was worth 12 francs in metal *jetons* (tokens) or 28 Nigerian kobos; but 5 francs in jetons were worth 10 kobos.[41] Evidently, the problem of value could not be consigned simply to the impuissance of paper. This was reiterated in 1951 in a letter to the colonial director of finances: "The Chief Administrator of the Region of Margui-Wandala complains that the cellars of the offices at Mokolo and Mora are glutted with metal money; money for which he has no use, the natives not wanting it anymore."[42] The administrator importunes that there is no use recirculating this money, "once so appreciated for its incombustible properties," since it will just be returned with the next tax collection.[43] Oddly, in this instance, the Cameroonians' wholehearted rendering of taxes was not embraced, since, according to the colonial authorities, it was inspired by the enigmatic "refusal of money" and the resurgence of the problem of value. For one, regardless of its enduring substance, the colonial authorities' analysis concluded that this money did not represent sufficient purchasing power.[44] The cost of living in the postwar economy had increased dramatically, with prices doubling. Small coinage fell into

---

[40] The ellipses at the end of the statement are his own.

[41] Citing Carras, Chef de la Région Chari, Rapport de deux tournées en septembre et octobre 1937, ANY/APA 11833/E.

[42] Letter to le Directeur des Finances, Yaounde, from the Trésorier-Payeur du Cameroun, 18 juin 1951, ANY/1AC 5507. The problem is evidently particular to the North, since, it is noted, southern merchants render exact change "using matchboxes and envelopes."

[43] Letter to le Directeur des Finances, Yaounde, from M. Latour, Chef de la Région de Margui-Wandala, Mokolo, 2 juin 1951, ANY/1A C 5507.

[44] Ibid.

disfavor as the 5-franc piece became the coin of reference, and rounding up to 5 francs became standard practice.

The administration sought to counter this tendency toward rounding up, since it was factored in as a contributor to the rising cost of living. In so doing, the rather less material problem of "mentalities"—both African and European—was posed:

> *In a period where all means are mobilized to work in an effective manner on the issue of the cost of living, the attention of the Financial and Economic Services of the Territory is being directed especially toward the problem of the circulation of metallic money. The fact of rounding up to 5 francs, for lack of divisionary coinage, results, for merchandise and objects of small value, in a significant increase in the theoretical selling price. One wonders, however, if a measure such as an increase in the amount of coins in circulation would have a sure effect on the cost of living for reasons having to do with the intervening psychological factor, that being the disfavor of the user. It would be most interesting if one could put an end to this state of affairs by modifying the manner of seeing the population.*[45]

A memorandum[46] requesting local officials to poll their communities to determine the reasons underlying Cameroonians' "disaffection" for metallic money obtained reactions such as the following: the money "represents only a weak purchasing power with respect to a quite heavy load"; furthermore, "we risk making errors with all these different models of coinage." The administrator of the region noted that what people really feared was that they would find themselves in possession of money that had been suddenly withdrawn from circulation, and hence having no value, "the quality and density of the coinage apparently play[ing] no psychological role."[47] Another response described similar reticence with regard to 1- and 2-franc coins: they are cumbersome given the high prices of goods and, moreover, "users no longer have confidence in a currency that has been taken out of

---

[45] G. Carlander, Direction des Affaires Économiques et du Plan, Service des Affaires Économiques à Tous Chefs de Région, 7 janvier 1955, ANY/1AC 7552. In the 1940s, devaluation of the French currency with respect to foreign currency (and not the metropolitan franc vis-à-vis the Cameroonian franc CFA) led to debate over anti-inflationary measures. This is gleaned from archival correspondance; cf., for example, Circulaire No. 481cf, le Haut Commissaire de la République Française au Cameroun à Tous Chef de Région, mars 1948, ANY/2AC 6377.

[46] Circulaire 500/CF/AE/DLA du 5 janvier 1955, referred to in the confidential note of G. Carlander, Chef du Service des Affaires Économiques to le Chef de la Région de l'Adamaoua, 1 mars 1955, ANY/2AC 6377.

[47] Letter from Granier, sous couvert du Chef de la Région de l'Adamaoua au Directeur des Affaires Économiques et du Plan Service des Affaires Économiques, le 17 janvier 1955. Arguments put forth by—or on behalf of—southerners are quite different; cf. Réponse du Chef de la Région Nyong et Sanaga, 14 mars 1955, ANY/1AC 7552.

circulation numerous times and which is [hence] seen as unstable."[48] No doubt, the history of successive waves of conquest by Berber, Tuareg, Mandara, Kotoko, Fulbe-Hausa, German, and French movements and the imposition of their attendant hierarchies of value in northern Cameroon certainly give credence to such sensibilities of uncertainty.

The 5-franc piece became a symbol of the law of the sovereign to the point where the high commissioner of the French Republic of Cameroon implored, "Effective action on prices can only be usefully engaged by the recirculation of 1- and 2-franc coins, which are presently disdained. Such a result presupposes a reminder to the merchant of the obligation to calculate prices to the nearest franc, and not by multiples of five, and to make change; a reminder to the Public Treasuries that 1- and 2-franc coins are still legal tender and must be accepted and returned in payment."[49]

Here the efficacy of colonial monetary power was reduced to a question of Cameroonian accounting techniques. Cattle (and perhaps cowries) are traditionally counted in units of five (*jungo*: a hand). Prices are often expressed in terms of *sunku*, which is a set of five if one counts the units involved according to the cardinal system of counting; thus sunku often refers to 5 francs, and *sunku jowi* (*jowi*: five) signifies 25 francs. In any case, for the colonial authorities, the problem of the *refus d'argent* was reformulated—and seemingly depoliticized—as a matter of pricing policy. One might wonder, in that regard, just what the "theoretical selling price" referred to previously by one of the chief directors of economic affairs might be.[50] Evidently, it was being (hypothetically) overshot by the practice of rounding up. But anguish over how to convince northern Cameroonians to produce material goods and, more important, to monetize them in francs was calmed by the rearticulation of the problem of the procurement of the impôt in terms of purchasing power. At this point, price and pricing were brought into the fold of the political technology of taxation as a means of rendering local people consumers of French francs. However, this did not imply a purely instrumental endeavor, or the application of pricing policy with the explicit intent to produce consumers and taxpayers. In the application of this policy, local people took up its political rationale themselves in their assumption of what was represented as logical economic action *for themselves*: consumer protection.[51]

[48] R. Crus, confidential letter to the Haut Commissaire de la République au Cameroun, 29 mars 1957, ANY/2AC 6377.

[49] Tirant, le Haut Commissaire de la République Française au Cameroun au Délégués à Douala et Garoua et Chefs de Région, 5 mars 1957, p. 1.

[50] See note 46.

[51] With more time and another grant, it would be interesting to trace the emergence of the idea of "consumer protection" in France so that debates about its uses and applications, as well as its role in social welfare, could be highlighted here.

It seems, then, that the materiality of Cameroonian subsistence (e.g., millet, cattle) had been dislocated by a more ephemeral target of regulation: price. And a new persona materialized out of that move: the consumer, who stood in as the link between l'impôt and price, being both the source of the former and the presumed cause of the latter's instability. The consumer was thus constituted as complementary to price, emerging as a new target of regulation—the lead part, then, in the enactment of *la politique des prix*, or the colonial administration's new pricing policy. That role can be gleaned from statements elucidating the politique des prix, which are worth quoting at length because of this policy's lasting effects on the contemporary history of regulation and the objectification of impôt-taxer-prix in northern Cameroon:

> *The continuous rise in the cost of living and the corresponding reduction of the purchasing power of consumers have rendered necessary the implementation of coherent and efficient policy with respect to prices* [la politique des prix]. . . . *(It seems . . . preferable to limit the objectives of this policy of price decreases to a restrained number of staples, avoiding at all costs the imposition of burdens on trade and useless hindrances. . . . As thus conceived, the control of prices simply reinforces and, if needed, supplements the regulatory action of competition. . . . [O]nly the prices of flour, salt, rice, vehicles, foreign-made refrigerators, motor fuel and lubricants [will be] subject to control. . . . [However], attention must . . . be given to the price of foodstuffs produced locally because . . . the prices of some of these goods are often higher in Cameroon than anywhere else on the African coast, without any justification for such disparities. Instructions have thus been given to the [colonial] chiefs of the regions to establish new market price lists and to determine the normal selling prices of foodstuffs. . . . The first price lists will soon be homologated and, with much publicity and vigilant control, it will be possible to register price decreases in the food sector. . . . The control of prices will naturally have an impact on [distribution], but it must be adopted so as not to engender scarcity of certain goods and clandestine commercial networks. To the contrary, it has been proposed . . . that we create true standardized stores in the big centers, where retail of a limited number of goods, all of first necessity, will take place according to the most just price. Selling prices will be calculated according to normal profit margins so as to obtain an indisputable reference of value.*[52]

[52] "Note relative à la Politique des Prix," Direction des Affaires Économiques et du Plan, 1953, p. 3, ANY/3AC 3040. The legal basis for this policy is stated as the Decree of March 14, 1944 and Ordinance No. 549 of March 6, 1954, both relating to the matter of establishing price controls.

According to the author of this memo, price controls were construed as protection, which hinged on the formulation of price not simply as corresponding to a set amount of wealth (1 cattle = x francs) or as a manner of expressing equivalents but as appropriate behavior, a method of evaluation that would lead to "the just price." The latter, to which I will return in the next chapter, could only be ascertained by eradicating alternative (unjust? in any case, "irrational") techniques, such as rounding up, bargaining, and instituting "normal profit margins," or margins that would ensure procurement of sufficient French money for tax.

Again, according to the author of the memo on instituting price controls, the "just price" and "normal profit margins" required an indisputable reference of value. Absolutely. But absolute value means the annihilation of alternative sources of value, which presupposes the capacity to render them illegitimate or unthinkable. And like absolute power, which might emanate only from the enlightened sovereign, absolute value can be fathomed only by the enlightened consumer:

> *The opening of such stores—in a very small number in order not to harm honest retailers—would contribute to a large extent to the education of the consumer, because he, through his negligence and bad habits, is often the principal cause of the rise in the cost of living. It has been noted frequently that the consumer does not try to compare prices practiced in different boutiques, but goes to the first boutique he comes upon. Also, there is a steadfast idea that the higher the price, the better quality the product; some merchants attest to this experience, having found that they were no longer selling a particular product when they reduced its sale price, and the simple fact of raising it back up provoked clients' demand. There is a psychological factor here which is difficult to fight against and which discourages serious merchants. It seems, then, that one of the main arms in the struggle against the high cost of living [la vie chère] must be the education of the consumer, victim of his own habits.*[53]

To be sure, colonial regulation of prices was more than an attempt to control the rising cost of living "to the detriment of consumers" who could not come up with tax payments. It was also a response to the historical traces of another mode of computation, which rendered certain signs of the sovereign ineffectual. The issuance of 5-, 10-, and 25-franc coins in order to inspire the usage of 1- and 2-franc coins (which "fill the coffers of the public treasury") involved interventions to prohibit the systematic rounding up to the nearest 5 or 10 francs. Administrators were to "establish prices to the nearest franc" and "make the population understand the advantages of this

---

[53] Ibid.

new mode of computation."[54] The task of educating consumers and merchants as to normal profit margins—or legitimate prices—was a matter of asserting "an indisputable reference of value." But since value is always produced from within a relative system, the pedagogical exercise became that of disciplining those other, alternative sources of value. The politique des prix was just such a modus operandi. It defined and constituted both price and the consumer as primary targets of regulation in response to the refus d'argent and the refus d'impôt and, in the last instance, in the face of alternative modes of valuation.

Tax as Price

Given the agenda of the politique des prix, it is not surprising that, today, sale price is often signified by the verb to tax (*taxer*) and that, when purchasing, one "buys a price." As I have pointed out, the politique des prix established and homologated prices for certain goods; it applied measures to induce merchants and especially consumers to evaluate goods according to certain standards and coinage; and it objectified prices as a target of regulation, problematizing them in terms of the combined matters of the cost of living, the circulation and accumulation of currency, and the means to render the impôt. The institutionalization of French colonial currency—of which the contempory franc CFA is an extension—as the materialization and mode of actualizing the impôt rendered it a necessary means of exchange and definitive signifier of the fiscal relationship. However, attempts to avoid its extractive power and the instability inherent in its articulation with the logics of the regional and international economies subverted its potential as a store of value, since the latter was substantiated via thesaurization in more stable forms of value (e.g., metal bars, merchandise), historical signs of wealth and prestige (e.g., cattle, cloth), and more fungible currencies of the regional economy (e.g., shillings). The first transactions in French colonial currency were thus essentially limited in terms of action and signification to tax payments and the procurement of the means to pay taxes. Tax was figured as a price.[55] Ultimately, price signified tax, since it was what allowed for the translation from private wealth to public wealth—in French francs.

---

[54] Mise en circulation des monnaies divisionnaires 1958, Lettre circulaire No. 1479/AE, ANY/2AC 7215.

[55] On this sort of "détournement" as an effect of the ambiguity of l'impôt and its historical practice according to the logics of *échange-don* (gift exchange) in the Sahel, see Nicholas 1986: esp. 91ff. He argues that this encouraged the emergence of sites of power that were subversive to the prior system. With regard to such logics and strategies of minimizing census counts in northern Cameroon, see Beauvilain 1989: 483.

Today, the idea and act of "buying a price that suits you" (*qui te convient*) is largely a reflection of the combined effects of the institutionalization of this form of currency as the preeminent signifier of the impôt, the institutionalization of price as the handmaiden of tax, and its representation in the politique des prix as something that is "normally" stable. Like tax, which was to be handed over to the authorities, price was a thing that emerged out of a whole set of precepts regarding its immutability and constancy. But the ideal of stability and the immutable quality of price, perceived as an economic object, was contradicted by experiences of the colonial form of monetary value, or the French franc itself. French colonial currency was inscribed in a social field and was marked by the commodity forms that preceded it. These included, as we have seen, diverse materializations of the money form (millet, beads, cowries, metal bars, cloth, cattle), as well as the generalized field of differentiated monetary signs, which included North African currencies, the abiding German mark, and the versatile British pound. The French franc's imposition as a universal form of exchange or referent that would potentially supersede all others entailed, in part, the abnegation of its value as substance in favor of its conceptualization as an equivalent to all other commodities or, more simply, goods. Because it was not gauged in terms of, for example, a stock of gold, a swath of territory, or the materiality of local production, the ultimate assurance of its value was the overdetermination of the French political guarantee (Vallée 1989: 53–59). Like other imported currencies (e.g., cowries, thalers; cf. Colvin 1971: 116), the colonial franc represented a potential source of instability and uncertainty that, with few means of control, local parties could only seek to avoid.

Following from that, the contemporary franc CFA "is not recognized or experienced as a credit or part of a credence [*la créance*], but only as an extension of a bill of exchange [*la traite*], the mode of transaction, the method of spatial exchange surviving from the installation of the state in the heart of the financial system" (Vallée 1989: 50). Long-standing practices of thesaurization prevail, as they do in all places, with cattle, sheep, cloth, jewelry, enamelware, automobiles, and general merchandise enduring as stores of value (Ekejiuba 1995; Dupré 1995; van Santen 1993; Zelizer 1997).[56] I was told, "The people in the village don't want to hold on to money." In all

---

[56] A woman twice married explained the logic of the avoidance of money as follows: "At Mayo Louti my husband gave 1,000 CFA as dowry and kola nuts, without cattle, without sheep, and four bolts of cloth plus shoes and pots. And here, in Gazawa, the dowry was three bolts of cloth and 500 CFA—because . . . my father was a marabout, and he said that he did not want to take money for the dowry, and if someone gave cloth I could take it, but money, you shouldn't take it. He said, if the man asks for his money back [in case of divorce], what would he pay with? And if he [father] is no longer living and the man wants his money back, what would I pay with? No matter the man I marry, I don't take money. And since I have been married, I haven't had any problems." Daada Haman, Gazawa, Cameroon, April 29, 1993.

67

households, I confronted accumulations of cheap wares from Nigeria and broken or unusable articles such as cars and transistor radios.

While the destabilization of, and quest for, sources of wealth in northern Cameroon is a point for further consideration, suffice it to say for now that the localization and very creation of those sources is bound up in the extroverted nature of the colonial money form (Vallée 1989) and its introversion in local circuits of redistribution and exchange (Geschiere 1994; Guyer 1995). In the region, the inextricable historical association between money and tax, and tax and price—or what I have depicted as their conflation—has persisted and yet been modified by local institutions and power relations. The institutionalization of the franc-impôt complex in one punctuated moment posed the problem of localizing appropriate sites of extraction and circumscribing value equivalents, which eventually resulted in the objectification of price as a relevant target of regulation. This manner of problematizing the matter of fiscal targets and, ultimately, fiscal relations has structured the way in which questions about regulatory authority and practice are asked today. Tax-price is still enunciated as an integral category, but, as we will see in the next chapter, its terms are inherently unstable, as they were during colonization. Consumer protection still figures at the heart of fiscal interventions, even though claims to the right to wealth are not, today, articulated in the name of the consumer. Curiously, although these constructs have been assumed by Cameroonians—who paid the colonial head tax (elderly men often dragged me into their homes, where they produced packets of old head tax stubs as points of pride)—the colonial maxim, "subjugate first," prevails.

During the last decade of colonization, regulation of the official price regime came under, among others, the jurisdiction of the Surveillance and General Security sections of the administration.[57] The Economic Police (Police Economique) are the forebears of today's militant Price and Consumer Protection Brigade. Thus the consequences of the articulation of the impôt as a problem of price and (with efforts at so-called consumer protection, or tax collection) a matter of security, are manifest in the present-day "selling" of tax coupons in northern Cameroon. Today, "descending on site" (*descendre sur le terrain*) is the expression used to signify tax collection. One civil servant told me that his agents "sell [tax coupons] . . . we wait to see what they got."[58] A remittance is then given to the tax collector–salesmen, since "it's a way of compensating them. We calculate the remittance on what they got in receipts, on the turnover. If you sell, you take back . . . it's a way of motivating them. In that way, they'll have a higher turnover."[59]

[57] Arrêté No. 5515, Yaounde, 10 November 1953, Article 2, ANY/3AC3038.
[58] Civil servant, Maroua, northern Cameroon, March 27, 1992.
[59] Ibid.

Of course, the question of variable turnover seems misplaced, since a census and a fixed number of stalls in the marketplace should imply fixed returns on tax. However, if tax is a price, variability is perhaps a relevant question. Both tax and price are something one buys, and there is much semantic slippage between taxing and pricing. The effects of the historical concurrence of tax and price are such that the Department of Prices, Weights and Measures (Service des Prix, des Poids et Mesures) conceives of its work in terms of maximizing receipts as opposed to controlling infractions. The two are linked, of course, with payment of infractions being the source of administrative receipts. However, while verification of price markups, and industrial and commercial instruments of measure is what I imagined to be the raison d'être of this bureaucracy, efforts to "realize its program" were quite forwardly stated as the "increase of receipts."[60] Ironically, the *elimination* of price controls that followed from application of the economic liberalization program in 1989 (mandated by the Structural Adjustment Program)[61] resulted in an even more prominent role for the Brigade of Prices, Weights and Measures and the National Gendarmerie. As expected, the bureaucracy's revenues sharply declined subsequent to price liberalization. This incited a vicious turf war between the Department of Prices, Weights and Measures and the Brigade of Prices, Weights and Measures, which required the intervention of the Ministry of Industrial and Commercial Development.[62] But recourse to "forced recovery" (*le recouvrement forcé*) reversed the trend toward bureaucratic impoverishment. The Provincial Service's 1992–93 report notes that from 60 to 80 percent of its receipts were collected with the assistance of the Brigade of Prices, Weights and Measures and the National Gendarmerie. This led to an increase in receipts from

[60] "*L'augmentation des recettes.*" This is put forth in correspondence between the Service Provincial des Prix, Poids et Mesures and the Délégation Departemental du Developpement Industriel et Commercial de L'Extrême Nord, as well as correspondence between those provincial administrations and their superiors in the national instances of those same bureaucracies in Yaounde.

[61] This was legislated on July 28, 1989 with Law 89/011. Goods still subject to homologation include grain and ground corn, and fresh or refrigerated meat, according to Arrêté 001/MINDIC/DPPM/SDP, January 22, 1990.

[62] Declines in revenues are described in Chef de Brigade des Prix, des Poids et Mesure, "Situation des recettes, exercice 1989/90" [confid.]. The bureaucratic turf war is detailed in Circulaire No. 044/MINDIC/CAB/CT1, October 11, 1988 [confid.]. This was—and still is—essentially a struggle over control of small retailers and itinerant traders, who make up the great majority of economic actors in the region, with most large-scale commercial entreprises run by northerners being based in the South (in Douala). The service, which is largely limited to regulation of commercial and industrial entreprises *in the region*, went so far as to obstruct the logistical support of the brigade, which has jurisdiction over local small-scale traders. The brigade responded to these tactics with many appeals, complaining, in response to seizure of the brigade's allocation of toilet paper, that this struggle had become antics more appropriate to a hospital [No. 05/L/MINDIC/SG/DPEN/DDD/BPPM/MRA, February 2, 1989].

115,000 CFA (1991–92) to 667,000 CFA (1992–93).[63] In fact, amounts collected by the Provincial Service itself were practically unchanged over the span of these two years (2,041,000 CFA to 2,072,000 CFA, respectively). However, amounts collected by the brigade in the city of Maroua for this same period registered a stunning change from 245,000 CFA to 1,945,000 CFA; in Yagoua they increased from 5,000 CFA to 532,000 CFA.[64] According to the Provincial Service, recourse to the police and repressive forces (*les forces de l'ordre*) for the collection of fees and especially fines was necessitated by the *culte de l'esprit d'incivisme,* or the "cult of uncivic spirit."

But the recouvrement forcé is not only a response to the cult of incivisme; it is also a method of governing, which derives its logic from the construct of tax as price.[65] The suspension of price controls hypothetically eradicated a large part of the material base of this administrative instance. But since prices have been institutionalized as a particular, historical target of regulation, price controls and the taxing of price persist, today, as a structuring political rationality. That rationality is figured with respect to what has historically been deemed problematic for governing: rounding up, bargaining, discussions, and speculation. Thus price controls, although formally terminated, have resurfaced in the name of the "failure to publicize prices"[66] precisely, although perhaps not only, because consumer protection has been construed as the principal mediation between private and public wealth. Initially, officialdom conceded that liberalization (mistakenly and tellingly noted in one document as "*déliberalisation*") means the end of price as a target of regulation. This was acknowledged as having consequences for tax "receipts," which were described as perhaps not "the end in itself" of price control. Nevertheless, they were said to be a measure of the "propensity" of the Brigade of Prices, Weights and Measures to now reprimand the failure to post prices (an infraction that the administration

[63] Correspondence relative to Rapport Annuel 1992/1993 of the Provincial Service des Prix, des Poids et Mesures, Extrême Nord, Cameroon.

[64] From "Tableau comparatif des recettes entre l'exercice 1992/1993 et l'exercice 1991/1992," in correspondence concerning Rapport Annuel 1992/1993 of the Provincial Service des Prix, des Poids et Mesures, Extrême Nord, Cameroon.

[65] Therefore, while the move to repressive means might be interpreted simply as a maneuver by an agency seeking to maintain itself, the point here is to seriously consider that the unintended consequences of structural adjustment programs have, in themselves, subsequent consequences. That is, not only has the historical institutionalization of "tax" and "price" implied very particular understandings of those notions, but the contemporary situation (as part of the genealogy of tax and price) likewise structures people's understandings of tax and price, as well as "liberalization." Today, tax and price continue to be figured according to the problematic of law and order; people respond to, and act upon, these concepts as political constructs as much as economic imperatives.

[66] Correspondence concerning Rapport Annuel 1992/1993 of the Provincial Service des Prix, des Poids et Mesures, Extrême Nord, Cameroon.

depicted, nonsensically, as "staring one in the face").[67] In the end, the legal injunction to post prices was brought back into the fold of maximizing tax receipts through its interpretation within the historical problematic of prices—and speculation—as a target of intervention. This is so generalized that, at the start of each school year, booksellers in the market are typically fined for "price speculation," having raised the prices of books in accordance with the increase in demand. The brigade argues, to the contrary, that their increase in supplies means that prices should drop, since "the politics of supply [are] superior to that of demand,"[68] a policy rationale that is construed ultimately as "consumer protection."[69]

Evidently, transformations supposedly prompted by economic liberalization and structural adjustment programs are in certain cases domesticated by institutional imperatives. The politics of supply and demand and the publicity of prices hark back to the historical objectification of "that which is to be governed." Today, the administration of prices is part of a disciplinary apparatus. Governing prices is postulated not only as "useful to the services of law and order"[70] but also as a method of facilitating, but not naturalizing, the putative forces of supply and demand. The desired effect is "to orient the decision of producers (suppliers or merchants) . . . and consumers"[71] The state has thus engaged in the seemingly contradictory project, in strict neoclassical economic terms, of "ensuring the best conditions for competition" by setting prices. Above all, this initiative is presented as an effective means to "install social justice" and encourage the beguiled consumer. An official document explains, "In fact, the varying price of goods often perplexes the consumer, who stands before a delicate decision. Many questions are presented that are summarized by doubt as to the quality of the merchandise, its provenance, quantity, and so forth—so many points that render most consumers indecisive. And in the end, the choices become difficult and sometimes interest in the thing dissipates."[72]

"Price" is still governed according to the discourse of consumer protection, which was theorized as linked to the elimination of local accounting techniques, or rounding up. The colonial authorities' efforts to establish the

[67] Chef de Brigade des Prix, des Poids et Mesure, "Situation des recettes, exercice 1989/90" [confid.].

[68] Chef de Brigade des Prix, "Contrôle tarif voyageurs et librairies," 1 octobre 1992 [No. 115/CR/MINDIC/SG/DPEN/DDD/BPPM/MRA—confid.]; Chef de Brigade des Prix, des Poids et Mesures, "Contrôle tarif voyageurs, gares routières et librairies," 4 decembre 1992 [No. 146/L/MINDIC/SG/DPEN/DDD/BPPM/MRA—confid.].

[69] Chef de Brigade des Prix, des Poids et Mesures, "Contrôle tarif voyageurs, gares routières et librairies," 4 decembre 1992 [No. 146/L/MINDIC/SG/DPEN/DDD/BPPM/MRA—confid.].

[70] This phrase, and pricing policy for the 1980s, is set forth in Enoh 1979: 1.

[71] Ibid., 3–4.

[72] Ibid., 3.

"just price" as a measure against the high cost of living (allegedly due to inflationary tendencies associated with the franc and habits of rounding up) and a means to ensure the production of surpluses in currency for tax payments supposedly required the elimination of negotiation in exchange. Then, as now, negotiation, discussion, bargaining, and rounding up have been construed as problematic for economic justice: "Finally, it is certain that people with low revenues will revert back to the discussion of prices, if they have the material means to tender the exact amount. The merchant will surely look unfavorably upon the return to the coin which, when absent, justified the rounding of prices to his benefit. But the big merchants can be made to toe the line. As for the others, we must hope that they will submit to the law of discussion with their clients. It is up to the latter to defend themselves and obtain the most just price."[73] The issue of justice and prices is posed at the level of bargaining. The stubborn "habits of valuation" (bargaining, rounding up, speculation) that induced "repugnance" for the colonial monetary sign have been equally righteous as to judgments about the truth of price today. The aggressive targeting of "price publicity" in lieu of price stability is a representational shift—because a manner of determining the truth of price—that conforms, nonetheless, to historical definitions of tax and price, or to the conflation between taxing and pricing. The truth of price in northern Cameroon and the problem of "the law of discussion" are taken up in the next chapter. Since I would like to consider how price, as a technique of government, is integral to both redistribution and regulation, or the constitution of relations of inequality, I take up this question of the truth of prices and pricing techniques through the lens of the subject of debt.

[73] R. Crus, confidential letter to the Haut-Commissaire de la République au Cameroun, 29 mars 1957, ANY/2AC 6377.

Chapter Four   *Unsanctioned Wealth, or*

the Productivity of Debt

Je lance dans le monde un livre qui va
trouver bien des résistences. *Eh quoi!* vont s'écrier la foule de petits esprits, *prétendez-vous ériger en profession avouée, en profession honorable, l'art affreu, l'art exécrable de faire des dettes, et l'art bien plus exécrable encore de ne point les payer?* . . . Eh bien!
petits esprits, cerveaux étroits, vues courtes, apprenez que *l'art de faire des dettes* et de
ne point les payer est l'un des éléments de l'ordre social.
                           —Jacques-Gilbert Ymbert, *L'Art de faire*
                              des dettes

When Is It Debt? When Is It Wealth?

Until now, I have been largely concerned with wealth: principally, the ways it has been figured as a monetary form within a particular regime of truth about regulatory relations, fiscal power, tax, and price. At this point, a conversation about debt might seem odd, since debt seems to be the flip side of wealth—that is, not having enough. And yet I would like to consider the ways in which debt is plenitude and not simply lack. Perhaps, as was suggested to me during my stay in northern Cameroon, economic debt is not just the constraint of society, the rubber stamp of a certain social status: being liable, a liability. Evidently, if debt can be described as a social relation, indebtedness involves a certain sociability: as we know, the gift is a debt (Mauss 1950; Derrida 1991). However, the simple affirmation of the social constitution of debt relations and debt itself runs the risk of a functionalist trap. Merely pointing out the social constitution of debt and debt relations in a given context is tantamount to declaring its functional nature in human society. Inspired by those I lived with in the Chad Basin, I prefer to explore how debt can be a mode of either affirming or denying sociability. In that spirit, I ask a series of questions: What is the difference between debt that disturbs and what one might call socially sanctioned debt? How is it that some forms of wealth are socially sanctioned in spite of their origins in debt relations whereas others are denounced quite flatly as "debt," being portrayed as a negative economic indicator, a disruption in the order of production and exchange? And in what contexts does debt mark out not negative space in the social imaginary but rather a critical and perhaps strategic stance related to claims to new forms of wealth?

73

Ultimately, these questions are oriented toward the matter of the productive nature of debt and debt relations, as opposed to their significance as merely owing. They are inspired by the situation in Cameroon today, and in Africa more generally, that forces us to ask how debt and liability square with productivity. As has been demonstrated elsewhere (Bayart 1989; Vallée 1989, 1999), debt relations are instrumental in the construction of an "extroverted" political economy. Debt is an essential mediation between the state and the global economy: an important resource for political and economic agents, debt establishes the credits that are new rents for redistribution in the national economy and for the management of internal conflict. Debt thus generates both economic and political rents, or resources and wealth that derive from commercial, political, and financial relations as opposed to agricultural or industrial production. Debt-seeking, like rent-seeking, is an economic and political strategy.

And yet, beyond instrumentalist tactics, the productivity of debt can also be understood in terms of a primary relation that puts debtor-creditor relations at the very base of social relations more generally, and hence at the heart of productive associations. This means positing debt as a fundamental social fact, as *already there*. In the social sciences, debt is most often construed as an economic or juridical category. When debt is apprehended as a social phenomenon—social debt—it is still most often construed as something contracted, exterior to a primary, original situation. Debt happens to someone or to some people, but it does not constitute them; it is, then, a perversion or deviation in human relations—an abnormal situation that needs to be rectified.

Since the "return" to Marcel Mauss in anthropological circles during the 1980s, the idea that debt is constituted through "the gift" (*le don*) has been reiterated and refined so that debt relations are now often depicted as constituting social relations through gift exchange.[1] For the most part, however, the productive power of debt is still denied its ontological status, since debt occurs through exchange and is not apprehended as an autonomous, effective power in the very constitution of human activity. In an attempt to reinstate the philosophical status of debt, Nathalie Sarthou-Lajus (1997) develops this argument, exploring the ways in which debt is the founding mark of social relations. For her, debt is inherent to the original situation of dependency in which subjectivity arises; it cannot be reduced to a problem of exchange. Following Nietzche over Mauss, she asserts: "The debt regime

---

[1] The return to Mauss in both Francophone and Anglophone literatures was inspired by the critique of utilitarian readings of economic life. See, most notably, the work completed by the Mouvement Anti-utilitariste dans les Sciences Sociales (MAUSS) in *La revue du MAUSS* and their edited volume, *Ce que donner veut dire: Don et intérêt* (1993). See also, among many others, Weiner 1976, 1992; Appadurai 1986b; Nicolas 1986; Strathern 1988; Humphrey and Hugh-Jones 1992; Godelier 1996.

renews our understanding of social relations insofar as it brings forth the structure of dependence that underpins such relations. Debt is in fact at the origin of a fundamentally asymmetrical social relation, which breaks with the logic of parity in exchange" (Sarthou-Lajus 1997: 2). The truth of the subject's condition is found, then, in this original state of dependence. And the ontological status of debt is recognized as the constitution of the subject in its relations with different figures of alterity (37). This is not, however, an argument for the reinstatement of the ontological status of debt that would ignore or deny its historicity. To the contrary, it calls for an understanding of the very constitution of the "truth" of debt as a particular condition in human relations, as inherent to the constitution of certain forms of subjectivity, and hence as a historical phenomenon. Inspired by Lévinas, Sarthou-Lajus notes, "Debt forces us to apprehend the other and time together, as a fundamental relationship to alterity, which deprives the subject of its foundational pretensions" (72).[2] The mediation between the ontological status of debt and the sociology of debt is, then, a matter of history, or the production of truths about the history of debt and indebtedness.

This approach implies that debt is productive of something and that the productivity of debt is not necessarily revealed in those moments when disorder confronts order. Debt breaks with the logic of exchange not because it subverts it but because it induces deferred exchange, or intervals of time, which reorganize such relations through the multiplication of possibilities (Sarthou-Lajus 1997: 18). *Not opposition, but diversion* of appropriate paths and modalities of exchange (Appadurai 1986a: 26), debt represents a moment when particular truths about social relations are revealed. This is the lens through which I would like to view certain economic institutions and practices in northern Cameroon today. Here, as elsewhere, there are many ways of instituting debt relations. Likewise, the state of indebtedness has become generalized, giving rise, most ironically, to modes of wealth creation based on debt relations. As Olivier Vallée (1999: 50) comments, "The external debts of African states have become one of the most critical dimensions of their economic and social crises over the last twenty years. But, at the same time, their integration into a globalized economy . . . has taken place largely under the banner of debt management."

Vallée describes this process of integration via mechanisms for the exchange of debt, or the emergence of debt markets that dominated international financial markets during the 1980s (the Baker and Brady Plans).[3] This

---

[2] The subject of time, as deferred exchange, is rarely commented upon with respect to debt. A notable exception is Derrida 1987 and 1991, who posits that the gift is a gift only if it is forgotten. On credit as a historical event and the instability of time and value, cf. Rey 2002.

[3] James Baker, the former U.S. secretary of state, was behind the initiative that established a list of middle-income countries, which were said to be of high strategic interest due to their

system, which is still crucial to African political economies—what Vallée calls "political economies of debt"—is based on the conversion of debt into investment credits, funds for development projects, stock options in newly privatized companies (electricity, telephone), rights to natural resources (gas and oil), and promissory notes that become objects of speculation and exchange. Such conversions—or the selling of debt—involve value transformations, or the reformulation of distinctions between public wealth and the private domain, that have allowed strapped public treasuries to access hard currency and, more typically, have ensured the enrichment of public personalities, who have placed such currency in offshore accounts and bought into, via their rights constituted in debt, recently privatized companies. Public debt has been converted into private wealth, making the state of liability a resource in itself. Thus the power of lending agencies, or the Bretton Woods institutions, to direct practices regarding debt reduction and to induce a novel discursive domain relating to indebtedness is largely mitigated (Hibou 2000). The displacement of public debt to the private sphere has neither dispossessed state agents from their margins of maneuver over local political economies nor altered their strategies of accumulation and redistribution, underscoring the point that debt is constituted in social relations and is not simply a product of unequal exchange.

This point is confirmed by the experience of the citizens of these states, whose capacities have been affected by these processes in particular ways since, as Vallée suggests, the notion of a guarantee has been modified with the transformation of public goods (debt, natural resources) into items of private exchange. The idea of an ultimate guarantor, such as the state or the central bank with respect to national debt, is no longer evident, since there is now a proliferation of sites of indebtedness that serve particular interests—public debt being the source of private fortunes. In that context, many exploit this ambiguity in the status of the guarantee, creating wealth out of liability and often attempting to invert the logics of debt relations and indebtedness through alternative economic practices and acts of theft and banditry.

However, wealth produced in this realm of economic activity—which includes transactions in arms, drugs, currencies, and stolen goods that flow through regional and transnational markets—is often not sanctioned as legitimate because it is generated through relations that most often escape official regulatory authority as well as recognized circuits of redistribution. Beyond creating new forms of economic value, those who participate in unregulated economic activities and theft or pillaging endeavor to exploit or rectify the situation of liability that pervades their lives. They articulate

---

very high levels of debt outstanding with commercial banks. In 1989, Nicholas Brady put forth an official program for "voluntary debt reduction," which would absorb these debts through market mechanisms.

claims to social mobility and incorporation, expressing a critical stance vis-à-vis what have heretofore been construed as the most legitimate ways of accumulating and redistributing wealth. These people are at the center of the debates that drove the incivisme fiscal movement. Typically portrayed as marginal elements by most locals, this category of people is often described as "predatory." They join those in the marketplace who are condemned for their unorthodox economic practices and subversion of what locals refer to as "market confidence" (*narral*).[4] These people are said to destabilize the market and even the local economy, since they come from "the outside" or "the bush" to prey on established merchants, ignoring customary economic practices and resisting long-standing modalities for ensuring authority relations and social redistribution. According to this view, the wealth acquired by recent entrants into the marketplace, like that amassed by those who plunder, is unsanctioned wealth, or wealth that contrasts representations of ideal economic practice and legitimate modes of redistribution.

The following pages demonstrate this point by first examining pricing mechanisms utilized in the markets of northern Cameroon. As in many other parts of the world, such pricing systems are a means of accounting for social obligations in exchange (Alexander and Alexander 1999). They are inextricably linked to a theory of value that generates concepts of "true" prices and "just" economic practice. In exploring these concepts, I argue that pricing, when seen through debt creation, and as I pointed out earlier with respect to the monetary form, is a mode of regulating society. However, as conflict in the marketplace and incivisme fiscal indicate, that form of regulation is now destabilized in Cameroon, where there is much strife over representations of just prices, market confidence, and redistribution. This conflict is often described, quite correctly, as the intensification of struggles over the pursuit of wealth that has ensued with the contraction of the local economy and the generalization of austerity. However, this depiction is insufficient: these struggles bring into question the significance, or very intelligibility, of economic concepts; they are not limited to economic competition but also refer to representations of the economy, economic practices, and social relations.

Today's struggle is largely about the problem of pinpointing stable sources of wealth. And this quest for the immutable foundations of wealth is taking place in a context where, over the last decades, the wealth of the

---

[4] In Fulani, *narral*, which was described to me as "confidence in the market," has little to do with the spirit that moves Western markets and especially Wall Street. However, while local references to narral are in no way influenced by the present-day preoccupation with market confidence in the West, the two notions are similar insofar as they both, independently, refer to that which drives exchange and the possibility for future exchange.

nation has been constructed out of a specific mode of national redistribution. As Jean-François Bayart (1979, 1989) has shown, since independence, the ongoing work of Cameroonian national unity has taken place through the constant management and incorporation of regional economic networks and a potentially autonomous economic class that might harbor a political threat.[5] In step with the colonial obsession with territorial integrity and the lurking menace of an independence movement, the postcolonial regime has also sought to harness the power of regional politico-economic networks through the (unequal) distribution of political positions (e.g., administrative, parastatal) that are primary sites of accumulation. This has resulted in a rentier apparatus that articulates with the national public sector as well as exterior resources. The nature of those resources is for the most part determined by Cameroon's membership in the Banque des États d'Afrique Centrale (BEAC) and the larger umbrella of the French franc zone, the guarantor of the franc CFA. This means that the CFA instigates particular modes of wealth creation and capital accumulation (cf. Vallée 1989: 62–76).[6] Unlike non–franc zone African currencies, the assurance of the franc CFA's universality and international standing—via the French franc—endows it with political value that is largely unhinged from its financial value. While some might argue that this value differential is typical of all currencies (Taussig 1997: 129–45; Aglietta and Orléan 1998)—since their financial values are mostly or ultimately determined by political and symbolic considerations—the specificity of the CFA is that its political value has induced strategies of debt creation that are extremely reliant on external financing. The guarantee of the franc CFA does not ensure solvency, but it does assure debt, which has become, as Olivier Vallée (1989: 62–76) puts it, the "signature of the Republic"—being no doubt French as much as it is Cameroonian!

Thus Cameroonians could easily describe the last two decades as the "ascension to debt" not only because the state survives almost entirely on international and bilateral debt but also because liability has become a mode of rationality (Mbembe and Roitman 1995). Attempts to subvert—or invert—that now generalized social and political relationship are most evident in the recent eruption of acts of pillage, seizure, and banditry. But what does it mean to seize in a context where liability is a prevailing principle of social

---

[5] The potential for the emergence of an economic class with a certain degree of autonomy from state-produced circuits of wealth was held to be most likely in the western provinces. Today, the Northwest and Southwest provinces are at the heart of the opposition, which includes a secessionist movement in the Anglophone (Northwest) region.

[6] Vallée shows how the management of money that does not issue directly from a centralized state guarantor produces a specific type of dominant class. For a critique of the "real" quality of the CFA and its role in preserving and promoting French interests, cf. Tchundjang Pouemi 1980; Nkuété 1980.

relations? As a means of reclaiming lost fortunes, enacting retribution, or diverting wealth, these acts of seizure seek, quite paradoxically, to restore loss through obliteration or dispossession. Through violence and forced alienation, they interrogate the very relations of dependence and indebtedness that found wealth and the productive relations of the community. They raise the specter of the impossible: as moments of diversion, or value subversion, they both utterly confound and generate novel instances of truth about power over wealth.

To address the topic of wealth, or debt as unsanctioned wealth, I present herein the complaints of many traders and merchants in northern Cameroon. When discussing the state of the economy and the political crisis of the state with me, these men consistently referred to the problem of "unsanctioned wealth."[7] That is, they deplored the supposedly recent emergence of what they described as wealth that escapes structures of authority. To them, unsanctioned wealth involves accumulation that is not authorized by the prevailing socioeconomic hierarchy, or both official and unofficial instances of regulation—be they at the state level, such as fiscal regulation, or at the local level, such as professional associations. When reflecting on their comments and observing the marketplace, I hesitated to claim a subversive quality for unsanctioned wealth in spite of its ominous tones. To learn more about this unsanctioned wealth, I inquired into the nature of sanctioned economic relations and economic categories, hoping to see how unsanctioned wealth diverted from the norm. I thus turned again to what seems to be the most objective of economic categories: price.

The Truth of Price

In northern Cameroon, people rarely say that a given item has a price. Instead of referring to an object purchased for a specific sum, they say that they "bought a price." It is, as I noted earlier, as if "price" is a thing. This has to do with the way in which price was institutionalized along with tax as a representation of a particular form of value that was posited, in a certain sense, as an item of consumption. Following from this, and surely in consonance with long-standing local practice, the stated price of a cup (*une tasse*) of millet, for example, is a constant; changes in value are registered and conveyed by sudden, leaping changes in established volumes. This is the general rule for almost all goods bought and sold in the market. The price of a tasse is unchanging, as is the price of a *tas* (a pile of goods). For instance, a tas of tomatoes always equals 5 francs. However, the number of items (or the

---

[7] For lack of space, I do not quote my interlocutors at length. See Roitman 1996 for their detailed opinions.

volume) included in a tas increases or diminishes as indicative of changes in value: three tomatoes for 5 francs; seven tomatoes for 5 francs, and so forth. One says, "I bought 2,000," which conveys more information than "I bought two tomatoes," the latter statement being potentially impossible depending on the given volume of a tas and due to the indivisible nature of a tas.

The validity, or legitimacy, of any one price is indicated by the term *gaskiiya*, the Hausa word for truth. Gaskiiya refers to a "real" or "exact" price. It is uttered when parties have come to an agreement upon a price or when one wants to insist on the only price that is acceptable. Sometimes, when one claims to be *taxé* (taxed), this means that one has paid for an item beyond gaskiiya. Regardless of the administration's price lists and homologation, and despite the existence of a kilogram system of measurement and evaluation that was instituted by the French administration, bargaining and negotiation take place among exchangees such that *le prix qui te convient*—the price that suits you—is established. Gaskiiya is thus best described as a social price that is determined in the bargaining process by factoring in various criteria pertaining to the consumer (age, race, gender, status, income), the nature of the relationship between exchangees (generation, kin, status, strangers), and the reason for sale or purchase (profit, hardship, marriage, funerals). A minimum, legitimate markup is part of this determination; on a head of cattle, for example, it is generally understood to be 5,000 CFA.[8]

According to those involved, the method of bargaining to achieve gaskiiya is often deemed nonexclusive or "just," whereas, given that a kilogram equals 800 CFA whether one can afford it or not, the kilogram system is frequently viewed as exclusionary and restrictive.[9] Before the kilogram system was instituted during French colonization, "no matter how much money you brought, they gave you what you needed."[10] Indeed, these two modes of representing value (tas versus kilo) are considered differently according to disparate registers of rights and obligations inherent in certain economic transactions: for example, between Muslims, with respect to widowed, women or impoverished families, and so forth. This is especially true for the head of a family, or baaba saare, who, regardless of age and status, is a married man held responsible for the well-being of an extended family.[11] As

---

[8] In the process of negotiation, the seller often indicates and attempts to substantiate the price at which the item was procured in order to establish the right to a certain minimum profit. The standard 5,000 CFA markup on a head of cattle was ascertained in the cattle markets at Maroua, Bogo, Mindif, Gazawa, and Mbankara in Cameroon.

[9] One has recourse to 250 grams, of course, but that is not, generally speaking, how the problem has been posed by locals, since they confront the purchase in terms of "buying a price" and not a quantity.

[10] Interview, Maroua, Cameroon, February 10, 1993.

[11] Older men who are not married cannot make claims to the same sets of rights under the title *baaba saare*.

Saïdou, a young butcher in the local market, told me: "I prefer [the kilo-gram system] but, with all that, they bring money and they cannot pay a kilo. I'll take the money, but I prefer fixed prices. I'll give it to him at 400 CFA, but I don't want him to spend the night without eating—and if I see that he's a baaba saare . . . well."[12] Likewise, his colleague Ndjidda said, "I have a customer [baaba saare] who usually buys two kilos a day, but now he only takes one kilo at 500 CFA. If he comes one day with 300 CFA, I can make him a gift of 200 CFA from my pocket."[13] That the representation of price according to the tas is deem "fair" or "just," inspiring the obligatory gift, is in good part due to its accounting of social obligations inherent in exchange.

Since relations of dependency are factored into price determinations, debt is almost inevitably at the heart of exchange. The pricing system creates debt through advances and the accounting of social status, but it also arises out of the states of indebtedness that inhere in all social relations. This is clear in the case of the baaba saare, who becomes indebted through advances and yet receives credit as a result of his social position and responsibilities within the community. The very position of the baaba saare as a figure of authority in the community is in many ways constructed out of this play on depen-dency relations that establish indebtedness before any exchange transpires. As Michael Taussig (1987: 70) has remarked with respect to a very different context, "What makes a man a man? Debt."[14] In his study of the coercive arrangements underlying the Putumayo rubber trade, Taussig shows how labor was produced out of debt peonage, which was shrouded in a fiction of trade. Through constant advances of goods, both local Indians and white workers became indebted, becoming peons who were often sold not as peo-ple but as debt itself between the rubber traders (69). As in the Cameroon-ian market, where the appearance of exchange harbors the negotiation of debt, the Putumayo "slave" system depended on "the *appearance* of trade in which the debtor is neither slave nor wage laborer but a trader with an iron-clad obligation to pay back the advance" (65, emphasis in original). Not commodity fetishism, but rather debt fetishism characterized the discourse of colonizers and colonized in the debt-peonage system, which operated through "payments" that were conflated with "advances" such that paying up amounted to establishing an advance for future work, or indebtedness. Debt was a social relation, or a particular representation of such relations, that produced labor along the Putumayo.

---

[12] Maroua, northern Cameroon, May 23, 1992.

[13] Maroua, northern Cameroon, May 12, 1992.

[14] Becoming *un homme comme il faut* (a real man) is the topic of Ymbert's *L'art de faire des dettes* (1999 [1825]) cited in the epigraph to this chapter. I am indebted to Béatrice Hibou for the gift of this book.

Such is the case in Cameroon, where processes of socioeconomic assimilation and exclusion have been structured through particular arrangements of production, consumption, and exchange,[15] as well as historical representations of just modes of redistribution and even the just price. Initially, for instance, the assimilation of former slaves into the market took place only with respect to certain sectors of the economy, such as the butchering and sale of meat. Historically, then, the butchers' market was a site of incorporation. But, as an elderly man remarked, with much nostalgia for an overly idealized past, "Now, they [the butchers] are all new. None of the old men are left. . . . The new ones are different. Before, there was no kilo. Now there is the kilo. Before, we used our hands. We cut bones, we laid it out. . . . Now work is different. Before, people got along, they had understandings. You sell, I watch. When you leave, you ask me to sell. And when you don't come one day, I can take up selling. That is how people intermingled."[16]

This representation of an ideal past in which incorporation took place peacefully, where people got along and even intermingled, is quite silent on the fact of the segregated aspect of the marketplace and possibilities for economic accumulation. Until today, the entry of recent converts to Islam and non-Muslims into the butchers' market took place by segmenting that aspect of the market. That is, recent converts were informally but effectively prohibited from selling meat using the kilogram means of measurement and were thus restricted to the sale of meat (in necessarily smaller quantities) and animal by-products according to the tas system. Consequently, the tas system came to be associated with the poor and non-Muslim. Today, for those who have made great gains during the 1980s, the high point of the Cameroonian economy, and thus have secure positions in the marketplace, segregation remains a legitimate setup. It merely reflects the alleged natural differences between the local elite and Muslims (most often referred to by the ethnic term Fulbe, plural; Pullo, singular), on the one hand, and the underclass or non-Muslims (referred to as Kirdi, Mofou, Guiziga, etc.), on the other.

In the beginning, the Fulbe were never butchers, a Pullo could never be a butcher because he'd never find a woman. Those who are butchers come from outside, those who were once slaves, or converts to Islam, they become butchers. . . . It's not a noble occupation for a Pullo. That is, people find no dignity in this occupation; it's considered as an occupation of the lowest class, for those who have nothing. It's for slaves, those who are always in blood. Here . . . it's the Hausa who, in the beginning, started; but today there are no Hausas in the butcher market in Maroua. . . . [Today] they are

[15] On this general point, see Bourdieu 1984; Baudrillard 1975, 1981.
[16] Interview, Maroua, northern Cameroon, February 10, 1993.

the Mofou or Guiziga who came from the mountains, who didn't know where to go, who never went to school, who came into town and, since there is no occupation where they accept the Mofou and Guiziga without a problem, they convert to Islam, they enter inside, they become butchers. All those you see, 80 percent of the market, that's them.[17]

These representations of the history of incorporation and exclusion in this sector of the market reflect the ways in which idealized representations of the appropriate organization of society have structured the organization of the economy. The tas system persists because of its association with the enactment of social obligations and certain rights alluded to previously (such as with respect to the baaba saare). It is likewise the point where exclusion and difference is inscribed. In that sense, pricing is inextricably linked to a theory of value that exceeds economic value or exchange value. While most often presupposed as the outcome of supply and demand or a means of establishing distribution through prediction, pricing systems, as social systems, are infused with politics. Profits obtain through the quarantine aspects of the exchange process.[18] Money, or surplus value, can be captured in institutional arrangements that are both external and internal to the market. External institutions, such as credit systems, are politicized insofar as the logics of inclusion and exclusion, and hence socioeconomic differentiation, depend upon a set of criteria that could easily be contested as arbitrary. Yet the pricing system itself is a political institution insofar as price, as a practice, is a way of discussing a social relation. Evidently, debt can occur via pricing because credit is extended. But debt, understood as a *relation of inequality*, also occurs because gaskiiya (truth) is established. It is perhaps ironic that gaskiiya means both "truth" and "price" in northern Cameroon, since it is the truth about certain social debts. It is uttered or agreed upon when prices confirm the allegedly natural quality of unequal relations. But when is this social relation called "debt"? When does this social debt—which is, as Taussig has shown, a form of credit—shift from its representation as sanctioned wealth to its representation as unsanctioned wealth?

Agreement about the Truth: Narral and Socially Sanctioned Wealth

In northern Cameroon, the truth of price—the enunciation at the termination of a transaction: *gaskiiya!*—is established according to the redistributive

[17] Interview, Maroua, northern Cameroon, October 16, 1993.

[18] I owe this expression to Paul Alexander, whose comments (June 11, 1999) on an oral presentation of these ideas have influenced this presentation of pricing mechanisms. On forms of enclaving, see also Appadurai 1986a: 22.

concept that the price should suit you (*te convenir*). In the marketplace, there is general agreement that a price is "true"—it is gaskiiya—because "it suits you." When asked how one can "know" whether a price suits you or not, almost all my interlocutors explained that this is a question of *narral*, or agreement, confidence. Narral was described to me often rather mechanically as agreement about the organization of the market, with entry into the marketplace being regulated by the chief of the market (*sarki luumo*) or the various chiefs of particular trades and heads of professional organizations. The authority of these regulatory agents was explained as the means to prevent what was called "mixing," or the increase in supposedly chaotic or random selling of goods by unauthorized people (which observers often misleadingly shorthanded as "the informal economy"). This manner of organizing the market was said to induce confidence between traders, as well as between buyers and sellers. Not limited to the discourse of advanced capitalist economies, the idea that confidence ensures the health of the market reigns as well in northern Cameroon. Through belief in the authority that establishes confidence (narral), the true price (gaskiiya)—that is, the price that suits you—is thought to account for one's social situation. Price should account for difference. And yet, of course it can only account for a particular representation of social difference.

Not a real state of affairs, narral is simply a representation that works to organize the economy. It expresses a particular way of construing mastery of the material world, such as rights over goods and transfer of goods. Most important, it establishes and refers to legitimate manners of appropriation. This representation of a certain order—a just order—has served to structure or legitimate a system of exclusion and inclusion such that acts of appropriation (via pricing mechanisms, for example) affirm that order. However, this structuring of the material world through representations was not evident to my interlocutors. While the definition of narral as agreement and confidence was offered up to me quite spontaneously and without much searching, there was nonetheless a strange silence about the ways in which narral is exercised. That is, *the actual process of accounting* for social difference was, for those I questioned, almost impossible to explain. How is it that a baaba saare assures his claim to advances and credits, or debt, so that he can ensure his responsibilities as the head of a family? This question provoked a hush. As Ndjiida put it: "You can't say anything; he is a baaba saare." Or, more typically, it triggered circular logic: "Before, there was narral because, even if you didn't have any money, the *sarki* [chief] gave you some. Before, he gave you what you needed to feed your family . . . there is narral."[19]

---

[19] Interview, Maroua, Cameroon, July 7, 1992.

The exercise of narral, or the establishment of confidence, is surely linked to hierarchy; it habitually invokes references to the chiefs and especially heads of extended families. The latter (*baaba calaadje*) are those who have a constitutive right to work and money. While often indebted, the baaba saare is a paramount source and retainer of wealth, being a linchpin in the organization of redistribution and the guarantor of the extended family's right to material well-being.[20] But while much of the wealth acquired by a baaba saare originates in debt relations, this is not viewed as an anomalous situation. Although the baaba saare generates debt, he is not held responsible for having created a liability. His is sanctioned wealth. As locals explain, it is so because it is produced according to narral, or a specific representation of a hierarchy of relationships and belief in the future of those relationships (confidence).

Narral is exercised, then, through this belief in the future and the conviction that certain forms of social relationships will extend in time. This is surely not a particularly Cameroonian way of approaching the idea that material wealth and social well-being are founded in debt (cf. Nicolas 1986; Aglietta and Orléan 1998), despite the silence about liable origins. This blind submission to the secret of origins (cf. Derrida 1992) is precisely what Nathalie Sarthou-Lajus attempts to excavate in her effort to reinstate the philosophical status of debt. Situating debt and debt relations in time is essential to this task: "Through debt, the subject is inscribed in relationships to both the other and to time that are equally unique. The indebted subject is effectively subjected to the double exigency of existing in the constant reminder of his origins as well as the opening onto a future that represents the *hope of accomplishing* that for which he is responsible with respect to the other" (Sarthou-Lajus 1997: 71, my emphasis). This hope of an accomplishment is confidence in the future. Debt is the equivalent of sanctioned wealth if, as has been the case until the early 1990s in Cameroon, the constant reminder of origins does not exceed the hope of accomplishing future social relations. This is the case for national debt, since the conversion of public debt into private titles and entitlements has given a new "luster" (Vallée 1999: 57) to the failing state, masking the origins of wealth in liability and providing for future redistribution. But this hope of accomplishment of future social relations no longer necessarily obtains for all Cameroonians. And though we might be tempted to say that there is debt in Cameroon today, and so people no longer have confidence in social institutions or in the future, this does not make sense because debt relations are constituted in those

---

[20] Hence the expression "You couldn't find 5 *sule* from Kousseri to Douala, not even on a baaba saare," which I encountered on many occasions in northern Cameroon. It means that times were so difficult that even a baaba saare did not have a dime.

same institutions and in time. That is, debt has always been there. Nonetheless, in certain circumstances, such debt has been legitimated and represented as sanctioned wealth, whereas in other circumstances it has not, thus raising the specter of an unconsummated future.

Today many northern Cameroonians no longer believe in the truth of price. A young butcher who spent several years in prison for his inability to resolve his debts complained of this incapacity to really "know" whether or not the price is "true":

> *I have no cash to pay for cattle. When you don't have any money, you become indebted. If I had cash, I could work. If something costs 40,000, they say 55,000. They don't tell the truth. The person has cash in their hand. You, you don't; you only have children at home. And the nontruth is going to continue because you don't have money in your hand. You have to take on credit. Now, in the market, those who have money in their hand hide it. If they say 50,000, you can discuss in order to pay 42,000 to 43,000. If you don't have any money—you take on credit—you're obliged to pay 50,000. You're obliged because it's the problem of the head of a family (baaba saare). If you don't have money and you don't want to take it, your children are going to eat what?*[21]

This sentiment that value is inherently unstable—that something costs 40,000 CFA, but they say 55,000 CFA—was expressed to me in many ways. As just noted, the truth of price can no longer be affirmed, since today paper money and not credit establishes confidence. The following comment reiterates this idea, communicating the sense that one can no longer pinpoint stable sources of wealth and modalities for assigning value. Even the tas, for instance, has become an unstable and changing entity, contrary to representations thereof: "Almost all the butchers are in debt. They don't have cash to buy cattle. The people who bring the cattle to market [escorts and brokers] are the people with money in their pockets. They know a butcher; the butcher will aim 50,000 [like a tas] with a profit of 5,000. The butcher tells the guy with the money to buy, and of the 5,000 he gives him 2,500 to 3,000. This [latter] money is for the owner of money [*propriétaire de l'argent*]; he'll earn 2,500. [As a butcher,] in buying like that, after slaughter, you can't find a market. [By the time you weigh the meat in kilos], it's not 500 CFA. . . . It's going to sell at 250 to 300 but you bought it at 400 to 500."[22]

Many of these men have been jailed for their debts, having been officially accused by local government tribunals of "abuse of confidence," or what might be described as the accrual of debt that is not created in the silence of narral, where redistribution takes place and debt is normally

---

[21] Interview, Maroua, Cameroon, October 24, 1992.
[22] Interview, Maroua, Cameroon, May 12, 1992.

Hamidou Bouba with Haman, the "oldest" butcher in the market in Maroua. Credit: Janet Roitman, 1993.

The cattle market at Bogo, northern Cameroon. Credit: Janet Roitman, 1993.

sanctioned. This change is reflected in people's manners of talking about redistribution. As we have seen, narral is typically represented as an ideal situation where the true price and confidence obtain. As noted earlier, silence habitually reigned on the subject of the originary state of debt and even the creation of debt as fundamental to exchange relations. However, I discovered that some people now refer to narral and debt in one breath. Young men especially often told me that narral was a *système d'endettement* (a system of indebtedness) or a *circuit* (a circuit). The latter has, of course, no end; it does not offer the possibility of accomplishing one's social responsibilities, like paying a dowry to establish a family, at a future point in time. According to locals, in this circuit, one is either "under cover" or "in rupture." The former means having recourse to an "owner of money," which, now essential to safeguarding a place in the market, means accruing debt. Being "in rupture," on the other hand, means being expulsed from the protective hierarchy, which implies facing up to debt—or debt that is no longer sanctioned as simply a founding social relation—and often doing time.

Indivisibility: The Basis of Accounting and Redistribution

Debt creation, as has been noted with respect to the logics of rent-seeking in Cameroon and elsewhere, is in itself a mode of regulating society (Bayart 1989; Vallée 1989; Taussig 1997). By questioning the arbitrary nature of distinctions between legitimate and illegitimate forms of debt, the men who serve time in jail and the alleged newcomers to the market—who are often one and the same—interrogate the legitimacy of a mode of regulation. The latter is based on a standing monopoly over claims to the logical necessity of a certain historical form of redistribution (gaskiiya-narral). The unstable nature of regulation is, then, provoked by the instability in representations of appropriate and legitimate modes of redistribution and their attendant hierarchies.[23] The crisis in truth value—or the truth of price and modes of redistribution—is lamented upon by some as a problem of the representation of narral and the hierarchy it founds. As one man in the marketplace lamented, "Before, people got along, they had understandings. That's not the case now because if you give something to someone, he'll take command of the thing. He'll say that it's for him. Before, we had confidence."[24]

[23] Regulatory authority, in its quest to organize socioeconomic space according to consistent—as opposed to a multitude of potentially incongruent—sets of equivalents, relationships, and principles, must be construed and perceived as the only possible way of expressing a relationship or representing value.

[24] Interview, Mbankara, Cameroon, May 20, 1992.

Command over things: a state of being and exercise of power that clearly go beyond the right to decide autonomously the fate or use of an object. Beyond, as well, the logics of social exchange—the tightly spun web of rights, obligations, and sensibilities that are dramatized in transfer. Command over a thing—as a state and a mode of power—posits the problem of the nature of the object over which it holds sway.[25] The idea that one could have transfer without transfer of command is predicated on the notion of the indivisibility of the object exchanged.[26] Narral, for instance, is a social idiom that, as an idealized representation, presupposes the integrity of the community, that confidence will obtain. While it legitimates a certain hierarchy and a structure of inequalities, I found that it was somewhat glorified by locals as a symbiotic whole: the whole ceases to exist without all the parts; possession for one is possession for all. This is reminiscent of the tas, which is conceptualized as a mass more than a collection of singular items. Likewise, in a community whose economic history is grounded in pastoralism, the herd of cattle is most often apprehended as a structure and not necessarily a collection of singular things. This conceptualization of the amorphous whole in terms of ordered relationships and series of groupings by category is a nonquantitative mode of accounting. Thus the herd (per the tas) is apprehended as a qualitative grouping. Accounting for the herd is signified in local parlance as "seizing" it. In Fulani, there is a distinct word, *waaso*, which signifies the act of a rapid seizure, both physical and mental, of a totality. The herder's ability to identify a stray animal quickly and precisely is based on specialized knowledge of the ensemble as a set of moving relationships, the animals taking positions according to specific categories (strength, age, mothers with young, and so forth; Pouillon 1988: 191–93).[27] Here, more than anywhere, we see the workings of the principle of indivisibility.

While one might wonder, "What could be more *countable* than a herd of cattle?" (178), in the Sahel, it is well known that the herd cannot be ascribed to one owner, since it is constituted in a complex of relationships that inscribe genealogy and family heritage, and a history of alliances and dependency relations. Likewise, the herd cannot be apportioned out among various owners, since these relationships cannot be reduced to simple correspondences between owners and singular objects. This situation has presented notorious problems for both researchers and regulatory

---

[25] See Foucault 1996 on the emergence of an economic object in the discursive field of the political.

[26] For an ethnographic account, see Weiner 1992.

[27] Indicative of the significance of that form of knowledge (seizure), an "idiot," or person lacking in mental skills, is said to be incapable of distinguishing things that resemble each other. It should be noted that my attempt at rendering visible the elusive problem of indivisibility is largely inspired by Pouillon's work.

authorities.[28] Since enumeration is the basic mode of intervention in fiscal practice, attempts to reorganize and render cattle herding and trade coherent to regulatory techniques have met with the laws of silence, which render the question of how many heads are in one's herd inestimable. But these are not simply veils of resistance thrown up against regulatory intrusions. Like pricing via the tas, the prohibition on counting can be understood only in light of the point that "enumerations translate something other than the things themselves" (Pouillon 1988: 200). For instance, for each animal, there are several claimants to rights of different degrees and according to varying interests of usage: relative to animals received as dowry versus inheritance; between the head of the family and his married sons; between husbands and wives in *bange*;[29] over animals received by children at birth (preheritage); between sons, daughters, and brothers in inheritance; and so forth. Apart from these assignations of ownership, there are also peripheral rights of usage ascribed to people designated as "guardians" of animals, which is a mode of diffusing costs, redistributing wealth, and avoiding fiscal responsibility.[30] Thus the question of property is not so much unspeakable as conditional, depending on which relationships are involved (i.e., between specific animals and persons, or between persons themselves) and to what degree ownership is implied (an absolute situation being practically

[28] Their own inability to explain "why nomadic pastoralists cannot count their cattle," the subtitle to Pouillon's essay (1988), is a point of irony in itself.

[29] *Bange* signifies "half." It also signifies a head of cattle that belongs equally to two owners. This is most typically the result of a gift to a recently married couple (usually by the father of the bride). Both husband and wife are co-owners, and all potential wealth derived from the animal (calves, milk, money) is shared equally by the couple. Informal rules ensuring equality exist, although they are myriad and, no doubt, debated.

[30] In northern Cameroon, *goffal* is an example such a situation. In this instance, a cow is given over to a "guardian." Most often, the latter is in need of a source of revenue or has recently lost most of a herd to disease or drought. All resources derived from the cow (e.g., milk, butter) "belong" to the guardian, although the question of calves is open to interpretation. The owner often claims to have given the cow to the guardian due to the cost of keeping large herds. But this manner of diffusing costs is also a mode of redistribution. And, as one herder reminded me, it is also a manner of diffusing fiscal responsibility: "For example, if someone asks you, 'Where is your cow?' you say that you put it in goffal. If they're taking a census, you say, 'That doesn't belong to me; it's goffal.' Everything that you keep with someone else, it's goffal." In response to my question whether or not goffal is the same thing for a head of a cattle and a clock, he explained, "Goffal is only for things that breathe" (*be yonki*: with a soul). I prodded, "If you give the guardian money while he's guarding, is it still goffal?" He answered, "Yes, but if I bring this clock and you take money while you guard it temporarily, it's *ran*. With *ran*, you return money. If you don't return money, it's *sigmugo. Ran* is for anything—that doesn't breathe" (*walaa yonki*: without a soul). It is interesting to note that *ran* signifies a guarantee; it is not used with respect to "things that breathe," since they, of course, cannot be guaranteed. For more general commentary on peripheral rights of usage, cf. Pouillon 1988: 190.

excluded). The process of the constitution of kin relations, genealogy and family heritage, rights and patterns of inheritance and redistribution, and obligations in alliance translates into complicated modalities of property and appropriation that, in order to be specified, must account for the particular moment and relationship at hand. Therefore, given its mode of constitution, subjection of the family herd to procedures of nomination and enumeration, which go hand in hand, would imply the dissipation and dismembering of the complex of relationships and alliances it establishes (see Gast 1987).[31] Production of the "head of cattle" as a fiscal base proves elusive, then, given the field of signification in which cattle are objectified. Plural forms of appropriation allow for the possibility of the contradictory status: for example, the host who is a stranger (Pouillon 1988: 202) or the debtor who is a creditor (Taussig 1987).[32]

The unstable nature of truth is thus, as always, a problem of representations: narral or confidence no longer obtains, since the principle of indivisibility that prevents any one person from "taking command of the thing," or denying claims to redistribution, is thought to no longer hold. As they say, these days, "things are mixed," and hence they cannot be "seized" (waaso). How is it, though, that long-standing modes of redistribution and regulation became unsettled? What brought on this "mixing" that confounds accounting and accountability? When asked, those I spoke with referred to "change." Generally speaking, this change is attributed to "modern life" and especially "newcomers" (les venants) and outsiders, as several merchants explained to me:

> Before there was no [sale by kilo]; they cut it on the table. Thirty years ago, the kilo was at 20 francs, and then 100 francs, 200 francs—up to 500 francs. It changed eight years ago because of modern life. [I asked, What is modern life?] Gendarmes, functionaries, people from Douala—they wanted to pay by the kilo. But at home, they found bones and not meat. The sarki pawa [head of the butchers] went from neighborhood to neighborhood to check scales and licenses. If there wasn't any scale, he confiscated the meat; he took them to prison. Before, it was sold by the tas—we arranged the meat by price—at 100 francs, 200 francs. People took the money that suited them.[33]

---

[31] An elderly man once explained to me his resistance in converting part of his family inheritance (cattle) by saying, "Je ne peux pas chasser mon *jawdi.*" By transfering his *jawdi* (literally, goods or wealth), he intoned that he would be dissipating, and even "chasing away," the "force" contained by it. Masa Kisiri, Maroua, northern Cameroon, February 16, 1993. On power residing in objects, like persons, see Cohen 1966.

[32] Pouillon (1988: 202) notes that the oversimplified notion of "collective property" is inappropriate to this situation. Cf. also Comaroff 1980 and Ferguson 1985 on the social construction of property. More generally, see Grey 1980.

[33] Interview, Maroua, Cameroon, May 11, 1992.

The guys have changed too, and now they're installed, integrated in society. The elite, up until now, has continued to say, "You, you're just a butcher". . . . Today it has completely changed, and yet even now there is a reticence among the Fulbe; you would never find one of them working as a butcher now. But there is one reality: that is, today, you can find a Christian selling meat in the butchers' market in Maroua. That was inadmissable. Today you can see Christians and even pagans selling meat, but not slaughtering—because, at the level of the slaughterhouse, that's still controlled.[34]

There is change because Maroua is a big city. People can't stay, and others come. [But] since the elders don't want it to change, it won't. The people are going to get bigger [in numbers], and so the market is going to grow [in terms of sellers]. The elders don't want a lot of meat on the market now. I'm from Maroua. A newcomer who is a butcher must be allowed to enter; he can't do anything else. But there are some who weren't butchers before. They are Guiziga, Mofou, Matakam, and even Muslims—that is to say, Fulbe—they're people from the surrounding areas. They come from Gazawa, Miskine, Mindif. They can't do otherwise, we can't stop them. They must leave [their villages]. They are children, they don't want to herd cattle at home because they don't want to suffer. There are too many of them in the butcher market because they find 500 to 100 francs [CFA] a day. Money comes fast, so they come.[35]

There has been a lot of change in the market. Prices are lower: from 600 to 700 CFA to 400 CFA. The rights of the sarki [head of the butchers] are no longer there. Before, there was narral (agreement): when meat was left overnight, we met, we decided that, tomorrow, we would slaughter less. Now there is no agreement . . . because there are a lot of newcomers [les venants], a lot of races—the Matakam, the Mofou, the Guiziga, the Fulbe. Before, there were only the children born in Maroua. They all knew each other. They grew up in the same town. Now, they come from Meri. They are authorized to work, and then they separate [from those who gave authorization]. They can't work together. And you can't do anything if you have debt on you. For example, if you have a young married man who sells meat [for you], he goes and sells, he takes at 400 and he sells at 500 [i.e., he takes 400 of 500 sold]; the profits are for him. If [there are no profits], he takes 1,000 CFA to eat and he gives back the rest. You can't say anything; he is a baaba saare [head of a family]. He's a butcher like you. It's a question of confidence. He didn't get [earn] anything . . . there is no narral [agreement].[36]

---

[34] Interview, Maroua, Cameroon, October 16, 1993.

[35] Interview, Maroua, Cameroon, July 2, 1992.

[36] Interview, Maroua, Cameroon, October 7, 1992. When asked what to do for the *venants* and the youth, this rather young butcher responded, "The best thing would be to give them bones with a little meat; and then give them some more meat if it's not sufficient."

These opinions all indicate that the assimilation of non-Muslims and people considered to be of ethnic groups other than the socially dominant Fulbe group no longer takes place via a segmented market. This change has destabilized representations of difference, which—while always constructed—were seemingly confirmed as "true" or natural in the division of labor, the patterns of redistribution, and the inequalities that prevailed. The exclusion of non-Muslims from certain aspects of the economy—such as the butchers' market, which is a historically lucrative site in this cattle-herding society—seemed to be a just arrangement, even to many non-Muslims themselves. Changes in this manner of representing natural or just socioeconomic arrangements could be described in terms of urbanization—or an increase in the numbers of "salaries eating meat," as it was put to me—and the influx of merchants into this sector of the market due to the relative declines in the cotton and groundnut markets, and the virtually nonexistent industrial and service sectors. At issue, however, is how the search for fast money in the context of a dolorous rural economy has upended the patterns of redistribution that have prevailed in this site of asymmetrical assimilation.[37]

Seizure: Enacting Claims to Social Mobility and Redistribution

As I have already noted, in Africa today, the process of maintaining exterior resources, such as debt financing, as the preeminent financial source for authoritarian rule (Bayart 1986) involves more than struggle between political or social groups for control over a given set of economic resources. The *very nature* of those resources is at stake, since debate over their most appropriate uses determines paths of redistribution. Throughout Cameroon today, the nature of "national wealth" is being challenged: claims about legitimate sources of wealth differ between regions due to variable resources and the fact that each area is part of a regional historical space that is not contained by the unified boundaries or coherent national history of Cameroon. The northern part of the country is less integrated with the south, where the political and economic capitals (Yaounde and Douala, respectively) lie, than with the regional domain comprising Nigeria, Chad, and the Central African Republic. Northern Nigeria weighs in heavily as a referent in the region, with its predominant financial networks and convertible currency, its cheap merchandise and black-market petrol, its centers of education and Islamic missionary groups, and through the historical trace of the Sokoto Caliphate, which once spanned the present-day confines of

---

[37] This is an allusion to *assimilation réciproque*, put forth by Bayart (1979) with respect to the political logics of socioeconomic and regional inequalities in Cameroon.

northern Nigeria and northern Cameroon. Chad also imposes itself through the effects of thirty years of war and factional fighting (see Issa 1997; Buijtenhuis 1987; Azevedo 1998), which produced refugees crossing borders and a war economy that spurred demand for provisions, arms, merchandise, fighters, and even services. More and more, Libya extends itself into the region through investment activities (centers of Islamic education, hospitals, real estate), charity works and schooling, and the arms trade (Bennafla 2000, 2002). These forms of regional integration are accompanied by international links that issue out of the small-arms trade, the drug trade, and the international ivory trade, as described earlier.

These sub- and transnational networks of commerce and accumulation define the dynamic axes of the regional economy. They represent a space of possibility and opportunity, absorbing the increasing throngs of economic refugees that now search the horizons for the last—or latest—bastions of wealth. Thus, while many people in northern Cameroon claim that the defining dynamic of the urban economy is the arrival of non-Muslims, uneducated rural folk, and undisciplined youth into the marketplace and various trading professions, one might argue that these people—and especially the youth—are at the forefront of wealth creation in the region. What we find is the odd pairing of dispossession and accumulation, to which I will return later. In brief, this parodox arises from a situation in which the demise of local agro-industry, the public sector, and private enterprise, combined with the insidious effects of structural adjustment programs, have made the economic strategies of the unemployed and dispossessed models of expansive techniques—be they capitalist or otherwise[38]—in a time of material contraction.

As I have argued elsewhere (Roitman 1999, 2001) and hope to underscore herein, this is such that the urban economy is now in many ways dependent on commercial, financial, and monetary activities taking place in the hinterland, especially on international borders and in frontier spaces.[39]

---

[38] I am not arguing that those who pursue these strategies are a vanguard of capitalist accumulation, nor am I maintaining that they represent "illiberal forms" of economic activity (as Duffield 2001 has understood them). Defining their activities in terms of capitalist accumulation is not part of my inquiry, which seems in any case a vain pursuit given that these economic activities exhibit both liberal and nonliberal forms.

[39] For a similar example, see De Boeck's (1999) interpretation of the economic activities of young Zairean urbanites, who have migrated to rural areas along the Angolan border, where the diamond and dollar economy prevail—the bush, as opposed to the city, becoming the very source of tokens of wealth and consumption. This does not mean, as De Boeck (1999) and Bennafla (1998) note, that investment practice has also been reoriented from the urban centers to the bush; revenues procured through commercial and financial activities transpiring in the latter are often invested or consumed in cities and major towns, a scenario that runs somewhat contrary to that depicted by Ferguson (1999) with respect to Zambia.

Those who partake in these activities trace out paths and poles of productivity through what seem to be languishing expanses of dusty farmland, barren villages, and arid mountains. In so doing, they contribute to the extension of regional and transnational networks of trade and accumulation, often latching on to the markers of distant cultural and intellectual movements (e.g., jihad, gangsta rap, environmentalism, nativism, human rights). Conflict over the economic activities and social obligations of *les venants* (which basically connotes—often mistakenly—"rural youth") is perhaps less an indication of their "chaotic" manners of "doing the market," or their rebellious attitudes toward regulation, as was suggested by many established merchants (who were not always elders), than their having etched out a space of economic mobility and taken up cultural and political idioms that either subvert or upend prevailing logics of redistribution and authority in the region. The venants have in some ways refuted the structure of exclusion and difference instituted by the tas system of pricing, specifically the truth of that price, the system's segregation of the poor and non-Muslims, and the idea that we are all in agreement about this structure of exclusion and its modes of indebtedness and social obligation.

Like others, the newcomers and those who endure these forms of exclusion are living in a situation of generalized debt. However, they apprehend that debt not as a natural fact of social relations and a sociopolitical hierarchy but as an insolvable situation. Their debt is no longer figured in a temporality that offers the hope of accomplishing or perpetuating familial and social links in time (cf. Sarthou-Lajus 1997: 71). As many men explained to me, they could no longer expect to marry and found a family, since they had no capital or credit to offer a dowry, purchase property, and take on the responsibilities of a family. Hence many of them cannot attain the social status of a "man" or a baaba saare; they remain "boys" regardless of their age because they are bachelors, implying a low social ranking in the hierarchy of value. Being unable to reproduce the web of dependencies that gives sense to and narrates local histories, these young men intervene to exercise claims to wealth, generating other narrative lines. And the ways they do so are frequently violent efforts to come to terms with the sense of loss that pervades their present.

Le Voleur Imprenable

Since the onset of structural adjustment programs, and in tandem with the exacerbation of the state's financial crisis, Cameroonians—dispossessed and well-off alike—have been making claims to appropriate conditions for wealth creation. Witness the Villes Mortes campaign and the government's

retort that the actions it entailed were nothing more than *incivisme fiscal.*
The people's claims to rights-in-wealth have been consistently ignored by
the state, and so some people have proceeded to exercise those demands
through seizure, contraband, banditry, highway robbery, and smuggling. In
turn, new forms of wealth have arisen, such as "spoils." Once associated
with war and asocial forms of wealth creation, spoils now signifies the dis-
avowal of particular social obligations, such as tax and debt. As with fraudulent commerce, what is seized cannot be taxed. For those living in a web of
international and local debt relations, seizure is a means of both reversing
and participating in the social order implied by such obligations. Thus, in a
recent conversation, a young man who works the unregulated border trade
insisted:

> *The government's latest policy is the struggle against poverty. In order to get*
> *money from the whites, Cameroon says that it is now a Highly Indebted*
> *Poor Income Country [HIPIC],*[40] *while we know that in our region we are a*
> *great power. People of all nationalities come here every day, to Mbaim-*
> *boum. . . . Cameroon is a HIPIC by cheating, by demagogy, in order to have*
> *the white man's money. So Cameroonians follow the example of the state!*
> *The state steals from the whites, the civil servants steal from the state, the*
> *merchants steal from the civil servants by selling them products at prices*
> *incompatible with their standard of living or by making them pay exorbi-*
> *tant rents on housing, and the bandits steal from the merchants and the*
> *civil servants, who, together, transformed the state into a criminal entity. In*
> *fact, me, I don't condemn Cameroon for having really become a HIPIC be-*
> *cause, if Cameroon steals from the whites, it's due to the fact that the whites*
> *always stole from Africa.*[41]

Spoils thus signifies a new sociability of exchange insofar as it is a new
means of redistribution.[42] But seizure and spoils are not simply a mode of
combating and inverting the general sense of liability in which northern
Cameroonians live today—for example, with respect to international donors,
former colonial powers, nongovernmental organizations, the state, and local
administrations. They are also a means to wealth, social mobility, and redistribution. Dispossession not only describes the state in which most Cameroonians now find themselves; it has become a site from which one realizes
the imagings of wealth creation.

[40] It should be noted that the HIPIC initiative was integral to debt management programs
described earlier. For another, detailed view of this initiative, see Callaghy 2001.

[41] Meiganga, Cameroon, November 15, 2001. I thank Saibou Issa for conducting this
interview.

[42] This is reminiscent of practice during the nineteenth-century jihad, when "spoils" was
articulated from within the discourse on legitimate property and wealth. For further commentary, cf. Roitman 1998a.

As Guy Nicolas (1996: 89) has put it with respect to *le sacrifice suprême*, or the case of political martyrdom in many violent politico-religious movements, these young men are "playing with loss." Beyond the mere fact of transgressing the law, the realm of seizure and spoils is part of the everyday imaginary of radical loss insofar as it constitutes the inversion of the state of liability. In the context of a largely undercapitalized or demonetized population, liability becomes a general principle or modality for most social relations. Those who work as runners, guides, and guards through the mountain passes and collaborating villages of the region, and as traders of stolen and hoarded goods in the marketplaces communicate and exchange their sense of loss and liability—their "loss of confidence" (narral)—by establishing new obligations and new ways of "commanding things." But what does it mean to seize in a context where liability is the prevailing principle of social relations?

As means of exercising claims to rights in a situation of dispossession and disempowerment, the ability to seize is strongly associated with notions of power and even efficacious forms of agency. As I came to understand, and as one can glean from ethnographies and oral traditions of the region and the Sahel more generally (Nicolas 1996; Vidal 1990), power over objects is most often conceptualized as the power to keep them in place, their natural state being both the movement of sets of relations and the mobility of the whole. In the Fulbe language of northern Cameroon, *nanugo* signifies to take, seize, stop, or trap. It summarizes the point that the power to stop things entails mastery over permutations between the social and economic qualities of objects. Thus one "stops" (nanugo) a person in the act of enslaving him (a physical intervention that implies an existential transformation, the person stops being who he once, socially speaking, was), and one "stops" or "catches" (nanugo) money in a material object. Nanugo also signifies the act of proposing a price inferior to that offered by a seller. Furthermore, while there is no specific proper noun form for the idea of savings, it is specified through the expression "so that money does not leave" or "disappear." The form of agency conveyed by this lexicon involves not so much the mobilization of objects as their arrest, or interventions that draw them down, if only temporarily, from their supposed constant state of motion. Interestingly, what is utterly unrecognizable, or radically different to the point of being "unseizable" and thus intangible, is often deemed to be a sign or source of power. This is most evident in the world of spirit possession, where the "spirit horse" is evoked as the "unstoppable thief," *le voleur imprenable* (Vidal 1990: 120).

One young man described this power of seizure in terms of life energy: "Road bandits are known for their capacity for erections [*de très grands bandeurs*] because they muster the greatest energy—that is, their life—to

97

struggle against poverty."[43] This statement echoes the beguiling idea that exchange is not the realization of demand or the need to acquire, but rather the consuming desire for sacrifice, expenditure, loss, and destruction.[44] In that sense, seizure initiates a path diverting from the supposed norm, being a transgression that does not correspond to a register of measurement, such as an economic or social calculation (e.g., price) or a social standard (e.g., the prevailing social hierarchy). No longer able to inscribe their experience of debt and liability in long-standing representations and narratives of social mobility—that is, no longer able to ascend to or maintain the status of a baaba saare, with all that implies in terms of the foundation of wealth and rights to wealth—those who seize exercise claims to wealth and express the desire for the means to imagine the possibility of a future. This imagined future includes economic mobility, social ascendancy, and assimilation, or the possibility of restoring loss, the "hope of completion" (Sarthou-Lajus 1997: 71).

Through violent means of appropriation and forced modes of alienation, such as theft and banditry, the very social relations and dependencies that serve to sanction some forms of wealth and their associated paths of redistribution are brought into question. The point is that seizure is not simply the negation of an extant order. While it may be a mode of subversion, seizure, like being "in rupture" or in debt, is not necessarily a moment of opposition between order and disorder; it represents a diversion that is produced out of the system of exchange itself.[45] In that sense, such moments of transgression are interpreted as such not simply because they confront order with disorder, but because they raise the specter of the impossible.[46] They are moments of value subversion in that they both utterly confound

[43] Meiganga, Cameroon, November 15, 2001. This was remarked to my collaborator, Saibou Issa, such a comment being rarely made by a man to a woman in northern Cameroon.

[44] A seductive idea, no doubt, because of its being an extension of the admission that the inscription of human history in the symbolic order is a consistently elusive endeavor, that history being realized, instead, in moments of transgression on the aesthetic order. Transgression in erotic aesthetics and as a matter of sacrifice is the animus of the economy of loss postulated by Bataille (1967).

[45] Cf. Nancy Munn (1986) on "subversive value transformations." With reference to witchcraft as "not simply another mode of value production, but a hidden world of its own" (witches being typified as the most radical of consumers, or cannibals), she examines the "specific construction of being that dissolves and disorders the overt, visible spatiotemporal order . . . even subverting the apparent, positive value potentials of transmissive acts" (13–14). Sorcerers and witches are perhaps the most widely studied "figures of disorder"; see, for good examples, Rowlands and Warnier 1988; Geschiere 1995; Ashforth 2000.

[46] "In counterdistinction to symbolic rites . . . [the principle of rupture] tends to render chaos acceptable; that is to say, not death, which is only an aspect of life and establishes exchange between the dead and the living, but the impossible: nothingness [*le néant*]" (Nicolas 1986: 167). Examples from Niger of moments that are understood by those involved to be symptoms of rupture, or transgressions of the laws of exchange and alliance, include jealousy, drought, jihad, and transsexuality.

and generate novel instances of truth. Through acceptance of what was once circumscribed to the order of the impossible (e.g., unsanctioned wealth, Christians selling meat, Cameroon as HIPIC), they challenge the established sources of truth. Paths are historical inscriptions; diversions from them are "always a sign of creativity or crisis, whether aesthetic or economic" (Appadurai 1986a: 26).[47]

In northern Cameroon today, the production of so-called unsanctioned wealth is the unsettling of the social and economic principle of indivisibility or, more concretely, the modes of exchange, incorporation, exclusion, and redistribution associated with and sanctioned by the representation of narral. The irreducible nature of this representation, or the inability of locals to explain just redistribution and the exercise of socioeconomic rights is what makes it, like power, utterly self-evident to those who live in its midst. This is what is sometimes referred to as the tautology of power, or the mode by which society conceals or masks its very foundations.[48] The truth (gaskiiya) established by this representation (narral) is, then, the power and necessity of a particular mode of redistribution and its attendant hierarchy, or their apprehension as "natural" sociopolitical instances. The relative stability of this representation of "society" and "economy" is of course always potentially disrupted: there is an ever-present plurality of political forms and regimes of accumulation that are constantly competing with those that seem to prevail at any given historical juncture.

Today, many of those who are dispossessed and indebted in Cameroon express an emerging sense of the possibilities of social mobility in a context of severe austerity. They often do so in violent ways and in marginal or frontier spaces where new forms of wealth are circumscribed. These peripheries of the periphery (Comaroff and Comaroff 2000) compete with the logics of economic redistribution and social mobility, as well as the political efficacy of the urban marketplace—or with gaskiiya-narral as a limiting truth and just representation of social relations. Although often constructing spaces of economic empowerment out of seizure, those who make violent claims upon a world of generalized debt and liability are often depicted by locals as the figure of the voleur imprenable, the unstoppable thief, the unseizable. The historical trace of those spaces and that figure can be gleaned in instances of physical mobility and in border zones, such as the bush.

---

[47] Who notes with respect to change in the cultural construction of commodities: "Diversions are meaningful only in relation to the path from which they stray" (28). This historical point is underscored by the commentary that "diversions . . . are not to be found only as parts of individual strategies in competitive situations, but can be institutionalized in various ways" (22), the instances of royal monopolies and enclaves being cited as examples.

[48] This is obviously a reiteration of Marx (1977 [1976]) on fetishism and reification. See also the chapter on the "fetishism of commodities" (1977 [1976]: 1: 163–77). These points are reviewed most plainly and interestingly by Pietz (1993: 129–30); and refer to Derrida 1992.

The Changing Foundations of Wealth

One of the most striking things about the landscape of the Chad Basin is the intense movement that takes place under the blazing sun and through the hot, dry air, along dusty paths aligned with thorny bushes, and down steaming tarmac roads. This physical movement stirs the otherwise listless ambience that sets in as the sun climbs in the immense, blue, dust-filled sky. The haze is cut through by the comings and goings of caravans of young men on bicycles and motorcycles, who ride along the long, blistering routes and cross the mountain passes between Cameroon and Nigeria in their quest for black-market petrol. They are joined by old-style camel caravans and more contemporary truck caravans which ply the Sahara piled high with merchandise, dry goods, foodstuffs, and men, the occasional Kalashnikov poking out from the mass of white robes and canvas bags. This incessant movement also involves other forms of ceaseless exchanges and transformations: constant currency conversions—mostly provoked by currency differentials between franc zone monies and the Nigerian naira, as well as the need to move from nonconvertible currencies to convertible ones—and the swapping and accumulation of birth certificates, national identity cards, voter registration cards, certificates, and diplomas. Although large towns and cities are terminal points for much of this activity, one must go "into the bush" to witness it in action.

But going into the bush does not necessarily mean simply driving out of town and toward the national border. It may be a question of visiting well-known border-town markets, like Banki on the border between Nigeria and Cameroon. It may also involve trips to places that look like ghost towns due to the fact that most activity consists of the comings and goings of motor-cycles and bicycles creaking from the weight of their loads as they make their way back to the cities, or it could involve a disappointing outing to once flourishing markets that have become dusty and barren. Indeed, the fortunes of these frontier towns and cité-entrepôts are typically deemed erratic or ephemeral, since they are highly dependent upon the whims of customs officials and the intensity or scarcity of government interventions (cf. Bennafla 2002: 71, 84). Nevertheless, their changing fortunes are born of a certain resiliency insofar as these frontier zones are constantly shifting configurations. Thus Karine Bennafla's perception of their instability is in some ways contradicted by her rather astute discernment of frontier zones as "moving configurations" (*configurations mouvantes* or *espaces-movements*, as coined by Fernand Braudel; see Bennafla 2002: 97–104). Her depiction, that of a geographer concerned with the spatial expressions of practices that define national and international borders, is worth reproducing here, since it relates so clearly to the genealogy of limit zones and frontier spaces put forth herein:

> *Emergent border zones are not homogeneous or polarized concentric spaces delimited within national territories, as the cartographic representation of frontier spaces in the form of circles or ink spots that straddle several countries would have us believe. [Instead,] new zones of exchange are formed by successive gradations and etch out distended spaces that are stretched along roadways, maritime routes, which are themselves dotted with markets (coinciding with cities or villages) that serve as collection points, depots or distribution points. Between these corridors of service are sometimes interstitial blanks (demographically and economically speaking): frontier spaces are more or less lacunary or incomplete. (Bennafla 2002: 99)*

Bennafla's point is that these frontiers are discontinuous spaces; their limits are not necessarily along a perimeter defined by a border, since they are constructed in relation to centers of consumption and provisioning that are often distant port cities (such as, for the cité-entrepôts of the Chad Basin, Douala; Cameroon; or Lagos, Nigeria) or economic hubs of international trade (such as Dubai).

The ways in which frontier zones etch out their discontinuities are significant insofar as they are expressions of their constitutive relationships to centers of consumption, commerce, and finance. This means that the bush is a space—albeit a discontinuous one—of certain forms of connection and integration, as opposed to outlying areas of negligible and even shady practice devised in a shadow economy. In that sense, in Cameroon, "the bush" is not just a signifier of a return to the past, a regression, or a step backward in the teleology of developmentalist history. Thus the frequent references made to the encroaching bush in conversations and debates about the

101

incivisme fiscal movement are perhaps not merely allusions to a traumatic past—or to the maquis associated with the 1950s anticolonial struggle that transpired in the southern part of the country, setting many communities against one another and leading to a wave of deaths that never resulted in proper burial. It is also, as the petrol sellers reminded us, commentary on quite distinct and contemporary events, the bush and the frontier having become elusive and yet promising domains of a possible future. This process, or the etching out of that future, is in many respects dependent upon novel definitions and key concepts, which contribute to mutations in representations of the foundations of wealth upon which economic regulation is predicated. However, the bush is an inherently unsettling space: its trace in the economic history of the Chad Basin gives insight into the ways in which it has been conceptualized as a limit condition.

In what follows, and in a fairly arbitrary cutting up of time, I describe techniques for governing and producing wealth that prevailed during the early nineteenth century. This is presented through my reading of secondary sources and oral traditions, which refer to both alliance and tribute as the primary means for mediating a heterogeneous social field. During this time, political relationships were for the most part established in a context of constant circulation and movement that defined nomadic and semi-sedentarized communities, as well as livelihoods structured by seasonal agricultural and pastoral work, and dramatic climatic changes. In that sense, dominion often took place through nonspatial or nonterritorial forms, such as tribute, various forms of alliance, and the constitution of dependents and retainers, or "sets of followers." These techniques of power and forms of power relations were critical to the nineteenth-century jihad, led by Usman dan Fodio, and the founding of the Sokoto Caliphate, which spanned present-day northern Nigeria and northern Cameroon. At that time, a large part of a pastoralist community (generally referred to by the ethnic term "Fulbe" or "Fulani") was transformed into a military and political force. This involved the redefinition of the ultimate foundations of wealth: that is, the slave came to be represented as the primary foundation of wealth, being procured through raiding—or jihad—and a system of military post–slave settlements. Production and procurement of the slave, as the fundament of power, involved the exercise of the right to spoils. However, debate as to the nature of legitimate appropriations, or seizure as a mode of producing licitly held wealth, was rife at the time. This was inherently related to the heterogeneous field in which power was practiced. The production of the slave was dependent upon "the bush," or the ambivalent space that traced out the limits of the expendable (unbelievers, slaves) and yet the indispensable (new forms of wealth and social mobility).

By setting out the trajectories of these historical representations of the foundations of wealth and legitimate modes of appropriation, we can see how shifts in the targets of regulation—brought on, for instance, by the institutionalization of French colonization and then, later, by postcolonial power arrangements and the enactment of structural adjustment programs— were not radical shifts insofar as they have drawn on long-standing representations of the foundations of wealth and modes of appropriation. We can also see, in contrast to these traces of continuity, how regulatory authority in this region, in its constant efforts to ascertain and govern the frontiers of wealth creation, has been a fairly unstable mode of power. The present chapter should be read as a prelude to the following chapter, since both contribute to an understanding of the ways in which this frontier, or the bush, marks the contemporary scene. They also show how present-day allusions to the "retreat into the bush" and the "return to the bush" are misplaced insofar as they occlude the extent to which the bush is a projected future and a space of somewhat novel forms of wealth creation.

Dominion without Presence: Political Mediation through Tribute and Alliance

Although the respective histories of the regions that make up northern Cameroon are shamefully slighted in this account, this part of the country enjoys a particularly diverse human landscape. This includes about sixty ethnic and linguistic groups; a politically dominant Islamicized population itself divided into various regional and linguistic categories (Fulbe or Fulani, Hausa, Choa, Bornouan, Mandara); and divergent affiliations with pastoral, nomadic, and sedentary agricultural lifestyles, religious groups (Muslim, ancestral worship, Christian, and heterodox practices), and geographic origins (the plains, the mountains, the primary river area, the lake, the southern forest, and neighboring countries; Boutrais et al. 1984; Roupsard 1987; Seignobos and Iyebi-Mandjek 2000).[1] This region is best described as a *terroir*, or historical regional space, following the use of the term by Paul Bois (1960) and Fernand Braudel (1986). In this sense, "northern Cameroon" refers to a geographic solidarity, which is the historical trace of the long-term trajectories of social groupings in the context of various demographic, ecological, and military regimes. This puts emphasis on the continuity of certain historical formations, which is not insignificant in a context where exogenous periodizations, such as "colonial" and

[1] The number of ethnic and linguistic groups is, not surprisingly, difficult to surmise; Boutrais et al. (1984) speaks of forty-some groupings while Roupsard (1987) accounts for sixty. They are noted herein only to give an indication of diversity. Also, the religious accounting generally estimates one-third Muslim, one-third ancestral worship, and one-third Christian; and the politically dominant Muslim Fulbe (Fulani) are said to account for 20 to 25 percent of the population.

"postcolonial," structure most historical narratives and political analyses (see Bayart 1989: 19–61).[2]

The plurality of domains that constitute a historical region include commercial, monetary, financial, and productive spaces; political regimes, warring territories, and no-man's-lands; linguistic communities and media networks; and religious, mystical, and mythic realms. The permanence of these is recognized most readily in, say, the etchings of long-term, gradual demographic movements and the deep tracks of long-distance trade.[3] Institutions issuing from these enduring spaces mark time through the *longue durée*, persisting and yet being incessantly transformed by the multiple temporalities of the myriad spaces that define historical regions, or what Braudel (1979: 193) refers to as "*le temps multiséculaire.*"[4] Changes— or what might best be thought of in terms of hybridization—in institutions, relationships, and practices result from the inflections brought on by exogenous representations. In that sense, change and discontinuities are variations, or the particularizing effects of appropriations, not dramatic aberrations in an otherwise stable historical terrain.

In light of the plurality of historical regions and their organization and deployment in the very long term, thinking about conceptions of the economy and economic arrangements in the conjunctural history of northern Cameroon[5] means attending to techniques of power that mediate plurality, as well as the flux and efflorescence of exogenous movements and relations that impact upon them. Two obvious and essential techniques of power in this region prior to colonization were—and in some ways still are—alliance and tribute. Their exercise was based on and contributed to the establishment of a regulatory apparatus that is perhaps best described as a military-distributional complex.[6] While this is both a generalization and a simplification, I want to think about the ways in which alliance and tribute were

---

[2] This is not to say that "colonization" is not a local historical marker. For elucidation of local conventions of periodization in northern Cameroon, cf. *Garoua tradition* 1980: 25 n. 7; Mohammadou 1976: 10–25.

[3] In the region of northern Cameroon, this is best portrayed, albeit with central reference to the neighboring region to the west, by Warnier 1985.

[4] On the irreducible plurality of time, cf. Pomian 1984, esp. 349 and Foucault 2001: 613–28. And on the plurality of what he calls contemporary "space-times," see Appadurai 1990. See also Harvey 1989.

[5] The school of historical geography associated with Braudel insists on the very long-term duration, which includes elements that impact upon human society most profoundly and transmogrify in incremental and almost imperceptible ways. The *longue durée* is distinguished from the social history of *conjonctures* and *l'histoire événementielle*. For an account, see Braudel 1972–73: 20–23. Evidently, while much of what I recount here is an effect of the longue durée, the limited scope of my research confines me to a history of conjonctures.

[6] While not posited in terms of regulation, elucidation of the military-distributional complex can be found in Burnham 1980b.

complementary techniques of power, both being associated with a predominant form of political organization based on "sets of followers," or *tokkal*, which I describe later. A look at the practice of tokkal gives insight into the ways in which power situations can arise that do not entail dominion, implying that dispersion is not necessarily problematic to the exercise of power.

This idea can be grasped through consideration of how the long-term historical constitution of the regional military-distributional complex was inextricably bound up in the elaboration of two concentric regions referred to as central and eastern Sudan, on the one hand, and the Chad Basin, on the other.[7] The former encompasses the latter and has been defined by the political and economic histories of the early kingdoms of the central Sudan from the tenth to sixteenth centuries. These include the former city-states of Hausaland (e.g., Kebbi, Katsina, Kano, Gobir, Bauchi, Zamfara) and important polities such as Songhay, Mandara, Bagirmi, and Kanem. Geographically, this comprises the area extending eastward from the middle Niger to the Lake Chad region, and running south from Aïr to the Niger-Benue confluence. The Chad Basin, on the other hand, while an intrinsic part of the central Sudan, has also been demarcated as a politico-economic zone unto itself (Last 1985a [1971]: 180–90). In this localized commercial zone, agriculture and intensive fishing and herding activities were coupled with the salt and natron industries to fuel east-west trade (Connah 1981: 190–96). This activity essentially generated the material wealth that was drawn into the eastern commercial networks dominated by the savanna kingdoms and the polities of the Sahel. And this local trade, which arose in part out of complementarities due to economic specialization, was accompanied by long-distance trade: by the ninth century, slaves plied the "Sudan Route" to Mecca, which extended from the Niger to the Nile, eventually stitching its way from Timbuktu through Bornu, Wadai, Dar Fur, Kordofan, Sinnar, the Funj kingdom, Shedi, and Sawakin (Fadl Hasan 1977: 207).[8]

From this point of view, the emergence and delineation of the Chad Basin

---

[7] This is important, since northern Cameroonian history is almost inevitably represented as originating in the nineteenth-century jihad, which gave rise to Fulani hegemony. This colonization of the region by the Fulani forecloses the significance of numerous populations and their various forms of political organization. It should be noted that the term "central Sudan" is vague. I am generally following the geographic definition and usage put forth by the contributors to Ajayi and Crowder 1985 [1971]. However, I pay less attention to the areas east of Lake Chad, including Wadai, Darfur, and Kordofan. For the history of that expansive region, cf. Fisher 1977. See also Cordell 1983. On the problem of defining the Sudan in terms of circumscribed geographic blocks, see Horowitz 1967.

[8] Jack Goody (1980: 29) dates this trade to prior to the second century. On the activities of the eastern network in the areas of Dar Fur and Nubia, as opposed to the more westerly region considered here, cf. Fadl Hasan 1971: 48–49.

was largely bound up in exchange.[9] From circa 700 to 1100, the Basin was known as Zaghawa, which included the so-called Sao people[10] and the polity of Kanem. The intense social diversity of the region, which comprised communities of the Chadic, Nilo-Saharan, and Benue-Congo language groups as well as sedentary and numerous nomadic and seminomadic populations, is a commentary on its significance as a hub of transactions. Indeed, the very terms Zaghawa, Sao, and Kanem are themselves probably derived from traders' terms for the areas, signifying economic zones as opposed to tribal or ethnic areas (Last 1985a [1971]: 186 and see 191).[11] Thus, at that time at least, the extreme heterogeneity of the region seems to have escaped an overdetermined definition in terms of ethnic or linguistic markers, or what we refer to today as "identities." From approximately the tenth to the twelfth century, an influx of linguistically diverse populations specializing in a wide variety of economic activities amplified the extent of exchanges and, in turn, contributed to political differentiation.[12]

But this differentiation involved fragmentation and fluidity as much as consolidation. In other words, the trade networks that issued from this amalgam of complementarities contributed only in an indirect—and even paradoxical—manner to the eventual rise, for instance, of the state of Kanem over neighboring dynasties. As Murray Last notes (1985a [1971]: 175], many states of the period prior to the rise of Kanem divided political authority between autonomous and often unequal groups, a characteristic that typified many polities even up to the nineteenth century. Furthermore, competition between the eastern and western trade networks centered at Lake Chad often fostered the instability of the various early kingdoms'

[9] This is not an assertion of the reducibility of transformation in this region to exchange. For one, I do not intend to privilege exchange value as an economic motor. While not entering into debates about the theoretical significance of exchange versus use value, suffice it to say that the question of the primacy of one mode versus the other evokes, in some ways, a tautology, since production presupposes a division of labor, which presupposes exchange. Braudel (1979: 11–12) remarks upon this in his work on exchange and the market economy.

[10] This term generally refers to the people who inhabited the southwestern part of the Lake Chad area, which is now mostly designated by Kotoko settlements and the more mobile Arab Choa communities. The classic references on the Sao are Lebeuf and Masson-Detourbet 1950 and Lebeuf 1969.

[11] On the Zaghawa as a people and their rather short-lived rise to predominance over other populations of the Kanem after the ninth century, cf. Barkindo 1985 [1971]: 227–29.

[12] Cordell (1983: 36–39) signals population mobility in the region up to 1400. However, in a critique of the use of oral traditions, he rejects the notion of large-scale migrations, insisting rather on frequent, local shifts of populations. On differentiation, cf. Last 1985a [1971]: 177, 179. The following section draws heavily from Last's work on the transformation of the early kingdoms of the Nigerian savanna as a result of increasing diversity and exchange, competition between trade networks, inflow of international trade, and the hegemony of Kanem over former kingdoms (110–1250).

settlements; the wealth and power of most dynasties and, above all, their out-lying settlements in which traders conducted business depended on vacilla-tions in the incessant rivalries between these networks (180).[13] The political instability of local towns and dynasties abated as these networks were mod-ified through incorporation into trans-Saharan networks and, concur-rently, the Zaghawa (or Sao) kingdoms devolved into a system of alliances within the international trade network (189).

In sum, and as has been well noted elsewhere, critical changes in the centers of the Chad Basin—and eventually the central Sudan—derived from trade, as opposed to the intensification of agricultural or industrial (e.g., mining) production.[14] Ultimately, this involved control of the ex-change of goods that were not locally produced: primarily gold and slaves, as well as alum, salt, and natron. In effect, the very transformation of the eastern and western commercial networks was a result of their having been increasingly linked up with north-south trade. But such incorpora-tion did not necessarily eventuate in control; North African Berbers and desert nomads (whether Berber, Taureg, or immigrant Arab) dominated trans-Saharan trade from the eighth to at least the twelfth century, if not later (Martin 1969; Fisher 1975: 62–64; 1977: 259–87; Fage 1987: 70; Lovejoy 1985 [1971]). They were able to do so because "control" meant not only disposing of capital used to establish credit relations but also and especially commanding camel transportation. The critical and often overlooked point, made by Ralph Austen (1990: 342), that "the economy into which camels were ultimately 'domesticated' was not that of the urban merchant but rather that of the desert nomad" had implications for the nature of merchant power in trans-Saharan trade, as well as for the trade itself.[15] These factors, and especially the inflated cost of pro-

[13] Last notes (1985a [1971]: 179–80) that these shifts are overemphasized in the historical record because traders of the eastern and western networks frequented different settlements in the same kingdom. Traders' references to settlement names, as opposed to kingdoms, has thus led to an appearance of change in settlement status when in fact there was continuity. He affirms, though, that this skewing of the record does not annul the matter of changes in dynastic fortunes and power due to competition between networks.

[14] It is extremely important to note that this is not an assertion of a direct corollary between long-distance trade and the rise of the early (e.g., Kanem) and late (e.g., Songhay) Sudanic polities. This commonly assumed axiom has been scrutinized, although not entirely discounted, by much recent historiography. The view of an apogee in the trans-Saharan trade during the period under discussion and subsequent decline due to warfare and the fall of Songhay has been revised; the magnitude of trade that transpired during the eighteenth and nineteenth centuries—when the European presence might suggest abatement of trans-Saharan trade with the rise of the Atlantic economy—is considered to have been in fact greater than in the prior era. On the process of consolidation, cf. Last 1985a [1971]: 167–226; Trimingham 1959; Hunwick 1985 [1971]; Lovejoy 1985 [1971]: 677–79. For debate, cf. New-bury 1966; Terray 1974; Johnson 1976; Austen 1979.

[15] On the critical role of desert communities, see Austen 1990: 347, who argues that the

tection, meant that the military dominated the merchants (Last 1985a [1971]: 223).

By the end of the fifteenth century, the resulting political arrangement was fragmented, being composed of several small states with a significant number of fairly autonomous settlements (Last 1985a [1971]: 225).[16] The fifteenth to the nineteenth centuries unfurled in conflict over control of trade routes and town-based markets as the traders and transporters of the Lake Chad region competed with those from Tuat, Ghademes, Fezzan, Kano, and Katsina, among others (Frantz 1977: 178; Newbury 1966: 235; Lovejoy and Baier 1975).[17] Permutations in this chain of antagonisms were accompanied by shifts in the statuses of the various factions, towns, and polities, which meant that the system of regional and long-distance trade proliferated in a differentiated, variegated, and not a unified, political field. It is no doubt possible, then, to narrate the economic and political histories of the Chad Basin or the central Sudan up to the nineteenth century in terms of constant circulation as opposed to increased consolidation and consequential state formation.[18] The role of nomadic populations, for instance, has been interpreted for the most part in terms of their incorpo-ration. But this has not dampened mobility; to the contrary, there has been a permanent quality to intense, if perhaps small-scale, population move-ments (Beauvilain 1989). More important, nomadic communities often dominated sedentary ones. The most notorious were the Arab pastoralists, Berbers, and Tuaregs (Frantz 1977: 177–79; Fage 1987: 62; Bonte 1998). Often their assertions of military and political power involved abdication of nomadic life, but the notion that their activities in the caravan economy led to their incorporation in its associated settlements is based on a general assumption that the desert economy was integrated into the regional economy by way of the trans-Saharan trade. In a more subtle reading, Ralph Austen argues, "The basis upon which the central and southern Sahara became more effectively integrated into growing Sudanic and world

---

transport and storage problems particular to trans-Saharan travel meant that only items with high unit prices—hence luxury goods, not staples—were traded. He also examines the much-neglected question of protection costs—a pertinent topic today, as we will see later.

[16] It might be argued that Kanem-Bornu was a more centralized polity than the states of the Nigerian savanna; by the sixteenth century, Bornu was said to dominate the Sahel and far northern savanna along with Songhay (Lovejoy 1985 [1971]: 648). But the eastern networks issued directly from the Lake Chad region, and political continuity based on trade and alliances existed in the area between Bornu and the Benue River (Last 1985a [1971]: 206).

[17] By the eighteenth century, local monopolies over salt and natron were established (cf. Colvin 1971: 113). Control over gold dust, slaves, ivory, kola, cloth, firearms, and gunpowder, among other items, was much less assured (cf. Lovejoy 1985 [1971]: 653–63; Austen 1990: 311–50).

[18] Fisher (1975) makes this point and then proceeds with the narrative of consolidation.

economies was not the expansion of imperial states but rather the growth of more stable and autonomous communities *within the desert itself"* (1990: 347, my emphasis).[19]

His argument is a significant clarification, since it attenuates representations of the history of political relationships in the central Sudan as a linear progression of increasing centralization and the inevitable expansion of states, and the gradual domination of sedentary peoples over nomadic peoples as a progression of history. While not denying the fact and import of the centralized nature and hegemonic positions of states like Kanem-Bornu and Songhay, volatility was as much a part of their political histories as aggrandizement. Furthermore, and most important, focusing on the role of desert populations in terms of the forging of stable relationships and organization, as opposed to mobility and subversion, has implications for our understanding of historical modes of governing in the central Sudan. Certainly mediation via alliance and tribute were the primary modes of negotiating the plurality of relationships that existed between the array of polities, settlements, entrepôts, and commercial factions that did business in this hub of trade and exchange.

By the fifteenth century, slaves were the principal objects of business in the trans-Saharan trade. In response to North African and Middle Eastern demand, states conducted raids on local populations on the basis of merchant credit (see Lovejoy 1985 [1971]). States thus regulated the supply of slaves but did not necessarily exercise monopoly control over trade. As an extraordinarily high-risk endeavor, great profits were to be had, and a network of credit relations developed through which profits were extracted at several phases of transaction (Austen 1990: 340, who notes, citing a Genoese merchant, that 100 percent commissions were obtained by desert-side agents). But the expertise required to domesticate and herd camels, navigate the desert, and ensure safety (along with the ambivalent position of Islamic commercial law on such risk-laden engagements) meant that the main caravan merchants maintained rather distant relations with their nomad counterparts (337–43). Caravans were brought together as temporary associations between commercial interests, and "instead of formal legal arrangements, the ties between participants in the various zones of the caravan trading system seem to have been based mainly upon various combinations of kinship, clientage, and slavery." (340, citing Peres 1937; see also Baier 1980: 57–78; Bonte 1998). Moreover, by the end of the sixteenth century, the diffuse nature of relations between commercial groups was aggravated by the Moroccan invasion and subsequent demise of Songhay (on the latter, see Hunwick 1985 [1971]). At this time, the Songhay state's part in

---

[19] Austen cites evidence for such communities from 1600 onward. Prior to that time, Sudanic polities such as Songhay and Borno prevailed over certain nomadic groups.

the coordination of credit relations and a monetary zone based on gold and cowries (cf. Lovejoy 1974) was curtailed. The merchant associations of the region formed a "vast, interlocking grid of communities," which defined the coordinates for the latticework through which politico-commercial relationships were forged (Lovejoy 1985 [1971]: 678–79). The autonomization of these groups reflected political fragmentation (i.e., the fall of Songhay) and the decentralization of Muslim commercial communities, but it was not without its own form of political organization. Alliances were the form of political and social mediation that prevailed; they were expressed and confirmed materially through credit relations and especially tribute (see Last 1985a [1971]: 194–95).[20]

Taxes, tolls, and levies were obvious sources of revenue for any political authority in the region. However, tribute gave material form not only to the power to extract, but also to subordinate status. For instance, tribute was paid to Borno (a primary terminus for trans-Saharan trade) by its more westerly and southerly trading partners: Bagirmi, Mandara, and the Hausa states. And the premium on slaves—which followed from the high level of international demand and the local institution of domestic slavery—had consequences for the objectification of the foundations of power. That is, slaves—or people—as opposed to territory, were the ultimate signs and sources of power (Kopytoff 1986; Guyer 1993).[21] One did not conquer land in order to settle it; rather, expeditions were undertaken and incessant warfare was waged to capture booty—or people who were enslaved—and to establish or confirm tribute relations. Furthermore, the local idiom of conquest did not necessarily predicate conversion of non-Muslim victims despite the exigencies of Islamic law. Non-Muslim territories were reservoirs of future slaves, and conversion would only sometimes alter their status as potentially enslavable.[22] Finally, slaves were the most lucrative of exports; could be converted into other forms of wealth through sale; were factors of pro-

[20] Although this is a well-known aspect of the politico-economic history of the central Sudan, I am extending Last's analysis of alliances in the founding legends of the early kingdoms and their significance as methods of mediation—as opposed to "government"—between "cult constituencies" and with respect to foreign traders' settlements. Evidently this is not to say that tribute relations were a novel aspect of relationships between merchants, settlements, and polities. Fifteenth-century tribute relations between Hausa states and Bornu are described in Barkindo 1985 [1971]: esp. 252; and Cohen and Brenner 1985 [1971].

[21] The extensive literature on slaves in the central Sudan prior to the nineteenth century includes, among others, Meillassoux 1975; Miers and Kopytoff 1977; Klein and Lovejoy 1979; Goody 1980; Willis 1985b.

[22] There is no clear consensus on the extent to which Muslims did in fact enslave other Muslims. Theoretically, the practice was forbidden according to Shari'a; while its occurrence is probable, its frequency is more problematic. Commentary can be found in Levtzion 1985 and Fisher 1975: 97–105, who reminds us that even a Bornouan prince was enslaved and sold in the trans-Saharan trade (102).

duction as agricultural, pastoral, industrial (salt mining, tanning), and domestic labor; provided manpower for both local and North African armies, as well as the trading caravans; were sources of reproductive power for nonslave families and dynasties; and were accumulated as wealth in and of themselves. The importance of the slave trade for the region can be gleaned from the fact that the trans-Saharan trade did not cease but rather accelerated after the seventeenth century, when the Atlantic trade intensified (Austen 1990: 321–28; and see Last 1967; Lovejoy 1978a; Goody 1980: 32–34). Slave raiding responded to both local and international demand, and slaves were transferred as the primary component of tribute between polities. Enslavement and tribute collection formed the crux of production and exchange in the regional economy. Moreover, tribute was a technique for extracting or, more correctly, producing wealth, a value conversion that occurred through the capture and delivery of people who became slaves, or an increasingly generalized form of licit wealth.

Spoils as Licit Wealth: The Rise of the Sokoto Caliphate

The nineteenth-century jihad—or the movement to establish the *umma* (community of believers) as governed by shari'a (Islamic law)—and the rise of the Sokoto Caliphate took place in this context of political differentiation.[23] Doubtless, the accession of Sokoto involved a radical reorganization of political relationships and social stratification. And yet that very reconfiguration was not without recourse to, and even the intensification of, tribute and slaving. That is, the centralization of the caliphate by means of an administrative bureaucracy and its extension of authority over myriad populations did not see the passing of tribute relations into the dustbin of desert trade history. During the nineteenth-century jihad inspired by Usman dan Fodio, tribute relations were established, like the principal forms of wealth (e.g., slaves), through acts of conquest. This was not exactly a new form of appropriation, since warfare had dominated the region from at least the fourteenth to the nineteenth century, and slave raiding was integral

[23] Standard usage of the term "caliphate" to qualify Sokoto, in contrast to prior references to "empire," stems from the work of M. Last in his seminal book *The Sokoto Caliphate* (1967). See also Kirk-Greene 1966; Abubakar 1977; Njeuma 1978; Mohammadou 1978. The seventeenth and eighteenth centuries have been interpreted as a "transitional" period in the history of the northern savanna belt, marking the moment between Songhay hegemony and the nineteenth-century jihad and the subsequent advent of the Sokoto Caliphate. Lovejoy (1985 [1971]: 673–87) characterizes these two centuries in terms of political instability and economic decline, noting that events in the region were inextricably linked to developments on the Atlantic coast or, more specifically, the Atlantic trade in gold and slaves. Economic decline, however, seems to be limited to the savanna belt, since the central Sudan emerges at this time as a point of growth. For a slightly different view, see Austen 1990.

to the pre-jihad war economy. During that time, appropriation through razzia and slave raiding was a constant endeavor, ranging from large-scale expeditions to small skirmishes. And since most tributary communities could rarely pay up in full, conquest was an endless and somewhat elusive affair.[24] Capture through war was the essential means of wealth creation, especially when the spoils included slaves, camels, horses, ivory, or weapons.[25] During the nineteenth century, when raids were conducted for the most part in non-Muslim territories, convergence between the act of jihad, or Muslim holy war against "unbelievers" (*haabe*), and slave raiding became more acute (Fisher 1975: 102; Lovejoy 1978b). This was increasingly the case at the height of the jihad, when the idiom of conquest was extended beyond acts of coercive appropriation in a manner that implicated it in political and economic transformation, culminating in the sociopolitical hierarchy of the Sokoto Caliphate (Last 1985b [1971]).[26]

The Sokoto Caliphate was edified through jihad over an extremely heterogeneous population, which was eventually incorporated in varying degrees into the emirate system and the patterns of social stratification it defined. By the end of the nineteenth century, this "centrally supervised federation" (Last 1985b [1971]: 27)[27] comprised about fifty lamidates (administrative centers) under the ultimate authority of the *lamiido* (emir; pl. *lamiibe*) at the head lamidate in Yola.[28] The 40,000 square miles it ostensibly covered included more than 1,500,000 people and entailed four months of travel from east to west and two months from north to south (Njeuma 1989: 9; Burnham and Last 1994: 318). This territory was typically defined on the basis of (potentially) raided populations as opposed to settled territories per se: "The Fulbe conquerors, and even those before them, were not primarily interested in dominating conquered territory, but in establishing

---

[24] On unpaid tribute, see Burnham 1980b: 53. A more purely economic statement of the point that tribute signaled power in raiding and conquest is made by Njeuma 1989: 17.

[25] With respect to slaves, this was equally true for nomadic and sedentarized pastoralists (cf. Stenning 1959).

[26] Last (1985b [1971]: 1) argues that "*jihad* should . . . be considered not merely as warfare against, but as a struggle for, as a constructive reform movement and not simply as the destruction of pagan peoples." While not denying the intentions of the nineteenth-century reformers, it is clear that reform required the subjugation of "nonbelievers."

[27] I insist on Murray Last's formulation, since it connotes structure without denying the divergent ways in which the various communities participated in the caliphate system. For review of the range of relationships, see Burnham and Last 1994: 318. See also Njeuma 1989: 7ff. More generally, refer to Last 1967; Kirk-Greene 1966.

[28] Or subemirates, if the capital at Yola is taken to be the central emirate. The term "lamidate," the Anglophone rendition of the Fulbe term *lamiido* (pl. *lamiibe*; chiefs of the localities) is now generally used in the academic literature to refer to the subemirates. The Fombina and Adamawa lamidates were part of present-day Cameroon. See Abubakar 1977; Kirk-Greene 1966: 15.

relationships which guaranteed tribute and levies, and at least respect for Fulbe authority" (Njeuma 1973: 5, my emphasis; see Njeuma 1989: 9, 28 n. 15; Mohammadou 1976: 29, 477; Adeleye 1985 [1971]). Those relationships were instituted through raiding—the primary means to attain slaves and spoils, and to assert rights to future appropriations—and jihad. One might argue, contrary to standard interpretations, that jihad was not simply the cause but rather the expression of the institutionalization of political and economic relationships through raiding and warfare.[29] Authority was exercised through this system of extractions and appropriations at various levels. Subjugated peoples delivered mostly slaves and grain to the lamidates, and the latter transferred slaves, horses, livestock, salt, and other items to Yola.[30] Slaves not retained by raiders as booty were delivered to the lamiido, or chief of the lamidate, where they were incorporated into the *baital*, or public treasury. They were also included, along with grain and livestock, in *zakkat* (alms, or the Islamic charity tax) and *jizya* (a levy on subjugated Muslims) paid by tributaries and allies. The local lamiibe transferred up to one thousand slaves a year in tribute to Yola.[31] And even though tribute was the material consequence of slave raiding and jihad, it applied to Muslims and non-Muslims alike. Apart from the lamidates, the predominantly Muslim states of Bornu and Mandara, while resisting defeat, nonetheless paid tribute to Sokoto as a mark of subordinate status. Also, because there was no standing army, military forces were mobilized in response to the call of the lamiibe; these levies were sometimes assimilated into tribute.[32] Through this, political relationships emerged out of an administration that was structured by aggregations of authority formed by the capital of the caliphate at Yola, the subordinate lamidates, small villages, and slaving reservoirs. The decentralized nature of the top levels of the administration induced much variation in organization at the local level

[29] Richard Fardon (1988: 77) maintains that the critical rupture in the nineteenth century was less jihad itself than the "extent to which many different people were either persuaded to turn to a way of life that relied on, in Jack Goody's terms, the means of destruction as much as the means of production." He shows how the terms "conquest" and "refuge" became idioms for social organization, and especially the construction of the predominant notions of "hierarchy" and "the past."

[30] Tribute was sent once a year, with the principal towns of each lamidate specializing in certain items: Maroua, Mindif, and Bogo sent chiefly horses, honey, and salt, while Ngaoundere and Tibati generally sent cattle (*Garoua tradition* 1980: 59; Njeuma 1973: 11).

[31] On *zakkat, jizya,* and tribute see Njeuma 1973: esp. 11; 1989: 9, 17–18. Slave acquisition and use in the Adamawa lamidate is described by Vereecke 1994. And see Abubakar 1977.

[32] The lamiibe exercised this authority on the basis of his role as "commander of the faithful." On levies and tribute, see Njeuma 1973. Eventually, military personnel were recruited, for the most part, from slave settlements, or *rumde*. On this institution, see my later comments. It should be noted that tribute is not like zakkat; it has no basis in Muslim law (Njeuma 1989: 17).

(Burnham and Last 1994). This led to an archipelagic project (Boutrais 1994b: 140), the geometry of which reveals, in some ways, the form of agency that engendered such a scheme.[33] Even during the nineteenth century, slave raiding, jihad, and tribute-alliance relations in the northern savanna and the Chad Basin resulted in a political entity that was not conceptualized in terms of exclusive control over geographic space.

This conceptualization of political space was not, of course, the expression of a generic history of conquest, alliance, and tribute. Its specificity derived, to some extent, from the predominant metaphor and organizing principle of the Fulani term tokkal (pl. *tokke*), which has been defined as sets of followers, a "political following" (Burnham 1980b: 47; Burnham and Last 1994: 320), or, more distinctly, "ties of affiliation to a local leader, without consideration of locality of residence" (Boutrais 1994a: 180). *The Garoua Tradition*, an oral history recounted in northern Cameroon, refers to this as follows: "Since, in the beginning, when they came here, they had not constituted villages, the ardo exercised authority only over people and cattle. The people who followed were family members, captives, and all other Fulbe or strangers who decided to live with them. This is the group that was called tokkal, and one spoke of 'the tokkal of Ardo so-and-so.'"[34]

Although I hesitate to insist on the concept of tokkal, since it could easily be taken for an essentialist or static construct that was the basis of meaning for the communities described herein—leading, therefore, to ineluctable paths of history—I will nonetheless elaborate upon it because I wish to consider how this notion of tokkal was practiced and how such practice in-

[33] Boutrais refers to the precolonial state system from Fouta Toro (Senegal) to the Adamawa. Burnham and Last (1994: 318–26, 340) also comment on the nonterritorial organization of the Sokoto Caliphate. They claim that territorial administration, strictly speaking, was in evidence closer to the capital at Yola (340). Typically, historiography has drawn heavily on the model of European feudalism to describe the Sokoto Caliphate, often defining the polity as such. The origins of this tendency in colonial representations is reviewed by Burnham and Last, as is the appropriation of that paradigm and consequent interpretation of the political sociology of the caliphate in terms of "aristocrats" and "commoners" by Azarya (1978). The tendency is confirmed in Adeleye (1985 [1971]: esp. 72–84). Burnham and Last argue persuasively for an understanding of the caliphate in terms of the range of political formations that it entailed, rejecting applications of stereotypical representations that are taken to be the norm. This also applies to recourse to classical Muslim models of government (cf. p. 337). A revisionist move has been made by a recent generation of northern Nigerian historians with respect to the term "aristocracy"; their critique has imminent political implications for the contemporary conservative elite in its rereading of the nature of pre- and post-jihad history. See, for example, Usman 1981. Njeuma (1973) rejects the feudalist model and yet offers a reading of Fulbe administration in terms of "districts" and "district governors" that smacks somewhat of British colonial order and, more seriously, overemphasizes the territorial basis of administrative arrangements. Cf., however, Njeuma 1989: 17. On the inappropriate use of "feudalism" in European historiography, see the work of Bloch (1989).

[34] *Garoua tradition* 1980: 147–48 (Fulfulde), 57–58 (French).

duced certain power situations. Of course, I can only hint at the variance of its practice, but this will give at least an indication of the historical constitution of the Sokoto Caliphate through jihad and as territorial discontinuity through long-term settlement patterns, which consisted of migrating bands that did not, over time, forge clear relationships between earlier immigrant groups and thus averted the consolidation of a single homogeneous territory (Boutrais 1994a: 181; 1994b; see Njeuma 1989: 2). Contrary to interpretations of the rise of the Sokoto Caliphate in terms of a confluence of preordained ethnic interests (e.g., Fulani-Hausa), processes of incorporation and exclusion operated in and through migration, or what Margueritte Dupire (1994: 267) has called "*migration-fuite*."[35]

Tokkal was contingent upon two primary agents of political authority associated with nomadic groups: the *jawro* (pl. *jawro'en*) and the *ardo* (pl. *ardo'en*). The term jawro comes from *jawm*, which signifies "he who masters," and *wuro*, which has come to mean village but actually named the often temporary site where women were located with children. The prerequisite determinant for mastery was not land but goods. The jawro was not the chief of the land; he made no reference to autochthonous status with respect to a spatial area. He did exercise authority over issues of settlement, but this was in relation to migration movements and not agricultural activity. The primacy of the metaphor of movement associated with this form of authority can be gleaned from the fact that *tokke* (the following) derives from *tokkaago* (to follow) and signifies the herd as much as the community. *Lesdi* (the land) was constituted by populations within its limits as opposed to its actual surface, the implication being that the groups it contained were legitimately subject to tribute and slaving. Thus the jawro was master not of a territory but of all that had assembled in a certain domain (see Kintz 1985).

The ardo, like the jawro, issues from the lexicon of migration. *Artaade* signifies to proceed, to walk at the head, to lead. The ardo is inscribed in pre-jihad historical memory as a leader of pillage and razzia as much as migration (Kintz 1985: 98; Seydou 1976). The ardo fulfilled essentially the same functions as the jawro, barring decisions related to questions of settlement. Because migrants were necessarily minorities in the areas they

---

[35] This means that tokke, or political followings, emerged out of the very process of lineage or "ancestry" (*lenyol*; pl. *le'i*). See also Dupire 1962: 21–26; Stenning 1957. As always, the process of ancestry or lineage construction necessarily involved "strangers" and, in this case, especially slaves. In that sense, the ambiguity of identity, lineage, or ancestry (lenyol), was—and is—more an idiom for political organization than a descriptive term indicating genealogical information. This is a generally accepted position in contemporary anthropological literature. *Garoua tradition* (1980: 147 [Fulfulde], 58 [French]) recounts the oral tradition regarding this process of tokkal. Likewise, Fardon (1988: esp. 79–89) shows how, for certain Chamba raiding groups, the concepts of movement and recruitment were the bases for certain rights.

moved through, they had no authority with respect to lesdi (the land), but only in *ladde* (the bush).[36] The spatial domain was conceived in terms of continuous movement, and the efficacy of this nonlocalized and nonstatic condition of power was borne out by the lamidate system of Sokoto. Political hierarchy and incorporation took place through application of this process of movement and the constitution of sets of followers. Burnham and Last (1994: 325) describe this as follows: "The number of specialized political titles attached to the courts of the Fulbe rulers of the states of Adamawa that were reserved for Fulbe freemen was relatively small, although in keeping with the *tokkal* concept of leadership derived from their experience of a mobile pastoral existence, Fulbe freemen could establish themselves as leaders of settled (in which case they were termed *jaoro'en* or *lawan*) or seminomadic (in which case they were termed *ardo'en*) agropastoral communities and thereby play a role in the life of the court and the state government." The network of tributary settlements that was to become the lamidate system of the Sokoto Caliphate emerged from the groups of followers, or *tokke*; their leaders became titled officials. Their ranks included many distinguished war leaders or mercenaries of jihad and slaves, who became prominent members at court. And "taking possession of unbelievers"—*be mari haabe* in *Garoua tradition* (1980), a recently published oral history of the region—often involved assignation of the tributary community to a tokkal already represented at court (Burnham 1980b: 47; Burnham and Last 1994: 339–40). The variety of political agglomerations that resulted basically either issued out of the process of tokkal, with differences in officeholders' residence (in or outside the capital) and use of intermediaries, or the association between bands of allies or slaves with an ardo or a lamidate.

This nonterritorial mode of dominion was likewise paradigmatic for the organization and regulation of material wealth and the relationships that defined such wealth. It had specific consequences for what was deduced as wealth and what were sanctioned as the most relevant objects of appropriation. Since tribute was an index of power, its size was indicative of mastery in warfare and conquest. Positions of power and status were signified by large followings, or "men in attendance" (Burnham and Last 1994: 334–35), the paramount sign of the very ability to redistribute. The diffuse nature of the political archipelago of tribute relations was such that wealth generated for the most part through raids and warfare eventually circulated through

---

[36] This may be the case for the *jowro* as well, but often the jowro was implicated in acts of installation no matter how temporary. Kintz (1985) makes the point that the distinction between the more sedentary connotations of the jowro's practice and that of the *ardo* is insignificant, since they both establish a myriad of intermediary possibilities between the two, both being caught up in the historical flux of migration and installation.

the *commandement* (commandment) of war leaders and titled officials, who periodically redirected wealth toward the heads of the lamidates through tribute, gifts, levies, and tax payments.[37] The lack of emphasis on dominion as entailing presence also meant that itinerant Muslim trading communities lived with their own political representatives in the towns of the lamidates and that long-distance traders maintained, as previously, a high degree of autonomy from political administration (Burnham and Last 1994: 340; *Garoua tradition* 1980: 84 and n. 126; see Abubakar 1977). Most important, the officeholders of the lamidates received no salaries per se. Heirs to the ardo and the jawro, the officeholders were rewarded for their guidance not through systematic reimbursement by the community or the lamiido but via prestations on goods falling under their jurisdiction. They partook in what might be called commissions, taking a share of captured booty, taxes (e.g., zakkat), and especially *gaisuwa*, which were gifts or "blessings." These commissions and gaisuwa received were subject to alienation in various forms, including charges on accession to office, recurring sequences of gifts to commemorate various events (e.g., official appointments, religious holidays), and levies on inheritance (Colvin 1971: 108–9; Njeuma 1989: 14, 18; Burnham and Last 1994: 334–35; Adeleye 1985 [1971]: 78–79). An entire apparatus of transfers, allowances, annuities, stipends, charges, and duties was constituted through the exercise of rights to spoils and booty. Through it, the subordinate statuses of those persons and communities that were the attendants or retainers of the Sokoto archipelago were forged and signified.

Given the exercise of rights to spoils, the transformation of groups of followers (tokke) into administrative powers (lamidates) could not have occurred simply through the mere accession or insertion of war leaders into an administrative bureaucracy. It involved, more profoundly, the conversion of pastoralist leaders into a reigning political and military elite (cf. Lestringant 1964; Mohammadou 1978; *Garoua tradition* 1980: 65; Njeuma

[37] War leaders included both nobles and mercenaries. Their role in the founding of military-frontier outposts is important, since it raises the related matters of property and forced alienation, which was a central debate of the Fodio-inspired jihad (for cursory remarks, see Last 1985b [1971]: 9, 13). My description of extraction and redistribution holds most particularly for the Adamawa lamidates (Ngaoundere, Tibati, Rey Bouba, Maroua), which are of special interest to me. I comment on the caliphate in a general sense but privilege the Adamawa case as the most relevant. Nonetheless, while the lamidates of the Benue and Adamawa plateau can be understood with respect to the Hausa system of government, the northern lamidates (e.g., Maroua) were clearly more influenced by Borno (Mohammadou 1976, 1978). Although now recognized, there is a problem of clarity in the historical literature, which tends to be structured by the quest for "models." Hence we read about Sokoto versus Borno and know less about the more typical hybrid forms. Burnham and Last (1994) provide useful distinctions between the Adamawa lamidates and those of the "Hausa-Fulani" states (Kano, Katsina, Zaria), as well as descriptions of the hybrid forms.

1974; 1989: 5–6). Until this time, the material welfare of the pastoralists-turned-leaders-of-jihad was bound up in cattle as wealth and as a particular form of property. Moreover, unlike certain groups who mastered the desert trade, such as the Tuareg, pastoralists had virtually no role in the regulation of trans-Saharan trade. Even after military conquest, they did not establish their wealth on the basis of commerce, nor did they exercise significant power over long-distance trade (Lovejoy 1978b: 351).[38] Capital transfers took place for the most part through the circulation of slaves, livestock, cowries, and gold or silver coins, as opposed to the alienation of tracts of land (Lovejoy 1978b). But conquest through jihad proved to be a quite forceful mode of social mobility and redistribution. The young men who were drawn to the emerging urban hubs of the caliphate were galvanized by common points of departure; having been "brought up by slaves and financed from the revenues of their families' private estates and public offices, their interests lay neither in Islamic learning nor in large-scale commerce," they shared a sense of purpose that was grounded in their being part of a "free-lance military" (Burnham and Last 1994: 330, 331).[39] The emergence of former pastoralists as a hegemonic military and political force in the region was contingent upon the emergence of the very notion of their rights to wealth through conquest. And this conversion was inextricably linked to the refiguration of representations of the very sources of wealth: from cattle to slaves.

[38] At this time, while Atlantic-based demand (which had been furnished, to a large exent, by the Hausa) was declining, North African demand (which had been supplied mostly by Baghirmi via Bornu during the eighteenth century) increased, especially due to the Turko-Egyptian conquest of Kordofan and Dar Fur. With conquest of the Hausa city-states and subjugation of the populations of the region through warfare, the Fulbe (Fulani) leaders came to be main suppliers of slaves to North African markets, but they did not base the crux of their wealth on commerce or long-distance trade. Cf. Colvin 1971: 113; Frantz 1977: 180–81; *Garoua tradition* 1980: 84–86; Burnham and Last 1994: 328, 340.

[39] Burnham and Last suggest the appellation "titled young" in counterdistinction to Azarya's "aristocracy." This description applies to Fulani men living in what were to become the lamidates of former Hausaland—those who are now known as "Hausa-Fulani." In accordance with the central point of their paper, this description cannot be generalized for all lamidates. In Fombina, for instance, where long-distance trade was not tightly regulated by the administration, opportunities in trade and warfare extended to those outside officialdom (e.g., Hausa and Kanuri traders; Burnham and Last 1994: 340, *Garoua tradition* 1980: 84–86). Generally speaking, the Fombina lamidates—and those who fought its wars and filled its ranks—differed in many respects from the lamidates of Hausaland, as did smaller lamidates relative to larger ones. Likewise, jihad and settlement among Muslims (e.g., parts of Hausaland) versus non-Muslims (e.g., Fombina) and the presence of neighboring Muslim-dominated polities (Bornu, Mandara) were contingent factors. The history of variations is summarized in Burnham and Last and can be pursued, with attention to failures of conquest (e.g., Bornu, Mandara) and resistance to conquest (e.g., Fali, Toupouri, Massa) in Brenner 1974. Consult also Tardits 1980, 1981; Adler 1981; Burnham 1980a, 1980b; Boutrais et al. 1984.

Here, it is worth recalling that the jihad campaign in Sokoto is sometimes referred to as the conspiracy of the religious scholars (*le complot des modibbe*). In Fombina,[40] in particular, the appointment of Moddibo Adama as an official leader of jihad (having received the flag of investiture from the hands of Shaikh Usman dan Fodio) initiated the substitution of other moddibe for ardo'en, who then became candidates for investiture, leaders of jihad, and titled positions as officials (*Garoua tradition* 1980: 26 n.11).[41] Without a doubt, the conjuncture of events that instigated warfare and jihad as appropriate modes of action for change was greatly inspired by the critique—developed by a group of religious scholars (modibbe) and judges (*alkali*) around Gobir in Hausaland—of pre-jihad authorities as "syncretists." To simplify somewhat, this established the terms for a war of Believers ("pure" Muslims who admit only the supreme law of shari'a) against Unbelievers (syncretists and "innovators" who tolerate non-Muslim practices in, and as a matter of, state).[42] Plotting aside, this resulted in the systematic substitution of modibbe for ardo'en as titled officials. Slave labor produced through jihad against unbelievers accorded the economic viability of this class of scholars and eventual administrators. But, over time, the modibbe's command within the regulatory apparatuses atrophied due to their inability to sustain sufficiently swelled ranks of followers beyond groups of loyal students (Burnham and Last 1994: 317–18; see Last 1967). This is significant, since senior men who received titles usually brought with them a coterie of junior followers and dependents, thus rendering the office and its associated titles "a corporate appointment" (Last 1985b [1971]: 27). Murray Last notes that Islamic inheritance laws prescribed the division of estates between all family members, thus mitigating possibilities for the reproduction of wealth over generations as well as engendering a class structure determined by inherited wealth. Administrative appointments were therefore important in the creation of family dynasties. Consequently, even though official appointments to the court and bureau-

---

[40] Fulfude for "South," and probably used by the Fulbe in pre-jihad Bornu to indicate territories south of Bornu (see Abubakar 1977). Unless quoting other authors, I use Fombina as opposed to the later term, Adamawa.

[41] *Garoua tradition* (1980: 124 [Fulfulde], 26 [French]) recounts how Modibbo Adama, who eventually became lamido of Adamawa, usurped power from the head of the Ba'en clan, going to procure the flag of investiture from Usman dan Fodio in the name of the elder leader and yet returning to claim authority in the name of dan Fodio for himself (ca. 1809). On this intrigue, refer also to Njeuma 1978: 30–31.

[42] The debates between Shaikh Usman dan Fodio, his associates, and the scholars and reformers of the time over the doctrinal problem of the relationship between syncretism and Unbelief are reviewed in Last and Al-Hajj 1965; Last 1985b [1971]. See Last 1967 for exchanges that occurred between Muslim leaders in the region more generally (e.g., between Muhammad Bello and al-Kanemi); Willis 1985.

cracies of the lamidates were clearly licenses to wealth and social mobility, they also impelled titleholders to redistribute, since dependents and allies were constituted, as described earlier, through gifts (gaisuwa) and ceaseless cycles of exchange. The emergence of a category of governing officials whose authority did not derive from expertise in Islamic scholarship and law in spite of the reforming character of jihad had much to do with mastery over newly appropriated forms of wealth created in the thick of a transforming economy.[43]

Producing the slave as wealth meant generating the primary form of capital and means of production; extracting surplus labor and converting slave wealth into other forms of wealth, such as cattle or horses; establishing settlements and military-commercial posts for the stocking of slaves and for their mobilization in intensive labor, trade caravans, and warfare; and accumulating slaves as retainers or signs of mastery. Paul Lovejoy summarizes this system of warfare, slaving, and tribute: "Under . . . *jihad*, slave raiding and war were institutionalized into a coercive system for the mobilization of labor and for the redistribution of peasant [slave][44] output. Slaves were 'produced' and resettled in areas around the emirate capitals and near towns along an extensive network of trade routes. Related to this was the collection of tribute from dependent communities, so that the production of peasant [slave] economies was siphoned off into the larger economy. . . . The dominant dimension of this sector of the economy . . . was the redistribution of commodities among the aristocracy and military through the state" (1978b: 348–49, and see 342, 351). The generation of power through jihad was, then, more than a simple matter of a change in leadership or control; it depended fundamentally on the production of "the slave" (*maccudo*) as a specific social category and *la masse servile*, or "slaves" (*maccube*), as the materiality of power.[45] In other words, by being objectified as a category of capital (in exchange), labor (in agriculture), and even a mode of being (as in "the slave," an ontological category), the slave gave positivity to the distinction that was crucial to the transformation of pastoralists into a gov-

[43] Nor was it grounded in the model of authority relations and interpretations of the very nature of authority propagated by the Sufi brotherhoods (here, the Qadiriyya). Burnham and Last 1994: 318.

[44] I prefer to maintain usage of the term "slave," since the notion that once slaves were brought into production they became "peasants" is problematic and raises questions that go beyond the scope of this discussion. For that conversation, cf. Hill 1985.

[45] While choosing not to review the ethnic aspect of the so-called Fulbe (Fulani)-led jihad herein, the point being made is that the very positivity of "Fulbe" ("Fulani"), or the binary term Fulbe-Muslim, was made possible by the third term, *haabe-maccube* (unbeliever-slave). Commentary and rejection of an ethnic reading of jihad and the rise of Sokoto can be found in Roitman 1996, chap. 2. Botte and Schmitz (1994) examine how the positive valence of Fulbe identity is established through representations of the "negativity" of *la masse servile* or haabe-maccube. See also Baumgardt 1994; Vereeke 1994.

erning, political elite: that is, between the "free" and the "unfree." And this distinction, to which many refer today, structured the very idea of licit wealth as spoils established in conquest.[46]

The Frontiers of Wealth Creation: Regulating the Bush

The problem of producing the slave (maccudo) through jihad posed, in Sokoto, questions of licit modes of appropriation and forms of property. For one, the production of slaves required raidable land. And since, theoretically, the enslavement of fellow Muslims was forbidden by Islamic law, raidable land was necessarily non-Muslim land. Hence acquisition of the preeminent form of wealth and property in the caliphate depended fundamentally on the frontier, or the boundary between *dar al-Harb* (the land of unbelief) and *dar al-Islam* (the land of Islam). Establishing and maintaining frontier posts was essential for jihad (Burnham and Last 1994: 322).[47] According to the distinction between dar al-Harb and dar al-Islam, "slavery became a simile for infidelity" just as "freedom remain[ed] the signal feature of Islam" (Willis 1985: 18). Those who could be legitimately enslaved were defined by the status of the territory in which they lived. Islam being the space of freedom, the religion of the land was said to be the religion of its emir (ruler). However, the clarity of this distinction was blurred by the heterogeneous nature of lands and the heterodox practices of rulers.[48] Moreover, the difference between acts of disbelief and acts of sin further muddied the ground between Islam and infidelity, or freedom and enslavement.[49] Finally, since the status of the land defined the status of the individual, conversion may not have sufficed as an assurance of freedom. At the time, only

[46] This is an abbreviated presentation of this point, which can be explored further in Roitman 1996.

[47] On Islamization, the frontier of Islam, and "violence on the boundary" in the region of Lake Chad, cf. Levtzion 1985. On belief and unbelief as the categories of enslavement, cf. Willis 1985.

[48] Areas where the majority of inhabitants were Muslim posed problems for this definition. The seventeenth-century Sudan, for example, was an area of slaving where shari'a in fact prevailed and most people were Muslim. On this situation, and the debates that ensued, cf. Willis 1985. For the equally problematic case of Bornu and review of relevant scholarship produced by dan Fodio and his son, Muhammadu Bello, see Masud 1986. Correspondence between Bello and al-Kanemi is presented in Last 1967, and the question of "syncretists" and the waging of jihad against fellow Muslims is treated by Last and Al-Hajj 1965.

[49] The idea that one was not a disbeliever because of having committed sin was much debated by Sheikh Muhammad al-Kanemi of Bornu, Sheikh Usman dan Fodio, and Muhammadu Bello. Dan Fodio's reigning position is stated in his *Ihya al-Sunnah wa Ikhmad al-Bid'ah* and *Bayan wujub al-hijra*. Useful commentary on the respective texts can be found in Masud 1986: esp. 69–74; Willis 1985; Last and Al-Hajj 1965.

hijra (migration, flight, withdrawal) from dar al-Harb to dar al-Islam and subsequent engagement in jihad against the former established an ostensibly authentic position of belief or freedom.[50]

In practice, or as a framework for appropriate action, the doctrine of hijra has been the basis for the historical association between war and migration in many places (Masud 1990). Hijra, or the obligation to migrate, involves the transgression of spatial definitions and establishes a new juridical existence. At the least, it entails rupture from familial and kin relations; during the nineteenth-century jihad, it removed the potential captive from the realm of property and wealth. As Masud (1990: 30, citing Watt 1971: 366) explains, "Hijra, an Arabic term, . . . literally means 'to abandon,' 'to break ties with someone' (such as a bond of kinship or other personal association), or 'to migrate.' " This migration is initiated through pacts of war or recognition of the obligation to wage jihad; that is, movement and rupture provoked by hijra constitute the very space of war. As a statement of belief, it involves dispossession through exile; through hijra, one enters into "the liminality of poverty and powerlessness" (Fisher 1975: 170). Nevertheless—and this is its constitutive role in the frontiers of wealth creation—hijra, or dispossession through exile, likewise bestows the right to "share in the spoils of war (*ghanima*)" (Masud 1990: 31). Thus dispossession and the frontiers of wealth creation become interdependent states. In the Chad Basin during the nineteenth century, exiling oneself from dar al-Harb into dar al-Islam meant removing oneself from potential enslavement: it was seizing oneself as spoils.[51]

This interpretation of the legal state of property extended beyond the realm of slaves as wealth and the question of rights-in-persons; it became a generalized theory of wealth and rights to wealth, the traces of which are palpable in conflict over wealth and rights today. Like disputes of the present day, one of the great debates of the nineteenth century was over the matter of seizure as a mode of official appropriation. Inspired by numerous formal claims to the courts issued to recover property confiscated and captured prior to and during jihad, this controversy revolved around Muslim and non-Muslim identity (read free-unfree). Many reclamations were made with reference to pre-jihad rulers, whose infractions included "the imposition of oppressive taxes, forceful seizure of the property of their subjects, disregard for *Shari'a* in their public expenditure, and misappropriation of the public treasury" (Tabiu 1989: 382). These were the crimes of the infidels against which jihad was waged, as its leaders asseverated. The legal position that prevailed in these cases was that property seized by corrupt

---

[50] This is dan Fodio's restatement of the doctrine of *hijra*, which became generalized in other parts of Africa. Cf. Masud 1986; Martin 1976: 34. On liminality and the symbolic act of hijra with respect to dan Fodio himself, see Fisher 1986.

[51] "Seize himself as spoils" is from Willis 1985: 21, quoting al Karashi.

rulers could be recovered.[52] Not surprisingly, judgment as to the "corrupt" quality of the pre-jihad leaders was based less on accusations and proof than on their status as governors of dar al-Harb. In his handbook on the treatment of the property and families of enemies, dan Fodio defined the latter as including " 'neutral' Muslims, hypocrites, apostates, rebels, bandits and 'robber-barons.' " As Murray Last (1985b [1971]: 9) comments wryly, "Clearly the Law could not be applied in the heat of the campaign."

This is especially true because war leaders were also tax collectors.[53] Just as the status of the person passing through the liminal space of hijra was eminently ambiguous, so the status of wealth created through seizure was also unclear. What was certain, however, was that the status of the land (or actually the status of the *leader* of the land) took precedence over the status of the individual in question: property in dar al-Harb could be legally seized even if its owner was Muslim (Tabiu 1989: 386, citing dan Fodio's *Najm al-Ikhwan*). But the definition of licit wealth and proper appropriation was constantly argued with reference to those moving, with captives, from dar al-Harb to dar al-Islam. In this instance, while the person making hijra attained "free" status, the status of captives remained radically uncertain. This dilemma arose out of the indispensability of the status of the slave for emergent forms of power. "True" Muslims, who exercised intrinsic rights over certain forms of wealth, made the move from the bush to the town—from ladde to wuro. Although tribute operated without recourse to dominion over territory, it materialized in the military-distributional complex. In particular, it was articulated through geographic points that are best described as combined fortified military camp–slave markets known as *sangyeere* (Burnham 1980b: 53). During the nineteenth-century jihad, conquered towns were rarely abandoned; they became military bases and entrepôts for traders (53; Burnham and Last 1994: 329). Many of these became capitals of the future lamidates. Through these geographic points, the limits of the space of lesdi—the land or, more properly, subjugated

---

[52] The claims were treated according to the nature of the aggressor, being either a "corrupt ruler," an "ordinary Muslim citizen," or an "alien." The ruling was argued by both Adb Allah (in *Diya al-Sultan*, 1812) and dan Fodio (*Najm al-Ikhwan*, 1812), who distanced themselves from scholarly positions that the value of the object must be submitted for reclamation. See Tabiu 1989 for further remarks.

[53] Their role as fiscal agents is noted rather bluntly in *Garoua tradition* (1980: 153 [Fulfulde], 65 [French]): "In the past, [the war leader's] work was leading war; after, they entrusted him to collect tax." A reference to the collection of cotton might mean that "they" entrusted him refers to white colonial authorities, the transformation then being post-jihad. This account might be dating the rise of the war leader–taxman in such a way due to a specific notion of "tax," as opposed to tribute per se. Most commentary concurs, however, on the fiscal role of war leaders in and after jihad. This was, as an aside, the principal way in which distinguished warriors of jihad were retrained from intensive mercenary activity and incorporated into the post-jihad arrangement of power (Last 1985b [1971]: 9, 13).

lands, which were often discontinuous—came to be defined by the ensemble of captives in a combined military and economic sense. On the whole, "a military and demographic strategy was pursued in which slave capture and slave production of foodstuffs were used to create and support larger and larger armies" (Burnham 1980b: 67), the slaves themselves being, in turn, primary recruits.

Sangyeere were the counterparts to *ribaadu*.[54] These were defensive centers established as (often temporary and shifting) outposts or strongholds to stabilize frontiers in regions marked by population mobility; ongoing raids by the Kebbawa, Tuareg, and Bogirawa communities and their allies; and effective resistance to jihad-tribute (Last 1967: 79–80; Lovejoy 1978b: 351). Like sangyeere, the ribaadu were combinatory as hinges in the junctures of the network of warfare and redistribution, serving to convert the spaces of the bush (ladde) both literally and figuratively into the land (lesdi). The mobilization of clan leaders, or heads of lineages (*hoore'en le'i*), and heads of tokke into leaders of jihad involved "baptizing cattle and herding camps . . . as ribaadu since, during jihad, what were called ribaadu were the sangyeere (military camps) of the *mujaddadi'en* (reformers). From here, they made war on the unbelievers and converted them, then returned to rest. When they had submitted the unbelievers of the region, they would take down the camp and push on further where they would put up another ribaadu from which to lead jihad" (*Garoua tradition* 1980: 131 [Fulfulde], 37 [French]). They were also the subordinate points at which slaves were produced, and captives and tribute transferred to superordinates. These were the constantly moving sites from which the city-states and towns of the lamidate system emerged, being the basis of conquest, conversion, accumulation, and commerce. They were essential for obtaining the primary means of production and the preeminent form of wealth for the lamidates.

And where there were ribaadu, there were also *ruumde*. The latter were "resettlement" points or slave locations. Often referred to in the relevant historical literature as plantations,[55] these were places where farming by large numbers of slaves was endured, along with other activities such as tanning, weaving, dyeing cloth, pottery production, iron smelting, and animal herding. They were the loci of productive activity and the form through which material production and its corresponding forms of labor

---

[54] The term *ribaadu* originates from the Arab *ribat* (fortress, fortified site) and corresponds to the verb *reenugo* (survey, guard) in Fulfulde, as noted in *Garoua tradition* (1980: 37 n. 64). The historical literature generally refers to these as *ribats*. Here, I will follow the use of the term ribaadu in the oral tradition to which I refer.

[55] The term was not used in the Sokoto Caliphate. Very involved debates on the pertinence of the term "plantation" can be followed in Hill 1976. On the microeconomics of Hausa *rinji*, cf. Hogendorn 1977. In-depth interpretations of rumde are found in those articles, as well as in Lovejoy 1978b and Hill 1985. For commentary on these debates, cf. Roitman 1996: 70–75.

were organized. While they were the bases of agricultural production, they were likewise intrinsic to the mobile, "frontline" military strategy and thus to the very definition of conquered political entities.[56] Even as organized jihad abated, military activity carried on, and this not so much to acquire territory as to realize commercial and demographic expansion (see, e.g., Burnham 1980b: 59, and more generally, Smaldone 1977).[57] The solution to production and accumulation varied in different regions of the caliphate, with some lamidates going military (e.g., the Fombina lamidates) while others went pastoral (e.g., Yola). At base, though, extraction was still enacted through raiding and tribute in both instances. Labor and objects of exchange and tribute continued to be produced as such through raiding and warfare.[58] And since methods of mobility existed for slaves—or a scale of statuses by which second-generation and manumitted slaves were gauged with respect to degrees of incorporation—enslavement was a constant endeavor, implying continuous movement as well as "continual violence" (Goody 1980: 41; and see Goody 1971: 32–36, 72). While rumde provided the productive basis of the caliphate economy, its consolidation and extension were wholly dependent on the tribute and slaving sector,[59] or conquest and the exercise of the right to spoils—spoils becoming public wealth in this emergent political order.

[56] On ribaadu policy as articulated by Muhammad Bello, the son and collaborator of Usman dan Fodio, refer to Last 1967: 74–80, 361ff. Ultimately, their contribution to large-scale organization of production was reconfigured as the tendency toward fragmented holdings intensified, being triggered by the combined effects of inheritance patterns, in which slaves were not divisible between heirs; the assimilation of slaves into families; their autonomization in the intermediate and oxymoronic status of the "free slave" (*diimaajo*); all-out emancipation; land tenure patterns; and the persistent association between slave raiding and distribution even after jihad. Therefore, rather than ineluctable, linear expansion from small- to large-scale organization of production, the nineteenth century was shot through with paths of mitigated reversibility: plantation agricultural production did not supplant production through enslavement and tribute. See Vereecke 1994 on how slaves are incorporated into society without fully acquitting themselves of their marginal slave status. On the institution of slavery as a site of incorporation, socioeconomic stratification, and redistribution, cf. Roitman 1996: chap. 2.

[57] Similar processes took place elsewhere in the region, as is documented by Reyna (1990) for Baguirmi.

[58] On the continuity of surplus extraction through raiding, cf. Burnham 1980b: 50–51, and 67–72; Lovejoy 1978b: 364. On the production of labor and exchange items through raiding, cf. Goody 1971; Terray 1973; Frantz 1977: 190.

[59] This last declaration warrants digression. In an effort to avoid the reductionism inherent in the idea of a slave mode of production, where slave labor is said to be the dominant form or very basis of production (Hindess and Hirst 1975: 109, 125ff.; Meillassoux, 1975), the emphasis here is on slavery as an institution; a mode of social organization; and a specific, historical social relationship of domination as opposed to an abstract ideal type or "mode" (refer to Watson 1980; Goody 1980). The counterpoint to the regnant view that commerce (i.e., long-distance trade), and not production, was essential to the formation of states in the western

Those who were given over to constant conquest, making claims to spoils and filling the ranks of the caliphate administration, transformed the bush (ladde), which was an ambivalent space, being both a source of wealth (slaves and spoils) and yet the land of unbelievers (dar al-Harb). As noted earlier, these men were not city dwellers prior to jihad, and they were generally not merchants.[60] Those who were scholars traveled between villages and often set up temporary rural residences where students came to settle and learn. Shaikh Usman dan Fodio, his brother, Abdullah, and eventually his son, Muhammad Bello, explicitly entertained the question of how to render pastoralists "men of the city" (or *yan birni*, in Hausa; Burnham and Last 1994: 333).[61] This made urbanization (read sedentarization) a great part of the meaning of "reform" and hence of the dynamic of jihad. Bringing pastoralists into the ranks of the military, judiciary, and bureaucracy meant liberating them from the tasks of herding and rural work. Slaves took up the role. And the cities of Sokoto were erected out of the spoils of captured towns and expanding ribaadu, where gaisuwa—the gifts or "blessings" of regulatory power—were amassed and organized. Muhammad Bello's policies were clear on the issue of ribaadu: they were considered essential to the establishment and expansion of a com-

---

Sudan is not being reiterated here. That critique gives primacy to use over exchange value, positing a productive system in which slave-based relations of production articulated with the then extant kin-based mode of production. Long-distance trade, according to this reading, was based on the procurement of slaves in war and their use by an aristocracy in production (Terray 1974: 339). And yet slaves were necessary to long-distance trade itself. They also worked as artisans and traders and were employed in some places (e.g., Sokoto) as administrators and political counselors. Furthermore, there is little reason to give primacy to use value over exchange value, since, for one, agricultural slavery in Africa (e.g., rumde) produced relatively small surpluses (due to technological limitations) which, itself, only allowed merchants and political elites to be free from labor. Second, the surpluses were directed to the market (e.g., caravans), and, through this, the foundations of wealth and power—women, slaves, retainers, dependents—were procured (Goody 1980: 32–37; Barber 1995: esp. 213–17). Thus the very notion of "production" becomes problematic in instances where slaves are primary producers and yet the extraction of surplus via their labor is not the prevailing mode of accumulation. What does one make, for example, of the maintenance of slaves who consume more than they produce? A productivist reading of their utility could be had only by considering their status as wealth (Watson 1980: 8, 14). They are, above all, necessary constituents in the production of power relationships.

[60] On the sedentarization of the Fulbe as a distinct element of dan Fodio's policy, cf. Burnham and Last 1994: 326–30. This is the crux of their critique of Azarya (1978), who extends a model of feudalism to the caliphate system and consequently considers the role of nonscholarly officials in terms of an "aristocracy." While not addressing that particular matter (which, following their intervention, is, I believe, now a non-question), I draw heavily on their insights in what follows, taking up, most specifically, the point that the policy of urbanization helps explain the pastoralists' success to the detriment of the scholars. On the policy of urbanization more generally, see Bah 1988.

[61] As an aside, the paradox proper to an "urban religion" being promulgated by nomads is noted by Abu-Lughod 1987.

mercial sector and would lay the groundwork for the integration of pastoral, agricultural, and industrial activities (see Last 1956; Lovejoy 1978b: 351–53, 363).[62] And yet the men who were incorporated into the fold of this novel, urbanizing military camp solution were eventually recognized as "men of the city" not foremost because of their personal accumulated wealth (cattle, horses, cloth, coins) but rather by their retinue ("men in attendance"), which signified a master of redistribution, a master of goods, a jawmu.

As the preeminent foundation of wealth, the slave, being derived from the mass of unbelievers (haabe), marked out a limit condition, which itself depended upon spatial and conceptual limits (Vereecke 1994; Roitman 1996: esp. 93–101). In material terms, the masse servile (maccube) was drawn out of what was defined as raidable land, or dar el-Harb, the land of unbelievers (haabe). Haabe, or the unbelievers, and dar el-Harb, the land of unbelievers, defined the frontier, both literally and figuratively, of the Sokoto Caliphate. More than that, as the mass of exchangeable, enslavable objects, they circumscribed the limits of social space. Raidable land was the space of ladde, or supposedly uninhabitable land: the bush. And yet raidable land was not simply apprehended in a passive manner, as a reservoir of slaves or as that which lay beyond lesdi. As Paul Lovejoy (1978b: 348–49) has remarked, raidable land was not just circumscribed through jihad as that which was beyond the pale, since, through jihad itself, entire regions were rendered uninhabitable for the local populace, the land being virtually cleared of autonomous farmers (see also Abubakar 1977). Appropriations of wealth and the regulation of people as wealth through sangyeere, ribaadu, and the system of tribute and titles that constituted the caliphate took place through the transformation of the bush—or the transformation of ladde into lesdi— an inherently ambivalent domain.[63] Movement between the two involved, as we have seen, hijra, or abandonment, exile, and migration to attain an ostensibly authentic position of freedom. The latter, sometimes described as "an ancestry not owned" (lenyol ngol maraka), is the position from which the ardo, who led people in ladde, could become a lamiido, or achieve political accession and social mobility in lesdi.[64] Nonetheless, not an ontological

---

[62] Nonetheless, urbanization did not eradicate pastoralism as an economic activity and specific lifestyle. Many Fulbe groups were not affected by these policies (cf. Dupire 1962; Stenning 1959), and even those who did become "men of the city" continued to accumulate cattle.

[63] Since it extends far beyond the concerns of this chapter, the ambivalent nature of "the bush" is not commented upon herein. I take up this topic elsewhere (1996: 93–97), referring, most specifically, to legends and tales recounted in northern Cameroon that reflect upon the bush as a space of uncontrolled forces as well as that which is necessary for the social word, such as the stranger who provides continuity for lineage or tokke, and knowledge required for reproduction and wealth creation. The oral traditions I refer to are "The Stepmother and the Orphan" and "The Jealous Sister Who Killed Her Younger Sister," published in Eguchi 1994b: 468 and 470, respectively. See also Eguchi 1994a: 282–85.

[64] "An ancestry not owned" is said to describe a pulaaku, or the state of being "Fulbe." The "true" Fulbe freeman is signified by dimo, which refers to freedom in the sense of unmixed

condition—as they say, "they are slaves because of their history, not because of their work" (kaigama [chief of war] of Adamawa, quoted by Vereecke 1994: 42)—the condition of the slave could be transgressed and overcome through marriage, inheritance, clientship, tribute, and titles. Some slaves eventually became titled dignitaries and courtesans, and at the court of certain lamidates there were *saraaki'en Maccube* (slave dignitaries).[65] Thus incorporation and sociopolitical mobility extended to the very category of people whose subordinate status—and objectification as labor and as capital—constituted the frontiers of power and wealth. Enslavement and the servile condition, being fundamentally the product of conquest and the capture of spoils, could be abrogated through heirs (for the female slave), claims to inheritance (for the freed slave), and titles (for the slave tout court). Inverting the principle of wealth as spoils, the slave revealed the extent to which its condition was both expendable, being part of the uninhabitable land of the unbelievers, and indispensable, being the very foundation of wealth and social mobility.

Over the last century, novel ideas about the foundations of wealth, the nature of licit wealth, and the most appropriate techniques of appropriation have been institutionalized in the field of power situations I just described. The logics of wealth through conquest and the principle of spoils as licit wealth were subjected to an alternative mode of conquest in European colonization. At that time, the exercise of power through the strict control of territory was brought to bear upon the military-distributional complex that had resulted from the practice of dominion without presence. Likewise, alternative theories about the nature of wealth, and hence what constituted the legitimate targets of wealth, were applied. As we shall see, mobility and displacement remained critical modalities in this new regulatory field, giving rise to a transformed historical template that eventually informed present-day debates about the foundations of wealth, the propriety of appropriations, and the status of the bush.

---

origins. The state of captivity implies a lack of ancestry, being "kin-less," or without lenyol, and hence outside tokkal. Thus both "freedom" and "Fulbe" are condensed in the state of lenyol. For elaboration, cf. Roitman 1996: chap. 2; and especially Vereecke 1994: 30–31, 42–43; Bocquené 1981; and Reisman 1998. Less detailed interpretations of the constitution of "becoming Fulbe" and "freedom" include Azarya 1978: 28; Burnham 1972; Schultz 1984. On "kinless-ness," see Watson 1980: 6; Goody 1980: 30.

[65] Who served alongside *saraaki'en Fulbe* (Fulbe dignitaries), *saraaki'en Kambari'en* (non-Fulbe dignitaries who had converted to Islam prior to jihad). This is what Burnham and Last (1994: 342) call "a legally defined system of differential incorporation," but which was much more than structured or legitimated by legalistic definitions. For a summary of the various titles, see *Garoua tradition* (1980): 63–76.

Chapter Six

The Unstable Terms of Regulatory Practice

SHIFTS in the targets of wealth, which were predicated on particular representations of the foundations of wealth, occurred in the region of the Sokoto Caliphate in the early twentieth century with the onset of French colonization, and then again in the late twentieth century through postcolonial power arrangements. These shifts were not radical, being based on extant conceptions of both that which is problematic for society and the economy, and that which is generative of new forms of value and new, productive relationships. But the continuity of the trajectories of representations has been mitigated or compromised by the fact that constant efforts have had to be made to ascertain and govern the ever-changing frontiers of wealth creation. With French colonization and the institutionalization of French currency as the preeminent form of wealth, the targets of regulation that posed distinct problems for power shifted: from the slave to what was called "the floating population" (the population flottante). Reminiscent, in many ways, of the figure of the slave—being both expendable and indispensable—the population flottante was represented as that which escaped and subverted public power and efforts to give order to the regulatory landscape.

Being on the frontiers of wealth creation, the population flottante became an elusive target of colonial regulatory authority. Following in the traces of the "sets of followers" (tokkal) and on the tracks of slave raids, the population flottante was—and still is—discerned in distinct spaces of circulation and exchange: borders and the bush. In some ways, it confirms that the bush can be apprehended as a projected future and a space of somewhat novel forms of wealth creation, as opposed to an outlying area of marginal and unregulated practices. This is such that, as during colonization, today's population flottante has been both criminalized and yet circumscribed as a potential foundation of wealth in this time of indebtedness and austerity. Nonetheless, generally interpreted as existing beyond the state or even anti-state, the activities and economic relationships associated with the population flottante have become new targets of fiscal power, its constituents becoming fiscal subjects in their own right.

The Colonial Census

In many respects, and as might be expected, the system of redistribution and regulation that had been established with the rise of the Sokoto Caliphate was reconstituted in the colonial context. This was facilitated by the fact that the French colonial authorities sought out the various chiefs, or, more specifically, the heads of the lamidates, to serve as political intermediaries between the colonial administration and the various local populations.[1] In this capacity, the lamiibe became colonial tax collectors. The endogenization of colonial institutions thus both perpetuated and transformed indigenous ones, etching out another path through the temps multiséculaire. This also impacted upon notions of the foundations of wealth. When we hone in on a limited domain, such as the institutionalization of official modalities for the regulation of wealth, we can see how this process took place in very specific ways. As we already have seen, colonial conquest and the imposition of its specific techniques of power, such as l'impôt, led to the redefinition of what constituted targets of wealth, transforming the field of regulatory intervention. In similar fashion, the colonizer's project of creating l'état civil, or civil status—which involved, both literally and figuratively, immobilizing or "fixing" groups that displaced themselves and structuring so-called acephalous or nonhierarchical communities—led to the production of new categories of fiscal intervention.

Since l'impôt, or the head tax, was at the heart of the colonial endeavor, this involved, of course, the classification or reordering of these communities to determine a census and hence a fiscal base. As much writing on the import of the census for colonial power has shown, the very act of enumeration and classification generated social difference and novel categories—represented

[1] Beauvilain (1989: esp. 360) shows that, even though the so-called Fulani community was politically dominant in the region, their role (and that of non-Fulani Muslim leaders of neighboring, independent polities) as intermediaries between colonial administrators and local people did not emerge out of necessity; it was a deliberate choice, and one that was much debated. The first wave of colonizers, the Germans, reflected less on the issue of who should legitimately serve their cause; delivery of the goods was the rule. But that policy was nuanced over time. While not impervious to the goods, the crux of the French debate rested on the abiding issue of French ambivalence toward Islam and the French desire to convert locals to Christianity.

by race, caste, gender, ethnicity, and so forth—that often became essential-ized in indigenous practices (see, e.g., Cohn 1987; Ludden 1993).[2] In an intervention that takes up this general conclusion, Arjun Appadurai shows how numbers, measurement, and quantification *themselves* informed the inscription of difference on the body and the objectification of group iden-tity, creating a situation in which "countable abstractions, of people and resources at every imaginable level and for every conceivable purpose, cre-ated the sense of a controllable indigenous reality" (Appadurai 1996: 117). This builds on Ian Hacking's extraordinary work (1975, 1983) on the emer-gence of statistics as one of the quintessential techniques of liberal govern-ment (relatedly, see Canguilhem 1989; Ewald 1986). Following in the wake of his concern for "number," or seemingly quantitative methods, I propose to reverse Appadurai's inquiry to consider how the practice of classification and the census—or, more distinctly in northern Cameroon, the drive to fix people in the quest for the census—served to structure conceptions of seemingly quantitative categories and especially the practices of price, tax, and even *fiscalité*, or the fiscal domain, itself.

As was generally the case for colonial empires, the problem for the order-ing and enumerating logics of the census was the heterogeneity of the social field. Initially, the French colonial authorities thought that this problem could be averted by singling out the leaders of indigenous administrations as sources of local knowledge and old hands at the art of distinction through homogenization (the former leaders of jihad having acceded to power by transforming myriad local communities into the undifferentiated mass of haabe). However, one perplexity that undid the colonists in their efforts to establish authority through indigenous chiefs was the precise status of populations that, while at least theoretically dependent upon such chiefs, belied, in practice, a rigorous definition of jurisdiction and even the very status of "dependent" (Njeuma 1973: esp. 5). This was due to the coexis-tence of the following arrangements: migration of once conquered com-munities and their subsequent refusal to recognize the authority of the Sokoto Caliphate; recognition of such authority by subjugated communi-ties that nonetheless refused certain acts of deference, such as tribute pay-ments; the performance of acts of deference by nonsubjugated polities; and the commodious incorporation of certain dependent groups that were still considered distinct communities. Generally speaking, what initially disori-ented the colonial project was the nature of the loose federation of varying political relationships and diverse modes of establishing and maintaining the rapport that constituted the caliphate, or what I have described as the

[2] For some reason, this work relates almost entirely to British colonization in India. For a slightly different view on Africa, see Pouillon 1988.

131

archipelago etched out of the mobile relations between "sets of followers" and "men in attendance."

And yet, beyond Sokoto, other polities and regions were equally troublesome: "If the Sultanat of Mandara is one [a territory] from a political point of view, it has neither ethnic, nor even geographic unity; the 'neighborliness' of people of the mountains and plains, pagans and Muslims, pastoralists and agriculturalists and all 'races' flusters the *commandement* (command; order)."[3] Still other, less hierarchical communities are described in like fashion: the Massa near Yagoua, for example, are described as a "geographical block," yet without correspondence to a political unit and exhibiting no "absolute identity from an ethnic point of view."[4] The drive to ascertain stable identities and geographic formations in terms of ethnicities was disconcerted by inconsistent practices, or the "Toupouri-ized" Massa, "Banana-ized Mousgoum," and "pseudo-Guiziga"—Massa, Toupouri, Mousgoum, Banana (the Fulbe term for the Massa), and Guiziga being names for supposedly distinct human groups.[5] Likewise, racial and linguistic commonalities failed to mask social divisions. As one administrator remarked, "We found ourselves in the presence of a cloud of small independent groups; in truth, they were hostile; although of the same race and speaking the same language, or closely related dialects, they considered each other strangers, even enemies."[6] On the religious front, a family of potential successors to power at Yagoua was described as such: "The older siblings are still Animists but the fourth son of Adap Toucia calls himself a Muslim; he speaks perfectly correct French and is an interpreter at the Post Office; the youngest also speaks French well, but he has abandoned the *boubou* [local gown] for shorts and a little shirt and he is Protestant."[7]

In this diverse human context, defining "civil status" (état civil) was problematic; colonial administrators lamented that the application of texts defining the "social characteristics" of such status met with "limited success."[8] As one official explained, a uniform definition of "civil" in colonial

---

[3] Lembezat notes that at Mokolo and Guider, "the Pagan mass was subjugated, more or less, to a Muslim minority—that is, the Fulbe, recent and detested conquerors." But at Mora, "Pagans and Muslims of the same origins . . . have lived in symbiosis for several centuries, the Muslim was not always and everywhere the 'enemy' of the Pagan." Cf. B. Lembezat, Adjoint au Chef de la Région du Nord, Rapport de la tournée, Subdivision de Mora, Nord Cameroun, 18 March–2 April, 1947, 50, ANY/APA 10418/A.

[4] B. Lembezat, Adjoint au Chef de la Région du Nord. Rapport de la tournée effectuée dans la Subdivision de Yagoua, 6–22 June 1947, 6, ANY/APA 110 418A.

[5] The French rendering is "Massa toupourisés" and "Mousgoum bananisés." Rapport Annuel 1950, Région du Nord Cameroun, Partie Politique et Sociale, 20, ANY/APA 11618.

[6] B. Lembezat, Adjoint au Chef de la Région du Nord, Rapport de la tournée effectuée dans la Subdivision de Yagoua, 6–22 June 1947, 60, ANY/APA 110 418A.

[7] Ibid., 10–11.

[8] Circulaire no. 1567/Cf/APA/2, 11 February 1950, 1, ANY/2AC 6888.

Cameroon was elusive, since "it appears that the populations of the three regions of the North of Cameroon are totally different from the populations of
the South. . . . The project . . . [cannot ignore] . . . the social characteristics
of the North, where the pagan populations live in a dispersed habitat and
where the Fulbe element makes up a large number of herders and even nomads (Bororo)."[9] To be sure, ordering the population to establish "civil status"
or a stable set of "social characteristics"—the basis for any census—was confounded by "extreme diversity" and what was apprehended as extreme disorder in the northern district of French colonial Cameroon: "235,827 Muslims
or Muslim converts [islamisés], 342,502 non-Muslims, that is to say, Muslim
groups mixed with pagans, isolated pagan tribes that are more turbulent than
hostile, Fulbe groups that are subjugated but not docile, chiefdoms to organize, lamidates and cantons that must be incessantly controlled."[10] Nevertheless, "The table established by race, tribe [and] clan permits an examination
of the demographic situation of the region (births, the elderly, pacified tribes,
etc.). It goes without saying that the names of the races determined in the
region are not very sure. The Matakams don't call themselves "Matakams";
the Kirdi of Mora (probably called Wandalas) must be studied. All the same,
the highest possible precision was applied to the preparation of the ethnographic table of the Region of the North so as to present a convenient relief,
capable of fixing ideas."[11]

Fixing ideas in terms of the particularizing category of "race," or the establishment of "racial chiefs," was endeavored—paradoxically, but no doubt
quite typically—in the generalizing name of "a people" and the idea of "the
nation":[12]

> *But the passage to direct administration of these pagan tribes cannot and
> should not be an intermediary step that permits us to better understand them
> to better penetrate; their regrouping [regroupement] in view of their unifi-
> cation should be achieved so that viable autochthonous, homogeneous politi-
> cal orders [les commandements] can be placed under the authority of racial
> chiefs [les chefs de race]—the final aim to which all our efforts must stretch.
> [This is a] long-term job with a distant payoff; [it is] arduous, uneasy, and
> delicate because, if the Fulbe were perfect organizers and, we must admit, our
> precious auxiliaries from the first days, they were also and firstly skillful
> detractors who knew how to flatter and exploit the independent, individual-
> istic, and even anarchic tastes that mark the pagan character . . . the great*

[9] Ibid., 1–2.

[10] Rapport Annuel 1940, Région du Nord Cameroun, 26; ANY/APA 11618.

[11] Ibid., 31.

[12] The constituting relations between, "race," "people," and "nation" are discussed in Fanon
1986, 1963; Anderson 1983; Balibar and Wallerstein 1991; Bhabha 1991; Ahmad 1994; Mc-
Clintock 1995.

primitive powers that we must try to restore today by bringing desirable temperance and humanity to them. However, no matter how far off this aim seems, we will arrive there progressively. Above all, a favorable political climate had to be established to permit the coming together of those whom the masters of the hour [the Fulbe] had dispersed, if not having made enemies of brothers, and, from the family cell that remains intact, revitalize customs, traditions, respect for the elders, in a word, what constitutes the force of a people, a nation.[13]

The force of a people and a nation presupposed, of course, "the social," or categories that are thought to represent the social, such as class, race, gender, and so forth.[14] This, in turn, was a matter of demography, and ethnographic fieldwork. And so the colonial quest for the "force of a people" was launched in the context of the combinatory and heterogeneous nature of identity and sociability in northern Cameroon. Producing "the people," and eventually the fiscal subject, involved a process of cataloging (ethnicity, gender, age) in order to conceptually immobilize. In this particular case, the organizational form this took was "the village," a territorially defined entity that had virtually no historical significance to local populations prior to European colonization (Burnham 1975; cf. Azarya 1978: 29). Through the policy of *regroupement* (regrouping), the French colonial administration attempted to resettle and reorganize people in an effort to decrease geographic mobility and set up the racial grid of the nation.[15]

This project rested on the assumption that "colonized peoples normally inhabited stable villages which were 'natural,' tradition-based units of political organization" (Burnham 1975: 585). At the time, French expertise on African societies held that "the village . . . is not an administrative creation. It is still a living entity" (Delavignette 1950: 74–75, quoted in Burnham 1975: 586). It was posited as the natural historical moment in premodern history, which Africans were thought to inhabit. This "sense of a controllable indigenous reality" (Appadurai 1996: 117) was based on a vision of African societies as manifestations of premodern history, which informed the political program entitled the Restoration of Pagan Powers (La Politique de restauration des pouvoirs païens), a supposed return to a more authentic (pre-jihad) state of affairs.[16] However, nonterritorially defined

---

[13] Rapport Annuel 1943, Région du Nord Cameroun, 8–9, ANY/APA 11618.

[14] This is not to say, in keeping with the science of sociology, that there is, in fact, a positive definition of the social, or a science of society. The point is that the objective nature of the social, is produced through representations of its constitutive categories. See Baudrillard 1983; Ellen 1988; Donzelot 1994.

[15] Reforms were enacted by decree in order to "decentralize the authority" of the lamiibe by "regrouping the multiple lawanats [sublamidates] into cantons." Rapport Annuel 1950, Partie Politique et Sociale, Région du Nord Cameroun, ANY/APA 11618.

[16] For commentary, see Roitman 1996: 201–12.

sets of followers (tokke) were the living entities of society. In the lamidate of Kalfou, for instance, a colonial administrator-cum-ethnographer noted: "[There are] 17 villages. . . . [T]hree of them have populations surpassing one thousand people . . . the fourteen others are not really large villages. They are still not very 'fixed.' These Fulbe are essentially unstable . . . they still have the temperament of a herder. . . . Take the case of Kalfou (village): there were 936 Fulbe in 1937. [Today] the Fulbe number 936 as they did two years ago. However, Kalfou exhibits significant movement back and forth for these two years: 31 Fulbe compounds have gone elsewhere; 34 have come to settle in their place."[17]

Other communities of the region also lived according to the rhythms of constant spatial movement between groups in alliance formation and marriage; segmentation of clans, extended families, and communities; and the displacement of entire hamlets. In the case of the Gbaya, for example, "On average, an individual . . . lives in five or six different villages during his lifetime, and villages themselves change location once every nine years on average" (Burnham 1975: 586). In the Chad Basin, this dispersion has been consistently inspired by ecological, economic, and social crises: drought, epidemics affecting humans and animals (especially cattle), wars and social movements, razzias, prestations, forced labor, the destitution of chiefs, the freeing of slave villages, pilgrimages, and long-distance trade (cf. Beauvilain 1989: 553).[18] The process of ordering implicit in the colonial policy of regroupement was obviously a matter of stabilizing this moving field, an attempt to extend the signs of European order (culture) over disorder (nature) or, ultimately, to redefine "the natural."[19] And this was a political question.

Throughout that effort, or at least for the good part of the first quarter of the twentieth century, the colonial authorities agonized over the extraordinary number of "incidents"—or *incidents kirdis,* generally referring to the non-Muslim populations[20]—that occurred among those who were thought

[17] B. Lembezat, Adjoint au Chef de la Région du Nord, Rapport de la tournée effectuée dans la Subdivision de Yagoua, 6–22 June, 1947, 55, ANY/APA 110 418A.

[18] "Dispersion" was the term preferred by locals to refer to the crisis of the 1920s. Beauvilain (1989: 556) notes that, even now, "villages of several thousand inhabitants can exist one year and completely disappear the next." The themes of crisis, violence, and population movements are central to Beauvilain's study. On population movements more generally, with specific reference to the Mandara mountains and plains areas, see also Hilaire 1991.

[19] A point reviewed, with reference to the colonial Politique de restauration des pouvoirs païens, in Roitman 1996: 201–12.

[20] The term "Kirdi" is used by the Fulbe and many Muslims to signify non-Fulbe, non-Muslims. Although supposedly introduced by the French via Baguirmi, "Kirdi," in practice, has come to be the equivalent of *kado* (pl. *haabe*), the Fulfulde term for an "unbeliever." The term carries heavy pejorative tones but has been recently recuperated by the non-Muslim movement in its quest for autonomization and political recognition. Its contemporary significance is remarked upon in Schilders 1994.

to have been previously subjugated by the caliphate administration. These incidents included rebellions, uprisings, refusals, agitations, thievery, fights, and ongoing wars (see Beauvilain 1989: 316–47):

> *The Bananas [Massa] and Toupouris steal entire herds after having assassinated the shepherds working for the Fulbe of Bogo and Mindif; the Guidiguis-Bongor route is impracticable for lone travelers who are inevitably robbed clean; the Kirdis of Lam and Doumrou steal the cattle from the Fulbe of Mindif and Doumrou; the Kirdis to the west close off the roads to Gazaoua, Gaouar, Bourha, Moda, Mitchiga; the Kirdis of Mandara steal from each other, reciprocally; those of Douré in particular make incursions into Nigeria.*[21]

> *The plague of this country is still the "Kirdis," who indulge in theft and pillage with almost certain impunity. A lone person cannot travel in this region without being killed or robbed. They still consider themselves the kings of their mountains. They have remained unknown to us for too long, and the subdivision officials do not always have the means to reprimand their heinous crimes.*[22]

> *The mass of Kirdis see our firm decision to not tolerate violation of our authority and to punish the wrongdoers and rebels, but only those. If, when a rebel is in flight, the head of the subdivision is obliged to burn his compound [saare], there is a very serious and fearful display of emotion in the village during this operation.*[23]

Fixing so-called rebels in flight was a colonial obsession, which reflected the ambiguity and efficacy of relocation and mobility as modes of political action. Historically, in northern Cameroon, "the lamidate system of command [*commandement*] often, to the knowledge or ignorance of the chiefs [*lamiibe*], led to the virtual fleecing of both pagan and Fulbe populations. The victims rarely issued complaints about the thievery and transgressions of the chief's [*lamiido*] agents. When the abuses became intolerable, the inhabitants abandoned the region and went to live in another chiefdom [lamidate]" (Lacroix 1952–53: 40, quoted in Ela n.d.: 16).[24] Mobility certainly confounded the quest for the knowable civil and fiscal subject—for a census and the head tax (l'impôt). The following

---

[21] Rapport Annuel, Circonscription de Maroua, 1919, 6, ANY/APA 12032.

[22] Rapport d'une tournée de prise de contact, 4–19 March 1929, ANY/APA 10036, cited in Beauvilain 1989: 356.

[23] Rapport d'une tournée, Subdivision de Mokolo, 11–27 December 1926, ANY/APA 11893/D, cited in Beauvilain 1989: 355, my emphasis.

[24] Although couched in different terms, the case for mobility as a mode of political action is well demonstrated by Burnham (1975: esp. 586–87 and n. 27; 1980) for the Gbaya people. See also the myriad examples offered in Beauvilain 1989.

description of signs of submission to colonial authority summates the point: "The head of the subdivision does not leave the village without having obtained from the inhabitants the material proof of their submission to our authority, which is: tax payment; restitution of people or animals taken in the course of battles between villages; repression of the slave trade; arrest or punishment of delinquents, wrongdoers, or warmongers; and a census listing names."[25]

Material proof of submission was in essence the impôt. But since its procurement and management were contingent upon fixing and immobilizing populations—through the census, in villages, in fields of export crops—the signs of subordination were no longer simply captive (or potential captive) status, as prior to the colonial conquest. While it might be true that the drive to immobilize the sources and targets of wealth in villages and fields was consistent with the field of signification that gave sense to precolonial slave camps (ruumde) and war entrepôts (sangyeere), the signs of power were nonetheless transformed with the practice of the impôt and the census. That is, colonial representations of the appropriate targets of wealth—or that which was to be governed—rested on a modified founding distinction: from free-unfree to fixed-mobile. From this, the primary source of disorder and consequent target of regulation became the population flottante (the floating population).

In short, the redefinition and expansion of the field of intervention, which came to refer primarily to the generalized category of the population flottante, was an effect of the colonial problematic of fixing demographic instability to establish the fiscal subject. In various contexts and historical moments this category has signified nomads, migrants, seasonal migrant workers, bandits, intermediaries of the caravan trade, traders tout court, highway robbers, itinerant salesmen, smugglers, speculators, marauders, refugees, foreigners, and so forth. In the nineteenth century, traders who circulated throughout the savanna, desert regions, and into West Africa were often construed in these terms.[26] Their designation as the "floating population" was not without political connotation, since their constant transgressions of city-states and emirates meant that they were deemed to have "weak political allegiances" (Burnham 1980b: 66).

Variability of allegiance was likewise registered during the colonial period. As already mentioned, natural disasters and economic and political crises gave rise to dispersion in the Chad Basin. But the procurement and

[25] Rapport d'une tournée, Subdivision de Mokolo, cited in Beauvilain 1989: 354. On nomination as a disciplinary technique during this phase of French colonization, cf. Roitman 1996: 211–12.

[26] As an aside, it is perhaps indicative that most of them were not Fulbe, or the leaders of the Sokoto Caliphate; they were Hausa, Arab, Choa, Kanuri, Jukun, Nupe, Wangarawa, and Mandara.

management of the head tax, while contingent upon immobilizing populations both conceptually and physically, also provoked movement itself. The quest for currency to pay the impôt—formally known as *la quête monétaire*—compelled people to move. Seasonal migration, in particular, increased significantly. In fact, contrary to expectations, the mobility of local populations increased with the installment of the colonial authorities.[27] Newly instated surveillance of roadways inspired travel by groups formerly intimidated by the possibility of capture and also led to "the descent" of communities that had sought refuge from razzia in the mountains.[28] This, however, involved incessant and incomplete patterns of movement insofar as migration was usually undertaken as a temporary or abridged act, not necessarily alternating seasonally because of drought, and most often resulting in situations of multiple residence.

Thus one cultivated food crops and labored in fields for monetary remuneration in the plains while maintaining residence in the mountains. Double residence—that is, momentary versus administrative—muddled the drive for territorial fixing. And beyond the spatial conundrum was that of "the social": since descent from the mountains was often equated with Islamization and the plains were demarcated as Muslim—or, more correctly, "Islamicized" (*islamisé*)—space, Muslim identity was grafted onto previous markers (religious, ethnic). Converting to Islam obviously did not require renunciations of past familial, ethnic, community, and even religious affiliations. One could be known as a Muslim merchant (using the title *Alhadji*) in one set of social and temporal circumstances, while attending a Catholic mission station as a catechist in another.[29] Double residence very often implied—as it does today—the very splitting and redoubling of selfhood (*dédoublement identitaire*), a subversive and yet complicitous movement

---

[27] Cf. Azarya 1978: 91.

[28] "La descente" has been—and continues to be—a topic of significant commentary and sociologically, developmentalist, and politically inspired research. Refer to Hilaire 1991; Beauvilain 1989: esp. 507–22; Gubry 1988; Iyebi-Mandjek 1993; van Andel 1992. On the difficulty of maintaining open roads prior to colonial surveillance, cf. Colvin 1971; Beauvilain 1989: 316–18.

[29] Beauvilain (1989: 521) refers to Alhadji Jean-Paul in Koma, who is a catechist in his home village in the mountains but lives as a pious Muslim, with a second wife, in the plains. Likewise, in 1988, I met Jean-Baptiste, a postal worker in Mokolo who, formerly a Muslim, had recently converted to Catholicism to ensure his position in what had come to be seen as a "Christian administration," the successor to the first president being Catholic. Jean-Baptiste attended catechism classes and continued to pray to Allah five times a day. The process of Islamization-Fulbeization has been commented on at length for the contemporary period, especially since it accelerated during the 1950s and 1960s with the rise of certain Muslim leaders in national politics. In the North, conversion to Islam has been the predominant means to social mobility (cf. Schultz 1984; van Santen 1993).

that engenders ambivalent power situations (best described by Mbembe 1992; Geschiere 1995).

The Population Flottante

The ambiguity resulting from states of dispersion associated with incessant physical movement, myriad and combinatory economic activities, precarious residential patterns, and overlapping identity references or political allegiances was carried over to the manner of signifying such persons, groups, and segments of the population. The colonial authorities' inability to seize, both literally and figuratively, these persons in social categories and as fiscal subjects led to their being defined as "antisocial": "a nonnegligible part of the population is floating, either because they leave the mountain to live in the foothills . . . or because they go from district to district according to conjunctures that are mostly psycho-sociological."[30] That the "psycho-sociological" might be economic and/or political is not suggested, although it is noted that these movements are mostly provoked by "conflicts between peasants and chiefs, between families or opposing classes, etc."[31]

Those who belied the process of nomination and territorial fixing (*encadrement*) were called "bandits."[32] As so-called robbers, they appropriated wealth in an illegitimate manner; and as members of roaming bands they lived in a constant state of circulation. Bandits and their counterparts, brigands, signified those who lay outside of, and undermined, the project of territorial fixing and ostensibly legitimate claims to wealth: the census and l'impôt. These were essentially people who assured their livelihood through the exercise of the right to spoils via conquest. The colonists recognized this, associating their activities with Muslim-inspired modes of capture and raiding, including jihad-like abductions and incursions, or various reigns of terror led by so-called religious or charismatic leaders (e.g., Rabah, Goni Wadaï) and "Arabs."[33] But these pursuits were likewise said to be propagated by the general populace; cattle theft and highway robbery were extremely organized sectors of activity:

[30] Monographie Departementale, Departement du Diamare, 1965, 12, ANY/1AA229.

[31] Ibid.

[32] Cf. the reports submitted by colonial authorities cited in Beauvilain 1989: 512; the annual reports for the years 1947, 1948, and 1950 (all in ANY/APA 11618); the annual report for 1952 (ANY/2AC 4206); and Note sur le banditisme dans le Nord Cameroun (Logone et Chari), 11 July 1952, ANY/1AC 1752/4.

[33] See, for example, Compte rendu de la tournée effectuée par le lieutenant Vallin, adjoint au chef de circonscription, 14–27 October 1930, 3, ANY/APA 11832/C. On the conquest led by Rabah in alliance with Choas (1893–1900), see Beauvilain 1989: 315–16; on the Mahdist uprising led by Goni Wadai, see Mohammadou 1992.

Following a razzia committed by the Kirdis of Bololo in the region of Gawell, a short visit to Mouda was made in order to punish the natives of this village who had taken an active part in the thieving and who form, on all occasions, a true association of organized accomplices, as storers of stolen property [receleurs].[34]

Pillage and theft [in] the region of the Moundang people [are committed by] influential, professional bandits; [they are] fairly aged and very respected. [But the entire population] gives asylum to accomplices to theft [receleurs].[35]

Efforts to undo the authority of these "professional bandits" and "storers of wealth" refer back to the problem of nomination, or control through classification: "In this region, we can affirm that the only ones who refuse to make contact are the thieves (who are more or less influential, unfortunately). In these cases, the burning of compounds, as a humanitarian measure, is necessary if we want our police to be efficacious. . . . By acting such that what is just is strength and that strength be just, our agenda corresponds to a distorted Pascalian idea."[36] But in spite of the (distorted) philosophy of justice as strength, as recently as 1950 the subdivision of Kaélé was described as "no less heterogeneous and difficult to command. A country of highway robbers, inhabited by half-servile pagans who are constantly engaged in guerrilla activities."[37]

In 1952 a French colonial administrator remarked:

We can say that the region [northern Cameroon] remains susceptible to the formation of organized "bands" of brigands, highway robbers, caravan pillagers. . . . We can examine in more detail the conditions of their existence: they are the same, but on a smaller scale, as those existing during the "Rabah years." First, there is a chief who finds himself designated as such by some unfortunate chance of fate, having committed a murder which induces others, linked as they are to the obligation of vendetta or pursuit. His renown spreads quickly; he becomes surrounded by people who were until then simple thieves. Audacity increases with numbers, and soon the band is known as such and lives only by brigandage; circling throughout a delimited zone, always on horseback on some frontier.[38]

[34] Rapport de tournée, Chef de la Circonscription de Maroua, 23–25 January 1930, 1, ANY/APA 11832/C.

[35] Ibid., 2.

[36] Compte rendu de la tournée effectuée par le lieutenant Vallin, adjoint au def de circonscription, 14–27 October 1930, 3, ANY/APA 11832/C.

[37] Rapport Annuel 1950, Partie politique et sociale, Région du Nord Cameroun, 17, ANY/APA 11618.

[38] Note sur le banditisme dans le Nord-Cameroun (Logone et Chari), 11 July 1952, 2, ANY/1AC 1752/4.

Audacity presented problems for colonial authority: "With the return of the dry season, the exploits of the brigands have recommenced. . . . The perpetrators of these acts are Arabs [Choas] whose audacity is extreme. I am reminded of one of my predecessors, M. Lenoir, who, wishing to personally pursue the bandits, was robbed of all his belongings by them during the night, being left, and for good reason, with only the bed on which he was sleeping."[39]

But more than audacity was the ever-present problem of frontiers, which were "a principle obstacle to repression. The police in pursuit of the bands cannot cross over."[40] Colonial strength was territorially bound, and colonial justice was often superseded not only by the sheer authority of professional bandits but also by their propensity for accumulation and profits:

> Other factors that undermine [police] action include, foremost, the (at least passive) complicity of a good part of the population. It is a regrettable but undeniable fact that in most cases the villagers oppose police action with silence and evasion. The explanation is as follows: the gendarme is far, he cannot be constantly on site; furthermore, he is not mean, he does not pursue the criminal and, when he does have serious presumptions [illegible]. The judge is farther still and only condemns with formal proof; there are notorious criminals who, when arrested, escape punishment simply by denial because there are no courageous witnesses to outpower them. Here, you need courage because the bandits are more fearsome and often more feared than the gendarme or the judge. It is dangerous to be exposed to their vengeance, while it is sometimes profitable to assure them of the means to escape.[41]

To be sure, brigandage and so-called banditry were the basis of a "true industry" that was "often patronized by the chiefs."[42] The organization of these enterprises depended on the chiefs' complicity, and in many instances, collaboration was quite formal. Famous brigands stocked their wealth in the villages of their patrons, and many heads of districts or cantons were likewise leaders of bands.[43] Known at the time as *sonngoobe*, these well-known

---

[39] Extrait du rapport de la tournée du Chef de la Circonscription de Maroua, 24 November 1930, 3, ANY/APA 11832/C.

[40] Note sur le banditisme dans le Nord-Cameroun, (Logone et Chari), 11 July 1952, 2, ANY/1AC 1752/4.

[41] Ibid.

[42] Rapport Annuel 1948, Région du Nord Cameroun, 13, ANY/APA 11618; and see Issa 1998, 2001.

[43] In the lamidate of Kalfou, "there are brigands among the inhabitants, at least one of whom is quite famous; a habitual offender who escaped from prison in Maroua and, it seems, is the brother of the Chief of Zaria. Summoned by the Chief of the region in 1943, the *lamido*, who had never tried to stop this dangerous man, decided to summon his brother whose 'status' as an accomplice (*receleur*) is unquestioned. The other [first] decided it was best to disappear" (B. Lembezat, Adjoint au Chef de la Région du Nord. Rapport de la tournée

men were celebrated by griots, who sung their praises, relating, as Saï-bou Issa (2001) recounts both the terror they inspired as well as their penchant for dilapidation and hence the redistribution of spoils. One former bandit thus states that "the famous bandit, the pretty woman, and the marabout all eat from the same bowl, which is then scraped by the lamido" (Issa 2001: 148, citing Saïbou Nassourou). As was suggested in the previous chapter, the admissibility of these appropriations and even the very right to appropriate were often judged according to particular interpretations of the material manifestations of power. As a colonial administrator observed:

> *A chief who wants to be a "great" chief must have beautiful gowns, a large following, horses and guards, ministers. . . . All these things are expensive. The villagers must share in these expenditures; it is legitimate and customary, to a certain extent; still, we must encourage the chiefs [installed by the French] to not try to compete in display with the Fulbe masters of Maroua [lamiibe]. . . . The chief is thus tempted, as is his entourage, to go beyond the permissible limits and many, very well known avenues are open. There is the traffic in titles, noted on several occasions; there is the traffic in matters of justice, which is, no doubt, less visible but no doubt also enormously profitable; finally, there is pillage, pure and simple, on a small scale no doubt, but frequent.*[44]

Historically, village participation in producing the materiality of power was tribute-gaisuwa. And since the impôt was incorporated into this register of rents, the colonial program of fixing, both conceptually and physically, a kaleidoscopic social field was also an attempt to domesticate and requisition the political power of tribute-gaisuwa. Because of this, those who were selected out as potential "racial chiefs"—or the "natural" leaders of so-called pagan villages and possible counterpowers to the lamiibe of the former caliphate—came to be politically problematic. As "intermediaries"—or those who depended on the interstices, serving as both tax collectors and brigand leaders, and essentially living off the right to spoils and rents produced in

---

effectuée dans la Subdivision de Yagoua, 6–22 June 1947, 56, ANY/APA 110418A). In the subdivision of Maroua, "Bandits, who are often armed, rob travelers clean and steal cattle after having disabled the herders. Sometimes protected by the Customary Chiefs who gain a profit, these criminals are very difficult to capture. An entire organization must be mounted to neutralize their activities. Gendarmes, mounted squads and especially action on the chiefs are the principal methods of struggle" (Rapport Annuel 1952, 43, ANY/2AC 4206). On chiefs as both district heads and brigand leaders, cf. Rapport Annuel 1948, 3–4, ANY/APA 11618; Rapport Annuel 1950. Région du Nord Cameroun. Partie Politique et Sociale, 17, ANY/APA 11618.

[44] Lembezat, Adjoint au Chef de la Région du Nord, Rapport de la tournée effectuée dans la Subdivision de Yagoua, 6–22 June, 1947: 63, ANY/APA 110 418A.

exchange—they thwarted colonial classification and its aim to fix the targets of wealth and fiscal power. The alleged problem of these chief-brigands was stated by the colonists in quite simplified terms as a matter of their "great need for money" (*leurs gros besoins d'argent*).[45] They financed power through fees and dues prescribed by Muslim law (e.g., zakkat, inheritance taxes) and, more troubling for French control of local administrators, the sale of titles and posts as local counselors and officials.

The power of extraction ensured by the intermediaries was deemed "unstable," then, since the rolls were frequently revised according to "the highest bidders."[46] This was aggravated by the intermediaries' strategies to increase their sources of financing, which included maximizing the number of persons paying for privilege and generating rents. In this context, the ambivalence of the intermediaries lay in their having brought *le signe de soumission* (franc–impôt) into the field of local power relations, submitting it, in itself, to the financial imperatives of regional organizations, and thus often subverting the preexisting system of political mediation and extraction that the French had hoped to employ. "Purging" the lamidates and sultanates of "useless intermediaries . . . whose essential preoccupations [were] collecting taxes and raising personal contributions" became, then, a political objective for the colonizers.[47] The autonomization of financially empowered leaders emerged as a primary concern.

With respect to one of these "chiefs," one administrator warned:

> We have thus arrived at this paradoxical situation: the chief of the Mousgou canton, who commands at least 3,000 Muslims in the plains (1,800 Mandaras), is considered to be the chief of 30,000 pagans and, as such, receives an allocation of 42,000 francs, equal to that of the sultan of Mora, the lamiido of Mindif or Bogo, and almost four times superior to that of the lamiido of Mokolo or the chiefs of the neighboring Mandara cantons. It will not be surprising, then, to see him, despite the prudence of the administration,

---

[45] Lembezat, Adjoint au Chef de la Région du Nord. Rapport de la tournée, Subdivision de Mora, Nord Cameroun, 18 March–2 April, 1947, 9, ANY/APA 1014A.

[46] This raises the question of legitimacy in stark terms. Sale of titles, or rights to succession, is contrary to the logic of succession defined by inheritance. Many disputes resulted from reference to these two registers of legitimacy. This was further complicated by the colonists' judgments about the quality and efficacy of local chiefs as administrators and intermediaries. Often, this was reduced to a matter of "appearance," a "mature" man being recognized as such by his white beard, elaborate clothing, and especially good health. Hence a chief who was a leper and hardly clothed was dismissed as incompetent in spite of his effective power over the local population and ability to manage conflict. On the problem of succession, cf. ibid., 20–23. On this question of legitimacy more generally, see Lembezat, Adjoint au Chef de la Région du Nord. Rapport de la tournée effectuée dans la Subdivision de Yagoua, 6–22 June 1947, ANY/APA 110 418A.

[47] This is especially true for the Mandara Sultanate (cf. Rapport Annuel 1946, Région du Nord Cameroun, 14–15, ANY/APA 11721).

sporting the title "lamiido," having the parasol of the great chiefs hoisted above his head; and I imagine he will find it difficult to accept being, from one day to the next, brought under the jurisdiction of [the sultan of] Mora.[48]

Such personalities were sources of wealth and commanded the circulation of rents in the region, yet they remained outside the bounds of official circuits of redistribution and affronted colonial techniques of regulation. Their industry of banditry and brigandage rendered them subversive to the system of the census, the circumscription of wealth in terms of colonial boundaries, and the thesaurization of wealth in forms recognizable to colonial authority. But their capacity to generate wealth made them critical targets of regulatory authority. They were especially important to colonial efforts to procure tax, since, while seemingly unnecessary and even troublesome, as speculators and highwaymen, their positions on the frontiers of wealth creation, as brokers and frontier traders, rendered them fundamental to the expansive designs of colonial extraction. This characterization of intermediaries as an ambivalent term—one that is essential to, and yet potentially subversive of, the creation of wealth and exercise of power—is such that the colonial authorities' statements about the evasive and untamable nature of intermediaries in the political sphere were generalized. "Intermediaries" came to signify the borders, the interstices, and undomesticated sites, a representation that was transposed onto the economic sphere.

In the latter realm, the "intermediaries" were specified as "market boys," who were deemed the ultimate source of economic instability and, in particular, the rising cost of living.[49] To be sure, the "market boys" were a significant economic force. They served as critical links between producers in the mountains and plains, and consumers and traders in the towns. Operating without significant capital and hence without licences, they evaded regulation but were nonetheless considered a "necessary evil."[50] And like the mobile brigands-chiefs, these intermediaries were often termed itinerant or "ambulatory" traders (*les ambulants*). They were the bulk of commercial activity, being approximately 361 in number in 1954 in contrast to 151 licensed traders.[51] Given the import-export monopoly established in the region by the R&W King company (which operated a flotilla on the Benue River), the ambulants were certainly necessary insofar as they delivered groundnuts from local producers for export and retailed the imported

[48] Lembezat, Adjoint au Chef de la Région du Nord. Rapport de la tournée, Subdivision de Mora, Nord Cameroun, 18 March–2 April, 1947: 68–69, ANY/APA 1014/A.

[49] French officials used the English term "market boys," thus hinting at their supposed foreign status ("Nigerians"). On colonial economic policy and the "market boys," see Rapport Annuel 1948, 69–70, ANY/APA 11618.

[50] Rapport Annuel 1948; Région du Nord Cameroun, 69, ANY/APA 11618.

[51] Rapport Annuel 1954, Statistiques, Région du Diamare, ANY/1AC 2204.

consumer items that kept the firm in business.[52] It seems, then, that their itinerant condition was practically required for commercial success in this context. In this sense, they were indispensable to wealth creation.

And yet they were baneful to the colonists because of their "vagabondage" and incessant transgressions of boundaries. Apart from district and lamidate frontiers, this included much travel to, and exchange with, Nigeria and Chad. The former was the primary competitor to R&W King, being a large market for cattle and hides, and a supplier of cheap manufactures.[53] The latter was the main market for grains (primarily millet) and a primary source of cattle imports. The significance of these frontier markets for itinerant traders was such that, in 1950, 1,503 cattle exports were declared while an estimated 12,000 to 15,000 were exchanged without being subject to colonial regulation.[54] In response, itinerant traders (les ambulants) were criminalized: "vagabondage," once defined as mere "wandering," became illegal. A government decree declared "natives who do not justify their regular and avowed means of existence and who do not have a specific domicile or habitual or variable residence necessitated by their profession" subject to official repression.[55] Ironically, mandated restrictions on traders' movements exceeded mere efforts to increase regulation of exchange in terms of levies, since they essentially reduced and even eliminated these exchanges. The pernicious nature of frontier commerce was evidently understood to be not only lost revenues for the colonial state but also unchecked politics. The introduction to an official statement on the political situation in 1950 thus reads as follows: "To a large extent, northern Cameroon is still untouched by the main currents and agitations from outside. This is not to say that it is not open to exterior influences. If the indigenous chiefs have little contact with their homologues in Nigeria, for example, the general populace has close relations with their neighbors, be this mountain dwellers who go to the markets and work yards in Nigeria and British Cameroon, traffickers and smugglers who exchange hides and cattle for cloth and kola, chauffeurs and

---

[52] In 1948, only three Africans are cited as having "proper" boutiques in town centers. In the early 1950s, almost all merchants were "satellites" of R&W King, to whom they sold groundnuts in return for pay or merchandise, which they then retailed. This situation is described in Rapport Economique 1948, Nord Cameroun, 28–30, and Rapport Annuel 1950, Partie Economique, Nord Cameroun, ANY/APA 11618.

[53] The "impossibility of restraining" this commerce gave rise to an ordinance (Arrêté du 17 Mai 1945) authorizing the importation and exportation of animals, produce, and merchandise upon condition that the value of exports be "reimported" in the form of either merchandise or currency. See Rapport Economique 1948, 30, ANY/APA 11618.

[54] Rapport Annuel 1950, Partie Economique. North Cameroon, n.p., ANY/APA 11618.

[55] Punishment was fifteen to six months' imprisonment or, for repeat offenders, prohibition from entering specific areas for five to ten years, with possible obligatory residence (Arrêt promulguant au Cameroun le décret du 6 mai 1924 portant repression du vagabondage au Cameroun, *Journal Officiel*, August 15, 1924, 357–58).

transporters, pilgrims and voyagers of all sorts. Frontier traffic has an utterly preponderant place in exchange; contacts of great distance remain exceptional."[56]

In sum, the ambivalence accorded to market boys, frontier traders, and itinerant salesmen—like that conferred upon brigand–chief tax collectors—ensued from their incessant transgression of boundaries, which was the very basis of their decisive role in the creation and distribution of wealth. With respect to the literal boundaries of the colonial state, this activity obviously collided with the limits of territorial jurisdiction. More than that, efforts to institute colonial law and constitute the legal subject via the "ordered knowledge of society" and enumeration were confounded by "unaccounted motion" (e.g., vagrancy), which, in subverting demographics, "also challenged the law" (Brantlinger and Ulin 1993: 45). For colonial authority, these prospects raised the specter of the continuity, formation, or autonomization of locally defined material bases, be they of brigands "always on horseback on some frontier" or market boys, smugglers, transporters, and pilgrims.[57] This political dilemma was carried over to economic policy itself, with lasting effects on manners of conceptualizing the foundations of wealth and, in consequence, appropriate practice with respect to profits and price.

The Intermediaries

This process of translation from the political domain to the economic entailed an important shift in representations of targets of power that accompanied the rise of the franc-impôt-prix trio. As noted earlier, "defense" against the law of discussion, or bargaining over value, was not limited to the mere protection of consumers, as was proclaimed. The colonial program of protecting consumers was organized according to prevailing notions as to the sources of disorder and even injustice that were to be governed such that the just price was obtained. The intermediaries were defined as problematic for propriety and price, not to mention the integrity of colonial determinations of value and colonial authority. Thus, in one temperamental flurry, appropriate economic

---

[56] The "main currents and agitations" issue from the South, where the nationalist movement was in full swing; the presence of an activist of the Union des Populations Camerounaise (UPC), Moumié, is mentioned earlier in the report. Rapport Annuel 1950, Partie politique et sociale, Région du Nord Cameroun, 8, ANY/APA 11618. On the UPC, cf. Joseph 1977; Mbembe 1996.

[57] This dilemma incited a response. For the colonial administration, "the essential point is to reverse, as it were, the situation at the psychological level, to make it such that people fear more for the gendarme than the brigand." For that, the gendarmes were to "live like the bandits" and be furnished with funds "for collaboration." Cf. Note sur le banditisme dans le Nord-Cameroun (Logone et Chari), 11 July 1952, 2–3, ANY/1AC 1752/4.

policy was officially declared by a colonial administrator as "that which would serve producers and not the more or less suspicious intermediaries who are used by this society to its fancy and convenience."[58] This rather imprecise policy position is found in more rigorous form in the politique des prix, which, ostensibly a general response to the rising cost of living, hones in on "market boys" as the source of economic instability.[59] Ignoring the monopoly effects of the concessionary companies, colonial authorities tagged these "boys" as responsible for price increases, since they "do not content themselves with reasonable profits."[60] As noted earlier, both rounding up and bargaining, the practices being stigmatized here, were said to be the primary causes of price increases.

However, the problem of these boys' taste for profits was perhaps less essential to inflationary tendencies than it was to tax, the ultimate source of colonial wealth. As I have argued, instituting tax went hand in hand with the institution of particular notions of price, such that Cameroonians became consumers of colonial wealth and generated a surplus in production and exchange that could be handed over to the colonial treasury. Their accession to, and (fairly nonviolent) assumption of, the logics implicit in the enactment of these relationships and the identity of the consumer was predicated on the force of certain representations not only of wealth but also of legitimate targets of regulation. The objectification of price as one of those targets coincided with the circumscription of categories of social and economic instability, which included the market boys. The latter were just one element of a whole category of social forces that colonial authority termed la population flottante. Their indispensability with respect to tax— and not necessarily inflation—lies in the disciplinary precept that tax requires a census, and hence immobility. In that sense, while in many respects the colonial intervention may have been an interlude (Balandier 1985), it had a momentous effect on these representations and on the forging of economic concepts, inducing a shift in the objectification of targets of regulation. During jihad and through the Sokoto Caliphate, power was exercised through and over circulation rights of conquest-spoils-slaves. Colonial power grafted onto this dispersion, giving rise to new objects of power and wealth: franc–impôt–prix–population flottante.[61]

---

[58] Rapport Annuel 1947, Région du Nord-Cameroun, 43, ANY/APA 11618.

[59] See, for example, Rapport Annuel 1948, Région du Nord Cameroun, 69–70.

[60] Ibid. On the effects of the European trading companies in northern Cameroon, cf. Beauvilain 1989, vol. 2. For another example, cf. Coquéry-Vidrovitch 1972.

[61] This is not to say, of course, that forms of money, tax, and price did not exist prior to the French interlude, or that these were not objects of regulation as such. It is to say, however, that a particular historical form of these categories was instituted with the exercise of French power, and that these articulated with extant forms of wealth, objects of regulation, and modes of power.

Given this modified notion of the foundations of wealth, colonial policy posed the question of "reasonable profits" as an interrogation of the larger problem of governing habits of valuation. As recent debates over the truth of price (gaskiiya) and social obligations inherent in debt relations reveal, intermediaries represent the interface between the mutually constituted and often socially problematic realms of the politics of truth and economic justice. This question of "reasonable profits" has resurfaced in debates over incivisme fiscal. They indicate how the colonial interpretation of consumer protection and the appropriate manner of, and reasons for, governing habits of valuation (price) has endured. In 1969, it was decreed that profit margins (defined as net profits applied to the cost price, or cost of production) on goods and services could not exceed 30 percent. Overhead charges could not exceed 8 percent, and wholesalers could not absorb more than 13 percent of total margins.[62] Purchasing power and, more significantly, legality of price have remained the centerpieces of state intervention, which was put forth officially in 1970 as an effort to moderate the "true state of anarchy in commercial activity," which "encourages disorderly and uncontrollable increases in prices to the detriment of the consumer."[63] Aside from the maxima decreed in 1969, establishing the "very lowest" retail price was a politico-economic directive against the intermediaries: "The number of intermediaries (various categories of vendors of the same type of goods) or commercial operations (wholesale, retail-wholesale, retail) should have no influence on overall profit margins. The price of an item, from the importer (store) or producer, can thus not exceed the two price limits, the intermediaries (not recognized, in any case, as true merchants), whatever their number and no matter the misfortune of their existence, must content themselves by 'nibbling' on the whole of the margins fixed by decree."[64]

"Illicit" price increases that were infractions of various decrees included prices that surpassed or undercut fixed limits, as well as "the remunerated intervention, in any form, of an intermediary who intercedes either occasionally or regularly and without qualification in the cycle of distribution, thus leading to the increase in legal prices of merchandise."[65] Thus the intrusion of intermediaries has been criminalized for its aberrant effect on a supposed norm—or its distorting effect on supply and demand—and in spite of the fact that, at the same time, administrators spoke of the very attempt to homologate prices as involving "much too much fantasy."[66] Quite ironically, the maestros of exchange have been indicted in the name of

---

[62] Enoh: n.d. [drafted 1979]: 31, with reference to Décret No. 69/DF/409, 2 October 1969.
[63] Lettre circulaire No. 10257/MIN FI/DCE/P, Yaounde, 12 October 1970, cited in ibid., 32.
[64] Ibid., 7.
[65] Ordonnance No. 72/18, Yaounde, 17 October 1972, cited in ibid., 17.
[66] Circulaire No. 144/MINCI/DCI/S8, Yaounde, 3 September 1968, cited in ibid., 40.

market equilibrium. Colonial concerns for the consumer as the ultimate source of tax resulted in the targeting of intermediaries in efforts to dampen the effects of competitive exchange practice. Significantly, more recent resolutions to eliminate "anti-competitive commercial practices" dictated by international funding agencies, such as the World Bank, have also located intermediaries as a source of economic deviance. Drafted in 1991, Article 11 of the Ministerial Order Number 008, "Defining Anti-competitive Commercial Practices," states: "To be considered of bad faith, the demander who presents himself as an ordinary buyer, buying to resell and to transform with the aim of realizing a profit while, in reality, he proposes to use the product purchased in a harmful manner to the seller."[67]

Of course, official price liberalization policy, one of the main tenets of the World Bank structural adjustment program implemented in Cameroon, caused both illicit price increases and the homologation of prices to be struck from the legal books. But intermediaries continued to be regarded as economically problematic. In northern Cameroon, the high proportion of retailers with respect to wholesalers is a result of a severe lack of capital and access to credit, as well as the related general demand for small-quantity purchases. Many regional districts have no wholesalers at all, and most large towns have only a few; hence the structure of distribution is shaped by the proliferation of "micro-retailers." In 1989–90, there were 82 wholesalers as opposed to 1,220 retailers for the five main towns of the area, not counting the very large numbers of unreported ambulatory sellers.[68] And the number of wholesalers has decreased since that time with the exacerbation of the economic crisis. In 1989, out of 1,693 commercial enterprises, there were 25 engaged in production (48 percent bakeries), 1,310 in distribution, and 358 in the service sector. By the next year, 92 commercial enterprises had closed, 11 of which were wholesalers. While small retailers and itinerant traders might in fact have been contributing to price decreases by increasing supply and undermining certain monopolies, they were consistently held responsible for price increases that were said to result from their speculative activities.[69] Regardless of their being a product of a shrinking capital base and certain effects of structural adjustment (e.g., salary cuts that induced a decrease in demand), the intermediaries (microretailers) are still condemned for "illicit" behavior with respect to price.

Here the intermediaries become part of a larger problematic. Apart from the colonial problem of nomination and tax, the legal status of the

---

[67] Article 11 of the Ministerial Order No. 008, Defining Anticompetitive Commercial Practices, 5, Arreté No. 008/MINDIC/DPPM, Yaounde, 7 March 1991, 5.

[68] Ministère du Developpement Industriel et Commercial, Delegation Provinciale de l'Extrême Nord, Rapport d'activité, Commerce, Année 1989–90: 13.

[69] See, for example, ibid., 13–14.

intermediaries, the legality of price, and the production of the legal (and hence taxable) wealth of consumers all have been bound up in the problem of debt. According to colonial theory, indebted consumers have no surplus for tax. And, as I illustrated earlier, the propriety of price in northern Cameroon has been judged, at least since jihad, in terms of socially sanctioned debt, or relations of inequality. The intermediary is the quintessential agent of debt, representing and creating the interstitial space and deferral for debt creation. Being defined as agents of bargaining, rounding up, speculation and, today, the failure to post prices (*le manque de publicité*),[70] this category is the unstable term that marks out undomesticated sociopolitical and economic space. As agents of exchange and producers of surpluses, intermediaries, and even traders more generally, were managed in the past as "guests of the state," a response to their uncertain political status (Alkali 1977: 258).[71] Under the legislative authority of the first president of Cameroon, Ahmadou Ahidjo, certain intermediaries were illegalized, such as cattle brokers (*sakaina*).[72] In northern Cameroon today, the intermediaries are joined by ambulatory sellers (ambulants), the clandestine (*les clandos*), street hawkers (*les sauveteurs*), "the informal" (i.e., economy), refugees, and foreigners (regularly signaled as "Nigerians," "Chadians," and, less often, "Nigeriens") in the capricious and often criminalized category of the population flottante. This category was circumscribed and given a name during colonization, when they became specified as targets of regulatory authority. By modifying what was deemed as properly within the field of "the economic," colonial power likewise redefined the economic status of limit zones, such as newly inscribed international borders as well as the bush. Despite constant mobility and acts of subversion or evasion, in many ways those who make their livelihood in these areas have emerged as a particular fiscal subject, both assuming their role as targets of wealth and becoming bearers of particular kinds of wealth, the rights to which are conditional and contingent. Today we can see how they have done so by observing their relations to regulatory authority, which gives insight into the very pluralization of regulatory authority in the Chad Basin today.

[70] With price liberalization, the failure to post prices has replaced price controls as the primary target of regulation. See chapter 2. I was given confidential documents ("CP" 9 August 1993 and "CP" March 1991), which informed me as to internal disputes over these matters.

[71] On the role of traders and raiders in opening up new regions through the establishment of Islamic centers, where those whose lives had been disrupted by raids served as slaves and clients, see Levtzion 1985: 192–93.

[72] Article 29 of Decret No. 76/420 portant réglementation de l'Elevage, de la Circulation et de l'Exploitation du bétail, 14 September 1976 reads, "The profession of cattle broker, or intermediary of sale [*sakaina*], is forbidden in interior commerce" (8). It is permitted with specific authorizations for exports.

Chapter Seven

The Pluralization of Regulatory Authority

IN A VERY GENERAL WAY, the incivisme fiscal movement expressed—and even served to develop—interrogations about the legitimate foundations of state wealth, the forms of wealth that are to be subject to state appropriations, the distinction between licit and illicit commerce, and the integrity of the contours of the nation-state. Ultimately, this debate about foundational terms like national wealth has occasioned cross-examinations of certain established truths, such as what constitutes wealth and work. People have interrogated the status of wealth produced through seizure and raiding performed by both agents of the state and the local populace. They have also probed the status of limit zones, such as borders and the bush, where wealth is produced and where targets of economic regulatory authority, such as the population flottante, have proved to be elusive and yet vital forces. In that sense, the past decade and a half has been marked by transformations in the ways in which the economy (or, more specifically, "the economic") is transcribed in national space—or the ways in which "the economy" is normalized as "national."[1] As a productive moment, incivisme fiscal, or the process of questioning it entailed, has given rise to transformations in the discursive field in which "wealth" and "work" are figured, as well as material effects of that discursive domain on contemporary practice. Among those effects are the novel arrangements between official and unofficial forms of regulatory authority that have become institutionalized in the region. In the Chad Basin, people now find themselves implicated in relationships with numerous

[1] Benedict Anderson (1996: 7) claims that the concept of the "national economy" dates from "as late at least as the founding of the League of Nations," being intrinsically linked to the very doctrine of self-determination. See also Mitchell 1998.

Moving contraband across the border between Cameroon and Nigeria. Credit: Gérard Roso, 2002.

figures of regulatory authority of both official and nonofficial status. This pluralization of economic regulatory authority (see Roitman 2001) issues from the multiplication of figures recognized as exercising legitimate authority over access to possibilities for accumulation and hence the right to employment and enrichment.

Unregulated Commerce and Road Banditry: A Day's Work

Circulating on the roads that link the various nation-states of the Chad Basin can be a treacherous affair. One is constantly swerving and veering to avoid the craters in the few main paved roads and to negotiate the ruts and troughs that mark the secondary dirt roads. Certain regions are particularly perilous, being well known for encounters with armed road gangs who set up roadblocks and brandish homemade rifles and especially Kalashnikovs in their quest for money and valuables. In the late 1990s, this phenomenon intensified, being labeled a true "war" by the press (*Le Messager* 1994; Pideu 1995; Soudan 1996; Dorce 1996). While limited in their scope, these road gangs, known locally as *les coupeurs de route* (those who cut off the roads), are nonetheless a regional phenomenon linked to transnational flows. They are composed of all nationals of the Chad Basin—Nigerians, Cameroonians,

Moving contraband across the border between Cameroon and Nigeria. Credit: Gérard Roso, 2002.

Truck overburdened with goods from Nigeria. Credit: Gérard Roso, 2002.

Chadians, and citizens of the Central African Republic, as well as itinerant Nigeriens and Sudanese.

These people and their activities are connected into regional and international markets in small arms, money laundering, and money counterfeiting. Moreover, they establish and participate in a network of economic exchanges and employment relations that found a significant mode of accumulation in the region. But that network of commerce and labor is not limited to forms of appropriation associated with organized gangs working the roads. It also consists of and is linked to a host of unregulated economic activities that have rendered the bush and international borders spaces of big business. The latter includes the smuggling of hardware, electronics, dry goods, and pirated merchandise, as well as the trade in black-market petrol, stolen four-wheel-drive vehicles, ivory, rhinoceros horns, gold, arms, and drugs. As one former military man, who was discharged and imprisoned for having allegedly sold his weapon to a coupeur de route, put it: "Over time, I understood that, even if the border zones are poor, one nonetheless makes big money there."[2]

No doubt, this realm of activity represents the only conceivable frontier of wealth creation in a region that has no viable industrial base and is not even an industrial periphery. With the severe economic hardship that was first noted in the 1980s, the application of World Bank structural adjustment programs, the contraction of bi- and multilateral aid, and the monetary devaluation of the franc CFA that occurred in 1994, the prospects for gainful employment have dwindled and purchasing power has diminished dramatically. This has been exacerbated by the demise of certain international markets, such as export crop commodities (cotton, groundnuts) and minerals (copper), and the recent rearrangement of industrial production, which has privileged labor markets in Southeast Asia, South Asia, and Latin America. This situation has given rise to large numbers of "economic refugees," many of whom have migrated to the borders, where they serve as transporters, guards, guides, and carriers in the domain of unregulated commerce. They are accompanied by "military refugees" born out of military demobilization programs and the inability of national armies to provide for their personnel. These people seek opportunities for accumulation in the emergent markets of the region. In Chad, for example, between 1992 and 1997, a military demobilization program involving approximately twenty-seven thousand men was put into effect (*Jeune Afrique* 1992; *Le Progrès* 1997; *N'Djamena Hebdo* 1997; Tiega 1997). This led to the dispersal of military personnel, who swelled the ranks of the unemployed, leading to the recycling of soldiers into the small-arms market, for which they have contacts and expertise. Many "deflated" (*déflatés*) soldiers collected their 30,000 CFA payoff, only to reinvest it in a Kalashnikov and a khaki uniform on the black market (Bennafla 1996: 67; Salomon 1997). Often they "enter the bush," as they say, working as road bandits with organized groups of under- and

---

[2] Ngahoui, Cameroon, November 17, 2001.

unpaid soldiers, as well as the unemployed from Cameroon, Nigeria, Niger, the Central African Republic, and Sudan. These men are joined by Chadian mercenaries who, after having entered Cameroon in the early 1990s to fight alongside their ethnic counterparts (the "Arabe Choa"), now roam the countryside.[3] This movement of men has transformed border regions and the peripheries of certain towns, both of which are now speckled with encampments and depots serving as warehouses, or bulking and diffusion points. While etching out spaces on the margins, these sites are not marginal. Like the activities they harbor, such spaces are dependent upon commercial and financial relations that link them to the cities.

Even though the problem of insecurity is recognized as the foremost challenge to governing the lands of the Chad Basin (cf. Zoua 1997; Seignobos and Weber 2002), the economic pursuits that prevail on international borders and in far-removed areas are crucial to the urban economy, as well as the financing of local administrations. The dramatic increase in the numbers of mercenaries and private security workers is a reflection of this situation. Since the late 1980s, on the continent in general, arms have proliferated from Eastern Europe, the independent republics of the former Soviet Union, China, South Africa, and Angola. Mercenaries and private security personnel also arrive from France, Belgium, South Africa, the former Yugoslavia, and Pakistan (see *La France militaire et L'Afrique* 1997; Friedman 1993; Ngangue and Salomon 1995; Harding 1996; Banégas 1998; Cilliers and Mason 1999; Mills and Stremlau 1999). In Cameroon, the spread of private security companies and their associated "securocrats"[4] has served to sustain the traffic in arms and munitions. As commercial fronts, these companies allow for the procurement of arms—such as 12-caliber guns, Browning or Baretta automatic pistols, and machine guns—and permits, which are not subject to quotas on imports (Kameni 1995). The brisk trade in munitions through the army also undermines official limitations on munitions per arm. Furthermore, the procurement of arms and permits through security companies is most notably facilitated by their being operated by former police commissioners or businessmen with high-level contacts in the Ministère de l'Administration Territoriale, which grants authorizations.

---

[3] For a historical perspective on these movements between Chad and Cameroon, conflict between the "Arabes" and the "Kotokos," and descriptions of the Zarguina, or bandits known for their blue-dyed clothing, cf. Bah and Issa 1997; Adama 1999.

[4] "Securocrats" is the local term for those engaged in the now burgeoning security business, including private security companies devoted to the protection of private firms, public buildings, political presonalities, and even public works sites. The final syllable (-crats) connotes the involvement of government bureaucrats in this lucrative private sector, which includes the mercenary business.

Generally speaking, the activities undertaken by the growing number of unemployed and dispossessed are very often financed and organized by military personnel, customs officials, wealthy merchants, and local administrators, such as governors, party delegates, and local chiefs. This was made clear to me in discussions with judicial authorities, police, and gendarmes, most of whom confirmed the financing and organization of the road-gang industry by local chiefs, well-known business figures, and leaders of political party cells. But it is also attested to by the sentencing, in 1996, of the *sous-prefet* (subprefect) of the town of Kousseri for complicity with coupeurs de route by a court in Yaounde, the capital of Cameroon. And, more recently, a group of coupeurs de route, who were arrested in the north, accused government officials of shared responsibility in their criminal acts before a military tribunal (Guivanda 2002). These denunciations testify to the web of relations that animate these forms of exchange and seizure. But they are also, according to Karine Bennafla (2002: 172), indicative of the increasingly blurred limits between civil servants, merchants, transporters, and bandits.

This blurring has perhaps always existed, but it has surely been exacerbated by recent changes in the regional political economy, which are of course linked to changes in the world economy. Like the more general populace, members of the local urban-based merchant class, which produced its rents largely through debt financing up until the late 1980s (Bayart 1989), were forced to reconfigure their economic activities with the contraction in bilateral and multilateral aid. In the Chad Basin, their past engagements in the import-export business, and as transporters and suppliers for public works projects have been reformulated in terms of the remaining or evolving possibilities for enrichment. Their convoys now plow desert paths and mountain roads running through Nigeria, Cameroon, the Central African Republic, Chad, Libya, and the Sudan, partaking in smuggling operations and unregulated commerce. And since privatization and the downsizing of public enterprises accompanying structural adjustment programs have inflated the ranks of unemployed youth, growing hordes of young men have followed in the wake of the merchants' convoys. Those who once found employment in local agro-industry, the health and education sectors, and development and public works projects now serve as transporters, guards, guides, and carriers along the Nigerian, Cameroonian, and Chadian borders. The intensity and expansiveness of their pursuits are such that the urban networks, which predominated over the countryside for several decades, are now becoming increasingly dependent upon economic strategies pursued by the unemployed and recently dispossessed. In many ways, the urban economy is now subservient to the "economy of the bush." As a report on the monetary situation of the franc zone in 1997 noted, the "urban exodus" of bank bills and coinage (notably

157

smaller denominations, which are virtually impossible to procure in large towns and cities) is largely attributable to the vitality of the rural sector (*L'Autre Afrique* 1997), and especially the "informal," or border and bush, economy.

Overall, the stimulation of economic activity in the bush is partly a result of the combined efforts of the economic refugees of structural adjustment programs and decreased foreign aid, on the one hand, and the military refugees of downsized and underfinanced armies, on the other. In the Chad Basin, those recently discharged during the demobilization campaign have joined up with unpaid soldiers from Cameroon, Nigeria, Niger, and Sudan, as well as the young guards and guides who have worked the bush trails trafficking contraband goods, and especially petrol, for almost a decade now. Their activities have transformed border areas, which are speckled with settlements that serve as depots, hideouts, and bulking and rediffusion points. Some "are quietly flourishing . . . as local entrepôts specialized in precision goods such as radios, cassette-recorders, watches, etc. as well as petrol retailing and currency exchanges" (Achu Gwan 1992: 23).

What is especially novel about this situation is that the dismissed, dispossessed, and unemployed who have taken to the bush, highways, and borders are making claims to rights to wealth. Many unemployed young men have some form of education, sometimes even having finished high school, and yet they find themselves obligated to scavenge and traffic for money. As we saw earlier, they often talk about their situation as a state of "war," where forced appropriation and seizure are the norm, being practiced by customs officials, police, gangs, armed bandits, and themselves. And those who normally benefit from officialized rights-in-seizure also complain about lack of compensation: regular soldiers protest (often through mutinies, as in the Central African Republic and Niger) against insufficient and irregular salaries, lack of basic infrastructure (e.g., sleeping quarters, food), and even essential equipment to carry out their duties (petrol, ammunition). Likewise, demobilized soldiers maintain that their indemnities are inadequate. For many, this, combined with lack of training for occupations in the civil or private sectors, is what compels them to "enter the bush," the implication being that the rationale of those who join road gangs and rebel groups is *alimentaire*—or about food more than politics (*L'Autre Afrique* 1997: esp. 14–15).[5] Thus, with great indignation, the soldier who had been imprisoned for selling his

---

[5] State resources for public spending have diminished as a consequence of structural adjustment programs and embezzlement. Nonetheless, presidential guards and private militias associated with executive power are paid well and in a timely manner, these outlays being mostly off-budget. Evidently, the right to redistribution is gauged according to certain representations of utility, be they well judged or not (witness Mobutu's Special Presidential Division).

weapon angrily cut off a question put to him by my colleague Saibou Issa about his reasons for sale in the following manner:

Q: . . . Why would a young military man, with a salary paid normally . . .

R: What salary!? What normal!? A settlement, yes! What salary allows one to live decently in Cameroon? You act as if you don't know that the salaries of state agents serve only to fool misery!

Q: Even the military? The state [le pouvoir] takes care of you, no?

R: The fact of not having reduced the military's salaries in 1994 does not necessarily mean that the salaries are good. When you have a big family—four or five people—you take the salary to reimburse debts! Do you know that the military are the most indebted, that they're all indebted?

Q: Because they manage their money poorly: women, drink . . .

R: That helps us hold on, to drown our worries. If not, instead of defending the people, we attack.

Recourse to the bush has given rise to hierarchies of bosses and workers that form and disband over time, creating a well-financed and yet fluid labor market—a sure source of employment and social mobility, and yet a fairly ephemeral entity. A self-described "ex"–road bandit described this situation as follows:

Q: Were you the head of a gang?

R: No, no! I played various roles in the attacks I participated in. I carried the sack of spoils [le sac du butin]. I assured the gang leader's security. I recuperated the arms after an operation. I participated in the planning of an attack. I never commanded. I didn't have my own group. You know, to have your own group, you have to have the means and the relations.

Q: What means? What relations?

R: You have to buy arms, give something to the guys before going to the attack, pay for their food, lodge them for days somewhere, pay informers who go to the marketplace to identify people who've made a lot of money, etcetera.

Q: And the relations?

R: (Sigh of aggravation) I told you that I don't know everything. The leader [le chef] of the team, sometimes he's someone I've never even

159

seen before. My prison friends would take me to him, and after an attack sometimes we'd never meet again, not even at the marketplace. In the Central African Republic, I had a chief [gang leader] who later became my neighbor in the [agricultural] fields! There were two guys working in his fields with whom we'd done operations. . . .

Q: What relations does the chief of the gang need?

R: Are you naive, or are you doing this on purpose? Do you think that you can do this kind of work without protection? For example, the chief who had his fields next to mine, in one operation we got a lot of money. I don't know how much exactly, but between the money we found, the jewelry, the watches, etcetera, the booty [*le butin*] came to something in the millions [of CFA]. We were fifteen or twenty people, I can't remember. I got 150,000 CFA. Since we attacked cattle herders and cattle merchants, well, it's sure that the leader got one over on us since, for himself, he kept millions. But afterward, when I saw him in the fields cultivating, I understood that it was the man in the car who kept most of it.

Q: Wait a minute! Who is the man in the car? This is not the first time I've heard people talk about a man who comes in a car just after an attack.

R: Oh! I can't really say. In any case, we threw all the arms and the spoils into the trunk of the car. Those who had military uniforms also threw them in. We dispersed, and then I got my part in the evening, at the rendezvous. . . .

Q: And the man in the car?

R: I never saw him again. But I'm certain that he went back to the city.

Q: Because he lives in the city?

R: Obviously! If it was someone from one of the villages around here, I would know him! A car in a rural area, that doesn't go unnoticed.

Q: What does the man in the car who comes from the city and makes you risk your life for a pittance represent for you?

R: You're the one who says that it's a pittance! Do you know what a civil servant's salary is in the Central African Republic? The 150,000 CFA that I got allowed me to spend a peaceful Ramadan and to clothe my family for the festivities. What job brings in 150,000 CFA for no more than a half day's work?[6]

---

[6] Meiganga, Cameroon, November 14, 2001.

No doubt, this work is well paid, as is attested to by a letter written by a man who describes himself as a "military personnel–coupeur de route."[7] This letter to the prefect of the Logone and Chari Department of Cameroon, which borders Chad, is supposed to be an official complaint regarding an unpaid salary of 120,000 CFA, the equivalent of a professional or "white-collar" salary in the region. Due to the transgression of nonpayment, the soldier–road bandit denounces his employers and warns the prefect that he is being sought after for his role in the deaths of nine Cameroonian soldiers. The letter reads as follows:

Chadian military personnel in the
Cameroonian territory aka coupeur de
routes in the Logone and Chari
Department

The bush, 17-1-94

To Monsieur the Prefect of the
Logone and Chari

It is an element of the Chadian military who is writing this letter to you asking [explaining] but why did I do this. Because we were paid each end of the month 120,000 F by month, but they did not pay me the month of December 1993 so I resigned. Their foolishness [error] of 1st month of 94, so I am informing you of the people who support us in the bush. They are: Alhadjji Mohammed Teiga aka Malham. There is Alhadji Lal Ghamat. There is Kanga Goudei. There is Alhadji Salam Collector-of-Everything-and-Nothing [choucou choucou], salesman of spare car parts in Kousseri. There is Alhadji El Amhadou, and then Christophe Pasteur, who delivers wine, "33" export [beer], Beaufort [beer], Castel [beer] and Wiskis [whiskey]. He is the owner of the Bar Gazelle in Kousseri. All the members that I just cited to you are those who furnish us with everything we need. Their special envoy is also a member who goes by the name Kanto. They rented us for 29,000,000 FCFA. Why? Because the Secretary of State at the Defense [Department] brought in the military to kill the Arabs ["Arab Choa"]. But we killed Cameroonian military, nine soldiers. Now they are looking for the Commissaire de la sécurité; 2nd, the Commandant of the company; 3rd, the mayor of the city [Kousseri], 4th, the subprefect. You are being sought after in the town of Kousseri at every hour.

I thank you for my information but I leave you. I am going to N'Djamena. I apologize for what is happening in Cameroon. I send you my photos as a souvenir.

D. M.

[7] Although I corrected the spelling and some of the grammar to facilitate reading, I reproduce a translation of this letter here so as to give an indication of the manner of speech and turns of phrase used by its author. Proper names have been replaced by pseudonyms. This letter appears in its original form as an appendix to this chapter because the translation evacuates the charm of the language of the French version.

The title "Alhadji" refers to powerful businessmen who supposedly made the *hajj* to Mecca. Certain Alhadjis referred to in the letter are well-known commercial and political figures in the region. It is also interesting to note the participation of "Christophe Pasteur," a Frenchman living in Kousseri. But the point is that this person would choose to submit such a letter to the prefect, which is indicative of the formalization of these activities and the idea that one has a right to claim unpaid sums of money through official channels, since they are viewed as salaries and involve officialdom.

Overall, the assertion that theft is work is not unique to road gangs. While the latter surely practice perhaps the most radical or brute form of seizure, such manners of expropriation are widespread. Chadian military personnel and customs officials find rents on fraudulent commerce more attractive than, and often a necessary complement to, their official salaries. They are now known as douaniers-combattants: customs officials–soldiers or fighting customs officials (cf. Abba Kaka 1997; Ngarngoune 1997). This has led to the blurring of the lines denoting civil versus military status, and even civilians versus administrators. For instance, when arriving at Ngueli, the bridge that spans the Logone River, marking the border between Cameroon and Chad and the entry to N'djamena, the Chadian capital, one is accosted by numerous people asking for identification papers and vehicle documents. Often, someone in uniform reviews these documents and then negotiates a fee for passage, which is formally presented as official tariffs. Shortly thereafter, a man in street clothes might appear, asking for the same documents. When you explain that you have just presented your papers to the government official, the "civilian" will brandish his official identity card, demonstrating that he is the "real" customs or security official. Who was the first man? Just some boy who had borrowed his uncle's uniform or, more likely, someone who had been given the uniform and told to go out and collect the day's pay. As one customs official said, those who cross the border "can be summoned by diverse people in civilian clothes or in uniform. These people pass themselves off either for gendarmes, customs officials, police, members of the presidential special services, etcetera. . . . The problem is that there is a sort of amalgam, and one doesn't know who does what. The multiplicity, the incoherence, the mix of uniforms brings on confusion. It seems that we're dealing with a blurring that is voluntarily maintained because it is part of a logic of accumulation created and maintained by the security forces who round up their monthly pay in this way."[8]

But summoning, assembling, or even supplementing—all connotations of "rounding up"—one's monthly pay is an economic strategy that is not

[8] Kousseri, Cameroon, December 8, 2001.

simply the ruse of unpaid or underpaid civil servants. For the general population, smuggling activities and large-scale banditry are forms of "work," which they contrast quite explicitly to "fraud" or "theft." The start of a conversation with a well-known smuggler who works the borders between Nigeria, Cameroon, and Chad highlights this point:

Q: *Thanks for having agreed to discuss your activities. To start with, what does the activity of a trafficker [traffiquant] in this region consist of?*

R: To start with—as well—what do you mean by "trafficker"? Are you insinuating that we violate the law or that we take advantage of a situation, or something like that?

Q: *No, no! Not that you take advantage, but, after all, you aren't ordinary economic operators.*

R: What is an ordinary economic operator?

Q: *It's someone who we can identify by his activity, his address, etcetera. He pays taxes, he has a boutique or a store at a specific place; it's someone whose life and activities obey certain norms.*

R: If I didn't have a specific activity and a specific address, how did you know that I master the route to Nigeria, and how did you know that at this very hour I would be here, on the Ngueli bridge?

Q: *I made some inquiries, and Abba Maïna led me here.*

R: So I'm well known, or else he would have led me to someone else; there are many people who go to Nigeria, to Chad, and elsewhere.

Q: *OK. You are definitely one of the oldest, most regular, and most well known in the cross-border commerce.*

R: *Voilà!* Cross-border commerce is the expression that fits.[9]

Another conversation with an "ex" –coupeur de route, who mysteriously escaped death by execution after having been arrested following the murder and "roasting" of a prominent police officer in peculiar circumstances, reiterated this reasoning:

Q: *How do you want me to address you?*

R: Why do you want my name? They told me that you want to write history! My name is of no use for that. And what name would I give you anyway? I've had so many; I changed my name several times. Only my mother calls me by my real name. So even if I give you a name, it's

---

[9] Kousseri, Cameroon, December 2001.

inevitably a false name, a name that I used at a given time or a certain place.

Q: Give me a name anyway. For example, a name that you used in an instance when you were robbing.

R: No! I wasn't robbing; I was working. . . .

Q: Yes, but stealing is not working!

R: You don't understand anything. The thief is like the liar. The liar wastes his spit for nothing; he talks to earn nothing. The thief takes by reflex; he takes everything that passes in front of him, even useless things. . . .

Q: You seem proud to have been a different kind of thief.

R: Are you trying to insult me? I'm telling you for the last time that, when there is a salary at the end, you are not a thief. Me, I work the roads.[10]

The idea that theft and highway robbery constitute work is more than just a rationalization of illicit practice; it is a reflection that is grounded in particular notions about what constitutes wealth, what constitutes licit or proper manners of appropriation, and how one governs both wealth and economic relations. As the participants in the incivisme fiscal movement have insisted, the materiality of the civil link between the state and its subjects is realized as much through taxes and welfare services as in wealth produced in domains that exceed the infrastructures of the state. Since the 1980s, structural adjustment programs, downsizing, and privatizations have displaced the sites from which the state enacts such transfers (Hibou 1999a, 1999b), and hence governs salaries, benefits, workers, and workdays, *as well as* economic rents, benefactors, clients, and syndicates. Hence the status of wealth, work, and state appropriations has come to the fore as a much debated set of referents. Likewise, in some ways the exercise of power over and in these domains has been modified, leading to a plurality of figures of authority over what constitutes wealth, work, and legitimate forms of appropriation.

The Contest of Regulatory Authority

Those who have managed to direct the financing, labor recruitment, and material organization required by regional and international networks

[10] Meiganga, Cameroon, November 14, 2001.

of accumulation form a military-commercial nexus, which involves leaders of factions or rebel groups, such as the Mouvement pour le Développement around Lake Chad;[11] the local merchant elite; and unofficially converted government administrators, including the douaniers-combattants. These are new figures of regulatory authority in the region insofar as their exactions and levies are often tolerated and even sanctioned by local populations—who achieve socioeconomic mobility and gain needed security—as much as those exercised by the state. As regulators, they compete with the state in its capacities to extract without recourse to force. And yet military-commercial alliances comprise renegade militias, demobilized soldiers, gendarmes, customs officials, well-placed military officers, local political figures, members of the opposition, and government ministers. This rather heterogeneous amalgam represents more than the mere involvement of national figures in corrupt practices perpetrated by regional traffickers, since regional regimes of accumulation, redistribution, and security are legitimated *alongside* those associated with the nation-state.

While it is true that transnational phenomena present notorious problems for state regulation, in the Chad Basin, as in other places, such networks become part and parcel of the political logics of the state itself, contributing to its ability to fulfill essential political imperatives such as extraction and redistribution.[12] This takes place, for one, through various manners of appropriation. For example, the Cameroonian administration has increasingly implicated itself in the recently established market town of Mbaiboum. In 1987, Mbaiboum appeared on the Chadian-Cameroonian-Centrafrican borders as a hub of unregulated commerce in local industrial goods (salt, sugar, textiles) and consumer items (clothing, cassette players, hardware, cement), as well as gold, drugs, arms, and diamonds. In the early 1990s, commercial activities in Mbaiboum intensified dramatically. In 1992, a Cameroonian customs station was established at Mbaiboum. Although the state has provided neither water nor electricity to this booming "town," in the late 1990s, it managed to take in 20 million francs CFA each year

---

[11] On the guerrilla movement around Lake Chad, see Faes 1997. Another rebel group operating in southern Chad, with incursions into the North Province of Cameroon and the Central African Republic, is the Forces Armées pour la République Fédérale, once led by Laoukein Bardé, who was recently assassinated in unclear circumstances.

[12] Some might argue that this is true for a regime or government, but not the state. That is, they understand the idea that the continuity of a regime may stem from appropriating the logics of wealth creation manifest in transnational networks but insist that state sovereignty is at peril due to the lack of authority exercised over such networks themselves. But if these networks contribute to the very viability of state functions (extraction, enabling productive economic sectors, redistribution), they perpetuate the viability of the state as a political institution as much as a particular regime.

through the sale of *droits de marché* (market duties or, literally, the right to the market) and licenses (Bennafla 1998: 54, 68; 2002: 85–88).

And yet, this formalization of once unregulated activity has not displaced unofficial regulators, who still exercise their "rights" on local populations: they collect "entry and exit" duties in the market (5,000 to 10,000 CFA per vehicle) and tolls on incoming roads (10,000 to 50,000 CFA for trucks), not to mention commissions and protection fees on the more lucrative trade in gold, arms, and diamonds.[13] As Karine Bennafla has demonstrated (1998: 66; 1999: 42–49), no measures are taken to quell these unofficial taxes, and Cameroonian customs policy has been described as "accommodating" or even "encouraging," with very low levels of taxation on goods, and a minimum amount of surveillance of the national identities of population flows through borders. Furthermore, military escorts have been established between Mbaiboum and certain outlying cities so as to protect merchants from the insistent pillaging of road bandits. In Chad, some claim that those who conduct such military escorts, such as the Garde Nationale et Nomade, are less concerned with protecting imperiled citizens than with securing fraud:

> *Unfortunately, in Chad, most of the laws governing the customs service are put to ridicule. The simple resolution stating that "a customs officer must not operate beyond the border" has not been respected. On the pretext of thwarting smugglers, the military and elements of the Garde Nationale et Nomade du Tchad—or alleged customs officials—ride at breakneck speed through the city crammed into their Toyotas [pickups], causing numerous accidents. The victims are most often peaceful citizens who have nothing to do with fraud. In reality, this chase between customs officers and smugglers is a pretense. It is, to some extent, a strategy that involves escorting the vehicle containing the smuggled goods all the way to the marketplace, for fear of being intercepted by other customs officials who amble along the roads. Without this tacit complicity, merchandise would not be imported from abroad. (Abba Kaka 1997: 8)*

Indeed, the Chadian and Cameroonian states have every reason to facilitate border traffic, which provides remuneration for under- and unpaid military officials, who convert to customs officials, and fills state coffers through licensing.

But this does not necessarily mean rendering "legal" unregulated traffic. The state can offer a legal structure for these activities without altering the fact that they are either formally illegal or based on fraud. This means

---

[13] On market and road taxes, see Bennafla 1998: 68. Information on the trade in gold, arms, and diamonds (and perhaps rhinoceros horns) is based on confidential interviews in Cameroon.

producing administrative paperwork for transactions without taking into account certain quantitative or qualitative aspects of the commerce involved, thus producing a false legal status for merchants. This is typical practice along the borders of all states in the Chad Basin—and perhaps all parts of the world—and represents one way in which the state is sometimes at the heart of the proliferation of sub- and transnational networks of accumulation and power. Evidently, this false legalization contributes to the economic well-being of under- and unpaid state administrators, who are reimbursed for such services. But it also contributes to the state's financial liquidity. Traffic between the Chad Basin and the Sahara has proved one means of accessing hard currency in a context of the nonconvertibility of local monies. In Niger, for instance, the state is central to the organization of the illegal trade in American cigarettes. As Emmanuel Grégoire notes (1998: 100): "The Nigerien state has, in effect, set up a legislative framework which organizes this traffic and obtains significant customs receipts, estimated at about 6 billion francs CFA in 1994 and 1995, or the equivalent of a month and a half of functionaries' salaries, which are six months past due (January 1998). Operators act in perfect legality in Niger, with fraud transpiring only at the cost of neighboring states which prohibit imports of foreign cigarettes to protect its own industry (Nigeria) or tax them strongly for the same reason (Algeria and Libya)." In this instance, state agents collude with, and are dependent upon, intermediaries (e.g., Tuaregs).[14] The latter control certain trade routes and are notorious for providing security in dangerous zones (such as southern Algeria and the Nigerien-Chadian border) not only for personal profit but also to respond to the insolvency of the state and its associated political risks (e.g., the demands of unpaid state bureaucrats, including police and "gens d'armes"). This scenario partially explains how insolvent states are somehow able to expand their administrative corpus: in Cameroon, for example, twenty thousand new functionaries were added to the rolls from 1987 to about 1997, despite the fact that there was new official recruitment during that time (Hibou 1997: 150). It also confirms the point that commercial policy in Africa (and elsewhere, such as Russia) is defined in terms of lucrative opportunities: "International commercial policy . . . is not designed primarily by the relevant [competent] administration (with its ensemble of rules on customs duties, quantitative restrictions, the standardization of regional commercial agreements, etc.), but by a certain number of influential actors, both public and private, who define such policy in function of possibilities for fraud and contraband, so

---

[14] Emmanuel Grégoire notes the special talents of the Tuareg of Hoggar as "passeurs" between Algeria and Niger (1998: 95), which is reminiscent of Austen's depiction of precolonial desert-side trade (see chapter 5). He also indicates that the Nigerien army often offers protection for convoys running illegal deliveries between Niger and Libya (p. 101).

as to ensure mastery of access to parallel markets and fraudulent practices" (Hibou 1998: 156).

The state thus benefits from profitable situations produced by competing regimes of power. It is sometimes also the instigator of proliferating unregulated, underregulated, or falsely regulated activities, and even becomes dependent upon those wielding power (e.g., regulation of access) and expertise (e.g., security) in sub- and transnational networks. While these endeavors potentially undermine state regulatory authority and national security, they also contribute to the viability of the state through the production of new rents and possibilities for redistribution among strategic military, political, and commercial personalities.[15] This results in a very contradictory situation. For instance, on the one hand, during the 1990s, the Cameroonian army claimed to be fighting "a war" against organized groups of highway robbers and the incursions of rebel groups from Chad, both of which included downsized and underpaid soldiers. Border towns had become rearguard bases as well as frontline posts. Cameroonian soldiers posted in the Extreme North to man "the front," as they called it, explained, "These bandits are men like you and me. Very intelligent. They are very well informed of people's movements in this part of the country since they have their accomplices everywhere. . . . Their heads [faces] are always masked in turbans and they are specialists in rearward combat. After every assault, they withdraw in cascade, sweeping the [Cameroonian] soldiers with gunfire, and they retreat to Nigeria where they know we don't have the right to pursue them" (quoted in Pideu 1995: 6).[16]

In the mid-1990s, over an eighteen-month span, "the front" was ravaged by the deaths of between four and five hundred civilians, with five or six times as many injuries. The numbers are, of course, hard to gauge, especially since graves were often uncovered in the bush (mostly in Nigeria) and many of the injured never reported to officials. In 1995, during a sixteen-month period, sixty "highway bandits" were killed, according to the Cameroonian military posted there. Five soldiers were said to have been killed over the same period, which is more than the number killed in the

---

[15] This is similar to the situation in Algeria, as described by Luis Martinez (1998), who demonstrates how the civil war in Algeria has not led to the disintegration of the state. The Algerian state found economic and political advantages through a specific manner of regulating conflict and control of resources. Recourse to the army and private militias as a means of ensuring exclusive control of certain resources (e.g., oil) is legitimated due to the state of war, thus permitting the state to finance the reconstruction and consolidation of essential alliances. Also, surveillance of the general population has been given over to militias, which benefit from accumulation via violence and increase their power.

[16] Interestingly, this soldier spoke of *le combat retardataire* (rearward combat); *retardataire* is used to refer to a soldier who overstays his leave.

military conflict over the oil-rich Bakassi region in the south (Pideu 1995: 6). "You're there with your comrades, you see them leave in a truck. Thirty minutes later, they come tell you they were all killed," was how one soldier (6) portrayed the impact of this "parallel army" that outpowered the Cameroonian forces. The latter had no telephone or radio links, were often immobilized for want of petrol, and suffered from insufficient funds for provisions. Their primary task of escorting convoys of commercial trucks, and bus- or carloads of anxious travelers was compromised by this lack of infrastructure and matériel. They were usually outgunned by attackers. But parity in firepower and organization were not the only attributes that made this a parallel army. "Every day, the military authorities in Maroua and Yaounde are informed about the zones in which the killers camp. In their villages, they work just like a regular army. They take guard every night and dispose of cars and motorcycles for their operations".[17] These regional contingents have their own villages in Cameroon; indeed, they have their own regions (e.g., Waza to Dabanga during the 1990s and the Cameroon–Central African Republic border during 2000–2002). Their interventions, though explosive, are not sporadic. In the late 1990s, they distributed tracts advertising the day and time of future attacks, warning travelers to be equipped with at least 2,000 CFA *nouveau format*, since, around the time of the 1994 devaluation, new bank notes were issued in Cameroon, denominated as "new format."[18] One wonders whether a truly marginal operation would insist on receiving only newly printed bills when, at the time, the old bills were generally recycled through informal exchanges without much difficulty.

As the independent press argued, this levy may be a form of spoils, but it is not necessarily simply haphazard theft: "Certain dignitaries of this part of Cameroon think that these attacks are knowingly maintained by authorities in Yaounde [*le pouvoir de* Yaounde], with well-defined ramifications for local administrative authorities. According to informants, a gold wristwatch belonging to an important person from Maroua [*un fils de* Maroua] was taken by highwaymen only to reappear later in the subprefect's possession in Kousseri. This provoked lots of commotion in town. Furthermore, locals complain that the bandits, once arrested and put in the hands of public authorities, are immediately released, thus inciting large-scale criminality in [the region]" (ibid.; and see Dorce 1996). In a conversation with Saibou Issa, who collaborated with me on this research, one "ex"–coupeur de route evoked the details of an incident that led to the

---

[17] Cameroonian soldier quoted in Pideu 1995.

[18] According to the tracts, failure to produce the desired sum in the proper form risked "loss of genitalia" (as reported in ibid.).

169

"roasting" of a high-profile police officer and the subsequent arrest by the "antigang" brigades (the former Groupement Polyvalent d'Intervention de la Gendarmerie, or GPIG)[19] of the band supposedly responsible for the crime. Our interlocutor was released from prison for unknown reasons, which he clarifies in an oblique way:

Saibou: What name do they call you by around here?

R: You want my name or the name they use for me around here?

S: I know that you won't give me your name; I mean the name you were given the day you were baptized.

R: How do you know [that I won't give you my name]?

S: I got information. Even people who recognize you physically don't know the name you went by before your exile to the Logone and Chari [department].

R: I'm not in exile. . . .

S: Can you go to Maroua, Garoua, or Touboro without worrying? Can you go in the day, go sit outside and have a drink?

R: I have nothing to do there. Anyway, how did you catch up with me [retrouver]?

S: Why do you say "catch up with"? Why don't you say "find"? Do you feel like you're not in security?

R: It's just a manner of speaking.

S: It's more like an unconscious reply. I'll tell you later how I caught up with you. We didn't finish with your name. How is it that a Mousgoum [ethnic group; generally non-Muslim] born in the Diamaré [department] is called Abba Maloum Bram [typical Muslim name]?

R: Is that all you have as a question?

S: Lots of people change their names when they want to change lives. Let's say that you're not the first. Maybe I'd even do the same. But I'm convinced that it would be difficult for me to change my identity so easily. For example, I'd have trouble getting a national identity card with my new name.

---

[19] The GPIG, accused of harboring corrupt elements, was replaced in 2001 by the Centre Opérationnel de la Gendarmerie (COG), which is housed in the Secrétariat d'Etat in the Defense Ministry. In the northern part of the country, the Bataillon Léger d'Intervention was established in 2001, with Israeli expertise, being subsequently renamed for mysterious reasons the Bataillon Rapide d'Intervéntion.

R: There are many people here who have three identity cards with different names, different ages, and different nationalities. There are salesmen [*démarcheur*] who can get you one if you're ready to pay.

S: *Is that what you did?*

R: I'm not seasoned enough to get you all you want, but I know that by splitting the payoff with one or two people, I can get things.

S: *What can you get?*

R: What are you looking for?

S: *Let's start with information. If I wanted to become a coupeur de route, a trafficker in arms or stolen cars, how would I learn the trade? Who do I need to see?*

R: That's the kind of merchandise you want to buy?

S: *To start, yes. Information is merchandise: it costs.*

R: You don't look like someone who wants to become a coupeur de route.

S: *Does the profile of a coupeur de route show on the face?*

R: To be a coupeur de route, you have to be fearful—

S: *That's paradoxical! I thought you had to be intrepid!*

R: It's the gun that makes force—

S: *So you were afraid—*

R: Wait a minute. You want the merchandise without paying?

S: *How much?*

R: 100,000 CFA.

S: *1,000 nairas?*

R: Do you think my nose is pierced? That's not even 10,000 francs.

S: *If I pay 100,000 F, what kind of information are you going to give me?*

R: Whatever you ask.

S: *Let's see what happens. Who was your boss [grand patron]?*

R: (Long silence) I don't know. Surely someone very well placed. Probably a big businessman or a high-level administrator. But I don't know.

S: *So you can't tell me the gist of what I want to know. I know that you were just a laborer [un ouvrier], which is why you escaped execution. If I pay*

171

you 100,000 CFA, it's wasted money if I haven't got the desired merchan-dise. I'll need to talk to five or six other people to gather the information I need for my work. If I divide 100,000 by five or six, that comes to about 15,000 or 20,000 CFA. You tick off your day and you tell me what you know.

R: On condition that you swear not to tell the people here my real name. They have confidence in me.

S: Of course. If you help me, I'll pay you and I won't reveal your real iden-tity, since you seem to be cooperating normally now.

R: OK. Thanks. But what are you going to do with the information?

S: I'm going to gather lots of diverse facts so that I can write the history of the coupeurs de route.

R: Ah! Afterward, they'll kill you!

S: Who?

R: Everyone. The coupeurs de route are everywhere.

S: What makes you think that I'm not also one?

R: You look more like a soldier, but who knows?

S: OK, to start with, what kind of weapons did you have? Who gave them to you?

R: The leader [*le chef*] told us that we would have more sophisticated guns than those of the army, or at least the minor soldiers [*les petits sol-dats*] who escort vehicles, and that they (soldiers) feared our arms. I think the guns came from Chad and the Central African Republic, and even the Cameroonian army.

S: The Cameroonian army?

R: Of course.

S: Those that you grab from soldiers during attacks?

R: Oh no! I don't know how it works, but me and my comrades, we had the distinct impression that they were arms coming directly from the arsenals of the army or the police! For us, the arms came and found us in the bush, and we left them somewhere after the operation. That is how it worked in some of the operations that I participated in.

S: Why did you roast the police officer, Koore of Maroua?

R: Wait! Wait! Who told you that this policeman was roasted?

S: In a conversation, like that. I didn't ask. The person I was talking to mentioned the bad elements of the forces of law and order. Is it true that the road bandits cut him up and put him to roast on the fire?

R: Let's just say that there is information in this sense. It's this kind of behavior that made us avoid aggression. In any case, I myself never shot anyone, and I certainly never burned a soldier. When you do such things, you have the authorities on your back for the rest of your life. There are limits to deviance. You have to steal to eat or to have capital for an activity that is, umm, more conventional. It's true that in this realm, you just can't decide to leave one day. You become an enemy. The person who brought you into this line of work is responsible for your honesty vis-à-vis the group. Confidence is important in a band of coupeurs de route because everyone [inaudible]. If I can talk about certain things now, it's because I know that big people [*de grosses têtes*] are now dead; the GPIG didn't miss them.

S: How is it that the GPIG missed you?

R: I was not executable.

S: You are protected [blindé] against death [through indigenous medicine]?

R: No, of course not. The elements of the GPIG knew very well who did what—

S: It seems rather that you know someone in the GPIG who saved you by simulating arrest—

R: (Long silence) OK. Let's get back to Koore.

S: OK, but I just want to know one last thing: Did the elements of the GPIG do business?

R: Do you know one Cameroonian person, an agent of the state, a holder of power [*un pouvoir de contrainte*] who does not do "illoffical business" (*du business illofîciel*)?

S: Wait a minute. What does that mean: illofficial business?

R: I don't know exactly, but from what I learned doing business in the milieu of trafficking in this region, illofficial business means, for example, that you traffic in illegal merchandise in plain view of the authorities, like the customs officials, who are responsible for controls, but, in reciprocity for corruption, these legal authorities close their eyes on this illegal activity. It's a system that allows everyone to live peacefully. They are activities repressed by the law, but those who are held responsible for the law let them pass.

S: In that sense, isn't it the law of the state that's "illegal"—insofar as what the state seeks becomes marginal?

R: From what I see here, it is difficult to apply Cameroonian law without creating problems. You have people coming from various countries, Cameroonians who go to Chad, to Nigeria. Here, if you don't speak Arabic, you are a foreigner; but if you speak Arabic, you're easily integrated. If the state wants to be the driving force here, that's going to create problems. People are Cameroonian by their nationality, but, on the economic level, Nigeria feeds them. Do you think that Cameroon could ever absorb all the fish that we get out of this region? Even if we created a state based in Kousséri [main town on the border with Chad], that wouldn't be a problem for the people who live here. A state covering the Logone and Chari [in Cameroon], N'djamena [Chad], and the zone of Maiduguri [Nigeria], that would be a good state. Business would work; people speak the same language.

S: Someone like you, who doesn't have an ordinary past, how do you manage to integrate yourself into this kind of economic milieu, where I imagine activities are initiated through well-known bosses [patrons]?

R: The thief is a man of confidence—I mean the ex-thief—because he knows the secrets of the thieves. The person who employs me knows everything about me—or almost everything. If you make an effort, you can weigh in as a partner. I need to change my life, the boss needs to have someone who is attached to him. I'm not the only one in this situation. We're numerous, each with his own story, his past. We go here and there to undertake precise tasks at the service of our patron. I think that my boss—or my bosses—are aware of this, since they've never sent me to Maroua. You know, if you delve a little into the lives of people here, you might unveil incredible stories.

S: What is the cement that binds relations between patrons and employees in a context of, as you say, illofficial business?

R: No, I don't say that; there are always words like that. I told you before that there is confidence. You can't entrust your assets to someone if you don't have confidence.

S: OK, but I don't understand how you can have implicit confidence in someone you don't know and, moreover, was a thief!

R: What could be more normal than to entrust your illegal activities to hardened people!

S: Is fish an illegal commodity? [This coupeur de route claims to now be a fisherman on the Logone River.]

R: (Laughing) You know very well that, in these things, there is not only fish![20]

The formation of the GPIG in the early 1990s put a halt to much road banditry, since executions deterred many of those working the roads. But reports—especially a significant one published by Amnesty International—about executions without trials, with images of bodies piled up on the roads outside villages, and claims that this special force was being used for political killings, and especially assassinations of members of the opposition, also put a brake on the alleged vigilance of the GPIG. And as the coupeur de route–cum–fisherman pointed out, the GPIG is not without its own motivations, be they "illofficial" business or maintaining political connections. During 2000–20002, road banditry increased significantly in the Adamaoua region of the Northern Province despite the conversion of the GPIG into the Centre Opérationnel de la Gendarmerie (COG) and the founding of the Bataillon Rapide d'Intervention (BRI), which was transformed, with mysterious nuance, into the Bataillon Léger d'Intervention (BLI). Descriptions of incidents usually indicate that attacks are extremely well planned, with information about the comings and goings of wealthy merchants, missionaries, or entrepreneurs with money for purchases and salaries; the transfer of funds between businesses, such as the brasserie or the cotton company, and their respective work sites or banks; and the movement of money between political parties and banks or high-level personalities. Recently, village chiefs and their private guards (*dogari*) have been condemned as patrons of gangs and one lamido is serving time in Garoua (see Oumate 2001–2). In a separate incident, government administrators, including a chief, a mayor, and a deputy to the National Assembly, were also all accused by a group of coupeurs de route appearing in court. In comparison, the only error of the chief who ended up in prison in Garoua was said to be his "having had the bad idea to go to the front himself" (Guivanda 2002). Like our pseudo-fisherman, the links between commercial and political networks are such that most of those who appear in court are ultimately protected. Not long ago, certain members of the police force were stunned when many of the accused requested that the procedures for bringing their cases before the prosecutor be speeded up. Evidently, the "protectorate" extends into the halls of the national judiciary. In exchange for a part of the spoils, the magistrates make sure that, if and when the accused are sentenced, the penalty will be as light as possible (Ousmane 2001).

These sectarian and entrepreneurial pursuits of aspects of the state bureaucracy, including district governments and the military, are part of strategies for the reconstitution of politico-financial networks. The latter

[20] Blangoua, Cameroon, December 26, 2001.

delineate autonomous political spaces vis-à-vis state power, but, more important, their activities serve to finance political clients and therefore prevent the emergence of a regional counterelite or counterpower. In Cameroon, the Biya regime's tolerance—lest we not say sanction—of high military officials' involvement in the arms, drugs, and counterfeiting sectors is well known and generally interpreted as a means of redistribution. This is a matter, then, of the very formation and maintenance of a dominant political class—or the stability of a regime.

But beyond political commissions and payouts, and the underwriting of political stability, rents (or wealth) thus produced are essential to "an extremely complex system of revenue transfers from formal and official circuits to parallel ones, from urban households to rural ones, from the richest to the most dispossessed (via allocations to families; social expenditures and diverse benefits such as school fees, health, funerals, participation in customary ceremonies . . .)" (Mbembe 1993: 367–68). These forms of redistribution are a primary mode of the exercise of state power. Appropriating rents associated with regional and international networks of accumulation—and thus collaborating with and managing their associated figures of financial power and regulatory authority—means creating wealth for off-budget activities, such as hiring private security companies as presidential guards or financing political parties, and state functions, like paying administrative salaries or financing external conflicts. In this sense, the regional networks described herein are a resource that contributes to the political logics of predation that define the historical exercise of state power in Africa (Bayart 1989).[21] Yet this is not to reduce this situation to a historical-cultural necessity: similar situations obtain in Colombia, Peru, Algeria, and Russia, where tributary relations between the state and sub- and transnational networks of wealth and power prevail.

As some observers maintain, state consolidation on the continent takes place via indirect, or nonbureaucratic, means (Hibou 1999b; Reno 2001). This has been aggravated by the emergence and deregulation of particular markets (e.g., in small arms, mercenaries, private security companies), as described previously. But is this manner of exercising power via indirect mediations a novel aspect of state power in Africa? Recourse to private, foreign agents, for example, is a long-standing manner of ensuring the effective exercise of state power. In Africa, this has involved the use of external alliances, such as the Cold War powers, or external resources, such as foreign aid, to manage internal conflicts and the demands of factions

---

[21] The multiple manifestations of the predatory logics of state power have been described by some observers as the *dédoublement de l'état*, which has taken form, for example, in the *conseils administratives* (Bayart 1997: esp. 64–67). On *dédoublement* as a mode of power, see Mbembe 1992.

constituting the basis of state power (Bayart 1989; Reno 1995; Hibou 1997, 1999b). In that sense, the reconfiguration of power on the continent today is less a matter of new practices of the exercise of state power than novel ways of negotiating the changing world economy, or managing extroversion. It is, as Achille Mbembe (1993) has argued in another context, an attempt to "redeploy networks of reciprocity, allocations, and compensations that were once amalgamated in the heart of the single party [state]." In the Chad Basin, sub- and transnational regimes of accumulation are critical connections to today's external rents; they are another means of insertion in the world economy. Figures of regulation associated with these regimes are critical to the consolidation of state power: they represent, through the production of wealth on the frontier, one place where the tentacular effects of state power are redeployed in its quest for the means to redistribute.

The Intelligibility of Seizure and Tax: Practices of Government on the Margins and in the Norm

In the field of state power, alternative forms of power—and regulatory authority—always exist because no form of power is effectively totalizing. But the question remains: Are appropriations, which found viable regimes of accumulation, giving rise to new figures of regulatory authority in the Chad Basin that are sanctioned in everyday practice? And this, in spite of their being associated with often extreme violence. Ultimately, an idea of the extent to which state regulatory authority is being displaced by other agents of regulatory authority means ascertaining the extent to which the economic and political relationships associated with the latter are institutionalized or apprehended by those involved as the most logical or "true" engagements.[22] Since commercial and financial activities that constitute regional networks of accumulation are among the few remaining opportunities for employment and enrichment in the Chad Basin, one of the main ways that regional elites—such as prominent merchants

---

[22] The methodological point implied by this entails a very specific approach to the political, which is spelled out in Roitman 1996: preface and chap. 1. It is reiterated quite elegantly by Barry, Osborne, and Rose: "The limits of the political are not defined in terms of the boundaries of an apparatus—the State—or in terms of the fulfillment of certain necessary functions—repressive and ideological State apparatuses—but as themselves discursive. Rather, politics has itself to be investigated genealogically, in terms of the ways of coding and defining or delimiting the possible scope of action and components of an apparatus of rule, the strategies and limits proper for rulers, and the relations between political rule and that exercised by *other* authorities" (1996: 13–14, my emphasis). This is, as Paul Rabinow (1986) says, a matter of studying the production of being "*dans le vrai.*"

and ex–military personnel—exercise regulatory authority is by controlling access to such possibilities for accumulation, thus determining the right to employment and enrichment. This takes place at the highest levels of business through commissions on deals, right-of-entry taxes, tribute and royalty payments to maintain political and commercial relationships, protection fees, and even payment for safe delivery of goods procured through customs fraud or for their "legal" passage through customs. And it transpires at the everyday level of business through levies on local merchants; protection and entitlement fees paid by young men engaged as guards, guides, runners, and wardens; entry taxes paid at unregulated border markets; and tolls on roads near these economically sensitive outposts.

No doubt, many of these payments are made under coercion.[23] Yet many people are often quite willing to make payments for access to privileged commercial relationships, international markets, and lucrative local sites of accumulation, since these provide the means for socioeconomic mobility in a time of scarcity. Furthermore, payments made to ensure access to markets, essential commercial and financial relationships, and protection serve to formalize the various kinds of traffic involved, be that of small arms across long distances or smuggled petrol through a mountain pass. This makes such activities less unpredictable in terms of both logistics and revenues. Moreover, contributions to those who regulate access to, and participation in, these commercial and financial activities are not without services rendered. These include protection and a formal cadre. In Cameroon, the role of the *commissionnaire de transport* (forwarding agent) is a good example of this. These individuals own or rent trucks for freight transport into the country. Through predetermined agreements with the customs service, they negotiate the freight's passage through customs, most notably for passage of the trucks themselves, and thus often irrespective of its contents. No particular documentation is needed to conduct this activity. Often being influential merchants, the commissionnaires' positions depend on informal relations maintained between themselves and the heads of the customs service, as well as political connections. In Maroua, for example, all the commissionnaires were members of the party in power (RDPC; for details, see Bennafla 2002: 165).

But, apart from protection and the formalization of supposedly irregular activities, payments made to nonstate regulators also involve the

---

[23] Cf. Bennafla's description (1998: 68) of payments made at barricades along the route to Mbaiboum, a flourishing, unregulated (until recently) market at the confluence of the Cameroonian–Chadian–Central African Republic borders. Even though the state administration recently attempted to regulate this intense center of border traffic by implementing official *tickets de marché* and licensing fees paid by merchants, unofficial "rights to entry and exit" are still also paid to regional henchmen at the market itself.

redistribution that takes place through the financing of schools, mosques, churches, and medical clinics. In northern Cameroon and Chad, prominent merchants are famous for building mosques and Muslim schools in home villages; today, these have begun to pepper the no-man's-lands and new frontier towns along national borders (Taguem Fah 2003).

Those who find themselves outside the bounds of national welfare and security come to judge prestations associated with unofficial regulators as justifiable and even rightful, since they grant access to possibilities for accumulation, protection, and services that are not secured through the state or public services. In this sense, the relationships that local populations establish with those controlling regional networks of accumulation respond to the claims to rights to wealth they have been articulating through the incivisme fiscal campaign and various acts of seizure. As those who work the economy of the bush insist, the expanding trade in unregulated goods is quite often a source of economic empowerment and freedom. These people have asserted rights to engage in commerce regardless of means. While state appropriations frequently take the form of seizure in marketplaces, on roads, and at border crossings, they have also become generalized as a mode of expropriation and enrichment, being presently perceived as fair game and taken up as an operative rationality by the local population. Ultimately, "tolls" and especially "taxes" can be effected in sites other than within the limits of the state-citizen bind. This was affirmed by Bakaridjo—the fictitious name of the coupeur de route from the Central African Republic who had a decent Ramadan thanks to his "road work"—in response to the following question:

Q: *I want to understand better. The man in the car allowed you to have a good Ramadan. Between him and President Ange Félix Patassé (of the Central African Republic), who is most useful to you?*

R: Patassé is a good-for-nothing [*un vaurien*]. A scared man who cries over the least gunshot. I pay my taxes to Patassé. The man in the city gives me the means to pay Patassé's tax. Patassé sabotages the state; he steals from the Central African Republic, which is already very poor, and starves the people. My employer [gang leader] both fills in and rectifies [*combler*] the theft created by Patassé.

Q: *With 150,000 CFA? (earnings)*

R: Patassé never gave me 15 CFA! In all of Patassé's offices [state administration], you have to pay for services! In any case, I don't give a damn about what you think. I deplore the deaths, of course. I've never killed anyone. In fact, once when a companion killed a passenger in cold blood because he didn't like the sight of him, the gang leader shot him after the operation and we split his spoils [*son butin*] among ourselves.

179

Q: So, in conclusion, you are unconditionally devoted to the man who allows you to take care of your family, whatever the provenance of the resources?

R: I was. I stopped now. I told you before; I paid by going to prison. Anyway, money has no color, no odor. A man should be ashamed of hunger. When one has all his limbs and all his senses intact, one must work. Me, I never attacked a poor man. What would I take from a poor man? I am sure that the merchants and others who fall into our attacks are people who earn their money illicitly.

Q: Illicitly?

R: Yes.

Q: Why?

R: They buy cheaply; they sell at very high prices, without respect for Islamic rules of commerce. They don't pay the charity tax. And we pray to Allah that we will fall upon such people [during attacks]. Moreover, when they negotiate cattle all day at the market, when do they have the time to pray? We see them at the market; they don't pray.

Q: And you pray before going to work the road?

R: What do you think?

Q: What prayers do you do? Which verses?

R: You also want to work the road? Allah exercises everyone's prayers. Those who don't want to pay the zakkat [Islamic charity tax], we take up the responsibility to take it from them. It's a charity payment on their fortune, a revenue tax.

Q: So you replace the state tax services! Is that legal? Is it legitimate?

R: Legal? Surely not! As for legitimacy, it is not for you nor anyone else to tell me how I should assure my survival. You, the civil servants, you have your "benefits" on the side. Is that legitimate? When people are named to a position of responsibility they bring along their close relations, members of their tribe. What happens to those who don't have relations in high places? In any case, for me, the ends justify the means, and long live the man with the car.[24]

For many, seizure is more than a brute means of accumulation. As in many parts of the world, violent appropriation in the Chad Basin is a modality not only of social mobility but also of social welfare, being intrinsic to the nexus of relationships that provides and ensures economic security. The

[24] Meiganga, Cameroon, November 14, 2001.

commercial-military bind is a site of transfers and redistribution; it is the realm in which forms of protection are founded and guaranteed; and it is a mode of sociability in remote and supposedly marginal areas that founds specific forms of productivity.

Having said that, we should exercise caution with respect to the idea that those partaking in seizure and theft are social bandits, as exemplified by Robin Hood.[25] The ultimate reference for such a thesis is, of course, Eric Hobsbawm's *Bandits*, which argues, as I do herein, that social bandits make up a professional class and that they are involved in acts and processes of economic redistribution as much as criminality. Where our depictions depart from one another is in the attribution of philanthropic qualities to these acts and their relationship to social justice and rebellion (see especially Hobsbawm 2000 [1969]: 18–19, 168).

As the many critiques of Hobsbawm's work on bandits insist, one cannot conflate the myriad myths and lore about bandits and banditry, on the one hand, and the lives of bandits or the lived experience of banditry, on the other.[26] While many griots have sung the praises of bandits in the history of the Chad Basin (cf. Issa 2001), then, as now, their status was extremely ambivalent, being both revered and feared. Moreover, during colonization, the "brigand-chiefs" constructed positions of economic accumulation by straddling the line between officialdom, as intermediaries for the colonial administration, and nonofficialdom, as leaders of well-known highway gangs. This ambivalence, which characterizes both organized banditry and unregulated economic activities today, is such that one cannot clearly delineate these endeavors in terms of a counterrealm, or as instances of rebellion, resistance to the state, or acts of social justice. Whereas Robin Hood is said to have stolen from the rich to give to the poor, bandits and those involved in unregulated commerce in the Chad Basin are financed by the rich and steal or traffic as a way of entering into the labor market and participating in a particular political economy. In that sense, rather than constituting an "anti-society" (Hobsbawm 2000 [1969]: 172) composed of a contained and oppositional moral universe— or what is more frequently referred to as a distinct moral economy— bandits, smugglers, and traffickers seek a certain mode of integration by partaking in recognized modes of governing the economy.[27] While critical of state regulatory authority, they maintain that those who govern them

---

[25] This clarification stems from queries put to me by Florence Bernault, Stephen Collier, Mirjam de Bruin, and Tobias Rees.

[26] Hobsbawm recognizes this point in the preface to the revised (2000) edition of his book. The classical critique of this work is Blok 1972; 1974: 97–102.

[27] Doubtless, these people develop special forms of behavior and argots, as Hobsbawm (2000 [1969]: 172) says. But these are modes of distinction as opposed to modalities of an antisociety.

act in ways that are justifiable and even licit, given the world in which they live.

In that sense, their exploits are a means for both reversing and participating in the social order implied by certain obligations, such as tax and debt. It is a manner of exercising power that partakes of practices of both freedom and domination. That is, practices of freedom and resistance are inherent to and devised out of power situations; they are not something constructed from outside the bounds of the epistemological grounds of power or its forms of knowledge (see Foucault 1990 [1978]: 95, 97).

The ongoing cycle of theft and seizure is often construed by local people as a marginal condition that is in fact the norm. The emergence of the debt markets that dominated international financial markets during the 1980s (the Baker and Brady Plans) became a crucial element of African political economies. As we saw earlier, this put precedence on debt as a commodity, making debt and liability assets insofar as they could be converted to certain forms of credits and assets (Vallée 1999). Such conversions—or the selling of debt—involve value transformations, or the reformulation of distinctions between public wealth and the private domain. This has in some cases replenished public treasuries with hard currency, but more frequently it has enriched the offshore accounts of local political figures. The latter have exercised rights to wealth constituted in liability, a rationale that has been taken up by the wider population, including those working the roads and unregulated commerce.

Thus the assertion that theft and violent appropriations are illegal and yet licit modalities—as noted by Bakaridjo, quoted earlier—is based on specific understandings about manners of rendering illegality a form of licit practice, habits of straddling the fine line between criteria that denote public versus private wealth, and ways of remaining both marginal and indispensable to productive systems. These statements extend beyond the circumscribed sphere of road banditry and smuggling insofar as they refer to a larger realm of knowledge that includes practices of government, such as the debt trade. Such practices are often dependent upon or generated out of the very ambivalence of certain statuses, such as "public," "private," "governed," and "governors." As was noted on a recent cover of a widely read African news magazine: "Cameroon: cop or hoodlum?" ("Cameroun: flic ou voyou?"; *Jeune Afrique économie* 2002).

Statements and interpretations about how illegality is licit practice are also widespread with regard to unregulated economic activities, such as those pursued by the taxi-motorcyclists, the original clandestine operators of the Villes Mortes campaign. In the late 1990s, and in an effort to quell incivisme fiscal and to capture this lucrative domain, the taxi-motorcycles were legalized through a series of regulations. These included a new tax (*l'impôt libératoire*), a driver's license, vehicle registration, vehicle insurance, a vehicle inspection sticker, a permit to carry passengers, a parking permit, and a custom's receipt for imported motorcycles. Drivers are now supposed to paint the motorcycles yellow and wear helmets and gloves, none of which I have ever seen. Most young taxi-men do not pay these myriad impositions, which might be described as a host of mini-seizures. But this is not because they do not have the means, since most taxi fleets are financed by merchants, gendarmes, police, prefects, and even governors. The motorcycle-taximen— who are often referred to as *les attaquants* (the attackers) or *les casquadeurs* (the cascaders)—simply refer to a different register of appropriations that, ironically, often involves the very same people who perceive official taxes. In response to criticism for not having paid his official taxes, one young motorcycle-taximan, a member of the Association des Moto-Taximen in Ngaoundéré, declared:

> We pay our taxes every day! Whether we have all the right papers for the motorcycle or not, we pay taxes to the police and gendarmes. In fact, it's become a reflex. The policemen of Ngaoundéré don't stop me anymore. I'm an old hand in the moto-taxi business. I've driven moto-taxis for people in high places, for men in uniform [who are owners of fleets of clandestine motorcyles]. Furthermore, often even when the police don't stop me, I go to them to pay the tribute [in monetary sense]. My older brother initiated me. He is a djo, someone who knows all the secrets, all the strings. He told me that, with the police, it's not enough to go tell them that they are big men [les grands]; you have to show them. It's like with the traditional chief, the lamiido. The lamiido doesn't work, but he has a lot of money because people come to give it to him. The lamiido doesn't ask anything of his subjects. His subjects come to give him envelopes out of respect, and they also pray to Allah to give him long life. Since the policeman is also a chief—in fact, we call him "chief" [chef]—you have to go toward him even when your papers are in order, especially when you are in order.[28]

During the same conversation, another moto-taxi driver added:

> People enter into the police force because they know that it pays. But it's not necessarily the monthly salary; there are a lot of "asides" [à côtés]. The police and the moto-taximen, we're partners. We know that if we are disposed to giving them a bit of money from time to time, we can work together. Together—that is, the police and the moto-taximen—we exploit illegality. Even when you have all your papers in order, you're in illegality because the motorcycle is illegal. Not even 15 percent of the motorcycles are painted yellow. We have imposed our vision of things on the authorities. The police themselves close their eyes; they can always find an infraction to ticket. That

---

[28] Ngaoundéré, Cameroon, December 2001.

way, they have money for beer. Today, we have representatives at each cross-roads, leaders who negotiate with the administration when there are problems. We parade in front of the authorities during national festivities, they solicit us during election campaigns. We've become an integral part of society through the force of resistance. That's power. So that the system can continue to function properly, it's important that there are people in violation because, if everyone was in line with the law, the authorities—the police—wouldn't gain their share, and then they would suppress the motorcycles on the pretext that they cause accidents, that we are hoodlums, etcetera. Today, maybe we are hoodlums, but we are hoodlums who help sustain families and contribute to the well-being of agents of the force of law. Long live the tolerant police [la police compréhensive]*![29]*

When pushed on the question of the relationship between the world of traffickers and the state, the utility and efficacy of the former, as an economic domain, were usually underscored, as were the mutually constitutive aspects of these two realms:

Q: So traffickers steal from the state, since they don't take the paths, I mean the roads, that the state has created for the movement of men and goods. They don't pay their taxes either. So doesn't the trafficker go against the social order, since we pay taxes to finance schools, hospitals—collective services and social services?

R: That's just talk. Ahidjo and Ousmane Mey [former state officials], didn't they massacre the Arabes Choas of Dollé, who wanted a school?[30] Didn't the Arabes Choas of Dollé pay their taxes, that is, since independence? Villagers who pay their taxes, do they get free medicine? Do they give schoolbooks to peasants' children? When people want to justify the embezzlement of funds, they should find other arguments. Taxes aren't for social services, they are for the personal works of leaders. It's like the right to passage that the men of the lamido take from those who do transactions on the river [Logone], or like the duties [*les droits*] that fishermen pay. It's a matter of tradition. We pay without seeking to know where the money goes.

Q: So you don't pay taxes, since you don't know where they money goes?

R. Taxes, we pay them, since now there is the impôt libératoire.

Q: Yes, but the impôt libératoire is for those who have a well-defined activity, a classified activity that corresponds to a well-defined tax. What is the profession indicated on your card?

R: Unemployed.

[29] Ngaoundéré, Cameroon, December 2001.
[30] See Issa 1997 on the Dollé massacre of 1979.

Q: But you just said that you're a cross-border merchant! Isn't that a job?

R: Yes, of course, but it's many temporary jobs. All of us here, we do many things at once: we sell gas, medicines, motorcycles, hardware—that we buy for ourselves or for those who send us across the border.

Q: Arms are part of hardware, and drugs are part of medicines?

R: Are you trying to ruin our conversation?

Q: We're talking about traffic.

R: Arms and drugs are the affairs of those who've recently come into the traffic—knowledgeable traffickers, people who act on command [*commandement*], who have networks to sell their medicines. The people who are accused of doing this type of trafficking, or who steal vehicles and attack expatriates, are well-placed people. We see them with luxurious cars that they sell quickly to get another one. They're always traveling, they have houses even though we don't know exactly where they work. Those are the people who create problems for modest people like us, who work outside the rules, of course, but we don't harm anyone. Arms are for aggressions and killing. Drugs destroy. The petrol we sell is to move people around, to help the moto-taximen work. The motorcycles we bring [from Nigeria] contribute to economic development. The motorcycles keep young people from begging and stealing. They have a future thanks to the motorcycles. And, in Kousséri, there are no taxis. The functionaries who don't have cars—like most of them—take the moto-taxis to work. Without the motorcycles, there would be no regular attendance at work; people would always go late. Schoolkids who live far away would always be late and even absent. During the rainy season, people wouldn't go to work under the pretext of clouds. Without the moto-taxis, women would walk long distances with children on their backs. So, are the moto-taxis useful or not?

Q: The state should thank you, then.[31]

When asked whether they considered their activities licit or illicit, there was general agreement among the moto-taximen that "anything that can move a poor man from hunger and begging is licit." But one young man argued:

We struggle in domains that force you to circumvent the law—with all the risks. For example, we sell contraband petrol and medicines, etcetera, which are officially forbidden. But what do you expect? Often those who are supposed to see that people respect the law are our sponsors; they give us our

[31] Kousseri, Cameroon, 23 December 2001.

185

original financing. A customs official who finances a petrol smuggler is not going to attack him [the smuggler] or the protégés of his colleagues! And without us, the work of the policeman, the customs official, the taxman, the head of the gendarmes, would have no interest for those who do it. Thanks to us, they have no financial problems.

Q: But that's corruption!

R: That's not corruption. When you give 10,000 or 20,000 CFA to a policeman or a customs official to get your merchandise through, what does that change for the national economy? Corruption is when one sells the Régie Nationale des Chemins de Fer [rail company], the SNEC [water company], the SONEL [electric company], etcetera. Everyone knows that that's negotiated; there are big commissions. One single person can earn in a privatization more than all of Touboro (a local town known for contraband) can produce, save in a decade. Us, we give with pleasure and the police receive with pleasure, just like the customs official. They've become family.

Q: What should be changed in these practices?

R: Paul Biya says that you have to beware of people who talk about change [*le changement*], without saying clearly what must be changed. Us, we're the solution to the crisis. Whether you like it or not, it's better to be a trafficker than unemployed. We send money to our parents. We pay school fees for our little brothers. We contribute to our sisters' wedding preparations. Some of us have even gotten married with our own resources. None of us here have ever gone to prison. When we have a problem with the gendarmes, we negotiate. When we have problems with the customs service, we negotiate. That way, government officials compensate their low salaries and don't go on strike.[32]

An older and well-known smuggler—who, as quoted earlier, insisted on his status as an "ordinary economic operator"—corroborated:

The civil servants are people who always have financial problems. They have needs that are not covered by their salaries, and so they become indebted to those who have money. In the end, needy civil servants and us, we have the same bosses [patrons], and this is not the government, but rather the merchants. Look! Since we have been here [on the Ngueli bridge], have you seen a single man or woman stopped by the Cameroonian customs agents or the gendarmes? All these hundreds of people who pass by here have their papers in order? The customs agents or the gendarmes who come here [to work] don't seek to be transferred elsewhere unless they have problems with

[32] Touboro, Cameroon, November 23, 2001.

the big merchants, or if they've amassed enough wealth. The passport for all that you want to do here, it's the franc CFA. Instead of paying for official documents at 200,000 CFA, it's better to just give 50,000 CFA with your own hands. That way, you have papers and protection.

Q: *Corruption?*

R: What do you call corruption? They say that Cameroon is the world champion of corruption. How can a poor country be the world champion of corruption? They say that in Arab countries, in France, and in the United States, there are people who have more money than the Cameroonian government. I imagine that those countries have several times over what Cameroon possesses! Giving 5,000 CFA, 10,000 CFA, or 50,000 CFA, what does that represent in the Cameroonian economy?

Q: *Someone else recently said the same thing to me. Explain what you mean by corruption. Giving 5,000 CFA to a gendarme or a customs official is illegal!*

R: I told you that every profession, like every religion, has its codes. Giving 5,000 is not giving 15 million. It's part of the code of trafficking: giving to continue to have.[33]

The code of trafficking, or the code of the route, was explained by another trafficker as follows:

The Koran and the hadiths have regulated the code of mating between a man and a woman, haven't they? There are rites and rules to respect even though it takes place in secret between a man and a woman. If this is not respected, Satan will interfere, and you will be three. The Koran governs the Islamic religion, the Bible governs Christianity, the Torah is for the Jews, the road manual is for those who drive. To drive a motorcycle and to keep it a long time, you have to respect the maintenance rules prescribed by the whites who made the motorcycle. You cannot take the Koran to adore Jesus, you can't go to church with the road manual. If you take the Torah to fix your motorcycle, you will soon end up with a carcass in its place. This is what my marabout taught me when I finished Koranic school. I say that a trafficker who wants to respect the law of the government cannot succeed because trafficking is not governed by the law of the government. It is governed by the law of the roads. If, when leaving Nigeria with petrol, you go see the customs officials to give them some money so that you can get through, they are going to arrest you. They'll say that you're suspicious, that you're not an ordinary trafficker, you want to tempt them, you're a spy. But

---

[33] Kousseri, Cameroon, December 2001.

if, while you're trying to evade them, they find you in the bush, then you can negotiate because you're in the normal order of the law of trafficking.[34]

These arguments all present the rationality of illegality, a disposition that is both economically strategic and socially productive. While "trafficking is not governed by the law of the government," traffickers and the police and customs officials have "become family." While obviously outside the realm of "the Law," and hence described by participants as obviously illegal, unregulated commerce and gang-based banditry are nonetheless perceived as licit activities. This is the case because, as one of the moto-taximen said, "So that the system can continue to function properly, it's important that there are people in violation. . . . [We] . . . help sustain families and contribute to the well-being of agents of the force of law." In the Chad Basin, maintaining states of illegality is a mode for establishing and authenticating the exercise of power over economic relations and forms of wealth, giving rise to political subjects who are at once subjected to governmental relations and active subjects within their realm. Thus, as was just explained, the code of trafficking refers to and engages with a larger code of power relations. As participants in the world of trafficking and road banditry recognize, this code may be illegal, since it departs from the codes and regulations of official law, but it is neither illicit nor illegible. It must be understood from within its own script, which, while circumventing government, partakes in modes of governing the economy that are fundamental to the workings of the various national states of the Chad Basin.

One might argue that this poses the problem of the efficacy of modes of governing, since it would seem that the various nation-states of the Chad Basin are not producing self-governing citizens, or people who enact the spontaneous payment of official taxes. But the problem of efficacy depends, of course, on the criteria upon which it is judged, or the register to which one refers. Government law and the "law of the roads"—or the code of officialdom and the code of trafficking—are deployed simultaneously, their conditions of emergence being both mutually constituted and yet in ceaseless autonomization. Their logics propagate certain forms of state power, being the raison d'être of security forces and customs officials, and specific practices of governing, being sources of the scripts by which forms of wealth are recognized and circumscribed as such.

In that sense, the military-commercial nexus that generates and harbors unregulated commerce and organized highway crime delimits the boundaries for modes of accumulation, social welfare, and security that represent both forms of resistance and manners of engaging in practices of government. As a realm in which one evaluates the nature of licit practices, as

[34] Mbang Mboum, Cameroon, November 2001.

well as representations of the self and self-conduct, unregulated commerce and gang-based road banditry establish and refer to a space of
ethics.[35] Yet this does not entail reference to a set of stable moral precepts
or an absolute authority that sanctions conduct. Nor does it entail an
autonomous and oppositional "moral economy" that has emerged in the
margins of state failure.[36] Those we heard from in these pages do not necessarily doubt the legitimacy of state institutions and administrations.
They do not confirm legitimacy crisis readings of their situation, which
maintain that the failure of state institutions to assure law and order or to
establish legality itself incites recourse to illegal activities as a mode of critique and resistance to the state. Such interpretations assume, evidently,
that a prior state of normalcy (legitimacy) has been transgressed and that
the project of modernity has been compromised and is being reclaimed
by social forces. To the contrary, state institutions everywhere in the world
participate in and even initiate illegal economic practices (e.g., the transformation of public monies into private funds through privatizations or
through no-bid contracts), which is part of the reason people living in
the Chad Basin deem them "licit." They say that their own activities are
illegal and yet licit because they are simply modes of economic accumulation and of governing the economic, or ways of participating in forms of
reasoning that constitute a particular political economy. Therefore, because evaluations of what constitutes licit practice and licit self-conduct
are not derived out of a set of ethical standards that are distinct from
those that make power legible, such resistance is necessarily generated out
of states of domination. This circumstance implies that this ethics of illegality is not simply comparable to "a set of moral principles relating to or
affirming a specific group, field, or form of conduct," as goes the classical
definition.[37] Morality involves a set of principles concerning the distinction between right and wrong or good and bad.

This is not the distinction being made by my interlocutors in the Chad
Basin. They are less concerned with whether or not their behavior is good
or bad than the ways in which their actions relate to certain forms of reasoning: the law of trafficking, the raison d'être of the forces of law and order.
Although they refer to a code (the code of trafficking), this is not described
by them as a moral code, which would set forth categorical foundations

---

[35] I thank Tobias Rees for engaging me on this point.

[36] Hobsbawm's revised edition (2000) of his 1969 book, *Bandits*, supposedly takes into
account the "context of politics," arguing that there are "historical conditions" for the emergence of social banditry. These include the disintegration of state power and administration,
as well as the failure of states to assure law and order (2000 [1969]: x). For another view of
social bandits and their role in state centralization, see Barkey 1994.

[37] *New Oxford American Dictionary.* Nor is it an ethos insofar as their practices do not capture the "spirit" of a particular time period or a given "culture."

regarding the nature of humanity and determine ethical versus unethical behavior. Moreover, they refer to several codes relating to state law, trafficking, governmental practices, and religious precepts, all of which inform various aspects of their own practice. This manner of referring to an ensemble of codes and precepts—and not a self-contained moral economy or a specific morality—contradicts the idea of morality as metaphysics, as a set of values and standards that transcend time and contingency. For one, the very idea of a moral economy raises the question of the limits of "the moral" or "morality." Its unspoken term is usually "culture," or whatever it is that is supposed to bring this economy together as a form of morality, or, to the contrary, that which makes moral practice an economy. That is, the concept of the moral economy often presupposes the ontological status of morality (Roitman 2000).[38] Furthermore, reference to a moral economy or to a realm of morality as a stable and authoritative realm that can be either preordained or located as an object of knowledge must be specific about the line between "the moral" and "the nonmoral." How does one recognize or define moral considerations versus human rationale that is not of the moral order?[39] And what does one make of the road bandits, smugglers, and *passeurs* of the Chad Basin, who, like us, refer to rules, codes, standards, and precepts that exhibit internal contradictions?

In some respects, this situation affirms the critique of the relevance of a moral code as a form of authority that takes on a "quasi-juridical form" to which the subject refers as "a law or set of laws" (see Foucault 1970; 1984: 32–39) or as being based on a metaphysical conception of truth that transcends human desires and practices (see Nietzsche 1974 [1882]; 1967 [1887]). The very possibility of making ethical judgments in the absence of absolute moral principles or rules was posited by Immanuel Kant (1965) in the instance of aesthetic judgments. However, typically with reference to Nietzsche's *On the Genealogy of Morals* and his *Beyond Good and Evil,* some commentators have challenged the assumption that, contrary to aesthetic judgments, moral, political, metaphysical, and ethical judgments require absolute criteria or universal standards. Thus, to conceptions of morality that entail such presuppositions, Foucault contrasted ethical practice, which, while involving codes and rules, consists of manners and exercises for self-understanding

---

[38] It should be noted that E. P. Thompson (1966, 1971), who first coined the term "moral economy" in his inquiry on the idea of working-class culture, was concerned with economic class as "an event" and sought to "describe this event as a process of self-discovery and self-definition." This is a far cry from many current uses of the term in the social sciences and is very much in keeping with Michel Foucault's concerns regarding the practice of ethics and *le souci de soi.* See Roitman 2001 for commentary.

[39] For elaboration, see Williams 1972 and 1985, which is one among many interventions in the debate over the possibility of moral philosophy. Lyotard and Thébaud (1985) ask this question in a quite different way.

within a nexus of relationships.[40] This ethics refers to manners of problematizing; it inscribes a mode of questioning about the self and the construction of the self in the world.[41] It is the manner in which I have understood the lives of those who are engaged in organized road banditry and unregulated economic activities in the Chad Basin.

Less concerned with the "truth" of the principles informing their practice, the smugglers, road warriors, and douaniers-combattants are very much interested in their own reasoning, and how it is constructed out of and within certain power situations, which entail an ensemble of forms of reasoning. In that way, they describe their relations to various truths (about the ways power is exercised over them, about the ways in which wealth can be procured, about violence, about indebtedness, and about illegality). They comment upon their reasoning or their relationships to these truths, and especially upon the ways in which they both question and live those truths. The ethics of illegality problematizes certain lived experiences and specific concepts, such as wealth, work, accumulation, and economic regulation, that are both critical to and unstable in that experience. Conversations with them give insight into the ways in which power situations are apprehended as such according to various, specific, historical codifications of the rationalities of power. In his explanation of the politics of unregulated commerce and Opération Villes Mortes, a young man expressed this sense of being both outside and in, the exception and the rule, insisting on marginality and integration in one breath:

> In 1992, when multipartyism started, we went in [joined] all the parties. The same people paraded on the streets in the official clothes of all the different parties celebrated the ideals of one party in the evening and then another the next day. We were really neutral; it was funny. We knew the slogans of all the big parties. We participated in the Villes Mortes—that was sincere since we took position against an order that has marginalized us, we, the youth. And then, at that time, everyone was waiting for a change [un

[40] Commentary on this point can be found in many places; a concise statement is found in Schrift 1995.

[41] As Paul Rabinow notes (1997: xxxvi) in his lucid and helpful review of Foucault's work on ethics and subjectivity, " 'Being' is given through problematizations and practices; it is not prior to them." In an interview with Stephen Riggins (Rabinow 1997: 131), Foucault refers to the way in which ethics is not a form of morality: "SR: Beyond the historical dimension, is there an ethical concern implied in *The History of Sexuality*? Are you not in some ways telling us how to act?

MF: No. If you mean by ethics a code that would tell us how to act, then of course *The History of Sexuality* is not an ethics. But if by ethics you mean the relationship you have to yourself when you act, then I would say that it intends to be an ethics, or at least to show what could be an ethics of sexual behavior. It would be one that would not be dominated by the problem of the deep truth of the reality of our sex life. The relationship that I think we need to have with ourselves when we have sex is an ethics of pleasure, of intensification of pleasure."

changement] *in regime.*[42] *Participating in the Villes Mortes, that was our way of saying that we are integral parts of the process of change, the precarious situation of the moto-taximen and other traffickers must be taken into account in the new Cameroonian society.*[43]

Power Is Not Sovereign

It is tempting to speculate upon the potential bases for this imagined "new Cameroonian society." Much of what I have described herein seems to suggest that new forms of power are emerging in the interstices of the world state system, transforming the workings of the state itself and potentially giving rise to new configurations of political power in the region. That is, if regional and international networks and newly constituted figures of regulatory authority can be defined as both national and nonnational, they might easily be described as "new spaces of power" insofar as they belie the assumption that the preeminent locus of power is the nation-state form. Moreover, beyond the literal geography of power, some might argue that the situation in the Chad Basin warrants reference to "new spaces," since novel manners of conceptualizing and arrogating wealth are being institutionalized in practice, giving rise to unprecedented power relationships. While these practices arise out of the historical templates of wealth, appropriation, and violence in the region—such as seizure and spoils in jihad— they are nonetheless driven by novel, transnational phenomena, such as emerging markets. The razzia has been given new élan with the diffusion of Kalashnikovs in the Chad Basin. Nonetheless, to say that power relations have been—or are being—transformed by transnational phenomena is to speak of a *qualitative* change involving not just new spaces and new forms but also transformations in the very *exercise* of power. Is the pluralization of regulatory authority in the Chad Basin an impetus for such transformations in the exercise of power, or does it induce such changes? Are they representative of new modes of governing the economy? More specifically, if the constitution of state power is dependent upon the power of nonstate regulators, do these latter instances represent new forms of sovereignty? Answers to these questions must first grapple with the very problematization of state power as sovereignty.

Since sovereignty, as a definition practiced in classical political theory and jurisprudence, is supposed to summate the founding properties of "statehood," it is thought to be constitutive of the state itself and *is thus*

---

[42] It is not clear whether he meant a regime change, as in a change in the form of political leadership governing the state, or a change in regime, as in a new political program put forth by the regime in place. I understood the former.

[43] December 2001, Ngouandéré, Cameroon.

vested with powers of its own. As a foundational politico-legal concept, sovereignty itself is assumed to be self-evident.[44] This is why most present-day commentary on transnational phenomena often confounds sovereignty and power. We end in a tautology: the state, as an abstract, unitary object of knowledge and a political subject in international political theory *is* such because of sovereignty; and yet sovereignty is simply the unrestricted and determining power of the state as a political subject in the system of states.[45] Sovereignty is thus a given as the foundational concept and defining property of "stateness" and the very presence of the state. The quest to define and, moreover, locate sovereignty stems from the presumption that sovereignty is the indivisible unit constituting the political system.[46]

From that conceptual point of departure, it is almost natural to apprehend the impact of transnational events and instances in terms of the potential displacement of the sovereign status of the state by emergent forms of power. These include financial markets or global capital markets and their associated legal regimes, agglomerations of nongovernmental organizations or institutions of transnational civil society (Smith, Chatfield, and Pagnucco 1997; Price 1998; Keck and Sikkink 1998), and, more generally, extrastate politico-economic networks (Cutler 1999; Cutler, Haufler, and Porter 1999; Nordstrom 2001; Reno 2001). In spite of its foundational relationship to the politico-legal concept of the state, many observers allege that sovereignty is not necessarily a form of power limited to the infrastructures of the state, postulating that there are now sovereigns other than the state.[47]

[44] "The more sovereignty is thought to explain, the more it itself is withdrawn from explanation. The theoretical sovereignty of sovereignty leaves sovereignty itself essentially unquestioned; the more constitutive sovereignty appears to be, the less unconstituted it becomes" (Bartelson 1993: 15 and esp. chap. 2, which has greatly informed my own thoughts). Very different critiques of the notion of sovereignty as constitutive of the modern state system can be found in both Wallerstein 1999 and Krasner 1999.

[45] On the circularity of sovereignty, see Foucault's writing on *gouvernementalité,* in which he establishes distinct understandings of the finality of sovereignty as opposed to government. While "to govern . . . means to govern things," and hence has a finality of its own, "the end of sovereignty is the exercise of sovereignty." He says: "Whereas the end of sovereignty is internal to itself and possesses its own intrinsic instruments in the shape of its laws, the finality of government resides in the things it manages and in the pursuit of the perfection and intensification of the processes which it directs; and the instruments of government, instead of being laws, now come to be range of multiform tactics" (Foucault 1991: 94–97). See also Bartelson 1993: 10–22.

[46] Bartelson 1993: 10–22, 25. See also pp. 23–31 on the problematic of sovereignty and space, or how space becomes an object of political knowledge, with sovereignty being the metaphysical condition establishing the unity of the modern state.

[47] For interpretations and commentary, refer to Strange 1996; Rosenau 1997; Walker and Mendlovitz 1990; Brown 1995; Camilleri and Falk 1992; Armstrong 1998; Shaw 1998. More subtle views and critique are put forth in Sassen 1998; Ong and Nonini 1997; Smith, Solinger, and Topik 1999; Reno 2001.

This viewpoint is, of course, based on a particular assumption: that is, that sovereignty *is* something. It is a form of power that we can define and locate in human sociopolitical and economic relationships. While sovereignty is less frequently taken to be a timeless essence of the state,[48] it is still referred to as a fixed reference; its ontological presence is assumed as constitutive of the modern political system. Hence, in keeping with its presumed constitutive conceptual and empirical power, sovereignty is treated as a timeless feature of political reality. Often, this form of power is defined as constituted by zones which produce new normative arrangements that give rise to differential regimes of civil and political rights (see Wapner 1995; Clark, Friedman, and Hochstettler 1998; *Millennium* 1994). It is often described in terms of domains of expertise over particular issue areas that engender new modes of governing and are grounded in what are alleged to be varying epistemic communities (Haas 1992). These structures, networks, domains, or zones are said to be generative of fields of social authority which produce codes, rules, norms, and significations that structure the practices and relations of those under its dominion. They are potential nodes of sovereign power, since they are construed as the predominant referents of the government of people and things, as well as value.

According to this general description, my regulators may be described as sovereigns. In the Chad Basin, relationships defining the military-commercial complex have been institutionalized over time, and this field of authority structures practices and induces certain rationalities for those in its midst. But to say that such an emergent domain is a predominant referent for action, understanding, and authority is to speak of the exercise of power and not necessarily sovereignty. These domains are said to be equally or more powerful than the state in the government of people and things, but this does not clarify the extent to which they are part of the same logical space as the nation-state. If their codes, rules, and norms are structuring in a determining way, or in a way that usurps or parallels state power, how has this become logically possible? That is, how have the claims to authoritative status and unqualified jurisdiction become normalized such that they are not contested as illegitimate (read illogical)? If we answer that question, there is no clear means to conclude that such power is sovereign.

Assertions that sovereignty exists in circumscribed domains where one is compelled to act or even think in a specific way, or where subjects are constituted in terms of particular (non-state-based) political and economic rights, are in keeping with a particular conception of power. This takes power as productive; it is a situation that gives rise to subjects who are, to repeat, "caught up in a power situation of which they themselves are the

---

[48] See, for example, Giddens 1987: esp. 263–64; some of the contributions to Czempiel and Rosenau 1989; Evans 1997.

bearers" (Foucault 1997: 201). Attempts to grasp the exercise of power understood in this sense have inspired acute attention to the structuring power of relationships and institutions, as well as the disciplinary effects of codes, techniques, and rationalities. However, the incorporation of much of this work into debates about novel transnational phenomena, or globalization, has displaced this analytics of power into the realm of an analysis of sovereignty *in spite of* the fact that this analytics of power was inspired by the very critique of the ever-present subject of the juridical sovereign in analyses and representations of power.[49] So much emphasis has been placed on Foucault's thoughts on power and knowledge and disciplinary techniques that his explicit preoccupation with the effects of the language of political philosophy on conceptualizations of power, the relational nature of power, and the seemingly insurmountable problems of origins and history devoid of subjectivity have been slighted.

As Foucault (1990 [1978]: 89–94) maintained, the abiding juridical representation of power is constructed out of the prohibitive thematics of repression and law; yet this manner of representation is "utterly incongruous with the new methods of power whose operation is ensured not by right but by technique, not by law but by normalization, not by punishment but by control, methods that are employed on all levels and in forms that go beyond the state and its apparatus." Yet this critique is not, of course, based on the mere point that the juridical mode of representing power is "outdated" or fails to account for new forms of power. Foucault's consequential move toward an analytics, as opposed to a theory, of power involved the formulation of specific domains formed by relations of power so as to comprehend historical practices of power.[50] For this agenda, an ultimate source of power and the possibility of its possession are irrelevant, since power is productive of relationships and subjectivities and not repressive or a simple matter of interdiction.[51] Thus sovereignty (if it *is* anything) is not a condition of unqualified power or absolute authority, since the omnipresence of power is not its unqualified unity; rather, power connotes a complex strategical situation in a particular social configuration. One might thus easily

[49] Foucault (1990 [1978]: 97) maintained, "It is in this sphere of force relations that we must try to analyze the mechanisms of power. In this way we will escape from the system of Law-and-Sovereign which has captivated political thought for such a long time. And if it is true that Machiavelli was among the few—and this no doubt was the scandal of his 'cynicism'— who conceived the power of the Prince in terms of force relationships, perhaps we need to go one step further, do without the persona of the Prince, and decipher power relationships." See also Foucault 1980: 102.

[50] This is possible only if the "juridical and negative representation of power" is finally disarmed ("cutting off the king's head"). Foucault 1990 [1978]: 82, 86–91.

[51] For commentary, see the chapter entitled "Thematics of State and Power" in Dean (1994: esp. 152–73). See also Foucault 1979a: 167–69.

argue that the networks and domains often described as new spaces of sovereignty or emergent sovereigns are new configurations of power, the question of their sovereign status being irrelevant.

In other words, if we accept that states of power are constantly engendered at the multiple points of its exercise, the question of sovereign status, understood as an instance of unqualified (normative) unity in any one domain, is nonsensical, since such situations simply do not obtain. Furthermore, this means that the infrastructures of the state, or the points of the exercise of state power, extend beyond the specific institutions of the state itself, or even the state as a unified and coherent entity. This is manifest in homes, schools, hospitals, factories, armies, and, I would add, world financial markets, international mafias, and nongovernmental organizations. While the latter may be defined as non-state-based, they are surely points of the exercise of state power (see Elyachar 2001, 2002, forthcoming)—and hence not potentially sovereign as "globalized" institutions.

In that sense, the precepts underlying apparently novel relationships, activities, and modalities most often issue out of, or are consistent with, those practiced in the existing political economy or sociojuridical order.[52] I have argued that the endurance of regional and international regimes of accumulation and power depend upon the normalization and institutionalization of new registers of value and the articulation of rights to wealth that were heretofore deemed asocial or irrational, such as spoils or rights-in-wealth through seizure. However, these seem to be perfectly consistent with those exercised by the nation-state; new ways of valuing and governing have emerged in the peripheries of the infrastructures of state power, all the while confirming the right and logic of extant modes of thinking and enacting power.

In other words, new figures of power—such as agents of regulatory authority in the Chad Basin—have emerged on the horizons without destabilizing extant manners of thinking and exercising power. Ultimately, while most who live in their midst view the activities of nonstate regulators, unregulated economic activities, and violent methods of extraction as illegal, they are likewise described as legitimate. Being part of the very legibility of power, these people and their activities partake in prevailing modes of governing the economy. The glimpse I have offered of their emergence and the institutionalization of their practices gives insight into "how different locales are constituted as authoritative and powerful, how different agents are assembled with specific powers, and how different domains are constituted as governable and administrable" (Dean 1999: 29). While produced in the

---

[52] This point is inspired by Giorgio Agamben's reflections (1997, 1998) on how the state of the exception is the very product of the extant regime of truth. He shows how the state of exception is normalized and how such arrangements endure even though—or perhaps *because*—they are devoid of "distinctions between outside and inside, exception and rule, licit and illicit." I thank Luca D'Isanto for this reference.

margins, the pluralization of regulatory authority is nonetheless at the heart of the problem—or the problematization—of power. Being one domain in which power is propagated through ways and means that exceed the infrastructures of the state, those who engage in the constitutive relationships and material manifestations of new forms of regulatory authority recognize this nexus as an intelligible site of power and governing, or as a means and mode of directing human conduct.

Therefore, instead of wondering about whether or not new types of sovereignty are in our midst, we should pay attention to the precursory matter of whether or not the intelligibility of the very idea of sovereignty has been destabilized with recent changes in the global political economy. Debates about globalization have spurred the problem of the intelligibility of sovereignty insofar as they raise the issue of the status of the nation-state in the international and transnational contexts. But this is not a new problem; it is, in fact, one of the founding debates of classical political science. The real question is whether we can discern changes in the organization of knowledge, or the production of valid statements about what the state *is*, or is not. This partly arises out of the kinds of interpretive struggles we have explored herein. But do new claims to sovereignty (e.g., indigenous peoples) come out of, or contribute to, the reorganization of knowledge? Or are they simply part of the history of "self-determination," and thus part of the existing template of knowledge?

To say that something has changed in a particular way—for instance, new figures of regulatory authority have emerged in the Chad Basin—does not address the question of *how* such change has become logically possible. For instance, certain figures of regulatory authority may be qualified as emergent in the Chad Basin simply because they were not there previously. But, as I have attempted to demonstrate, this in itself is dependent on qualitative changes in various domains (e.g., the international economy) leading to the definition of new realms of logical thought and action (e.g., the military-commercial nexus). This gives rise to unprecedented possibilities for the organization of economic and political life (e.g., the "bush economy"). The ultimate question is whether such changes across domains are the result of transformations in the organization of knowledge, or the prevailing manner of producing valid statements such as "this is (legitimate) regulatory authority" or "this is a (legitimate) sovereign."

In that sense, what is important here is not the actual emergence of regimes of regulation or even structures of power that supposedly counter or undermine state sovereignty, but the extent to which these emergent figures of power produce or partake of new forms of knowledge that work to destabilize the concept itself. As Jens Bartelson (1993: 224) has shown in his genealogy of sovereignty, "Sovereignty does not merely mean different things during different periods." It is transformed with transformations in epistemic arrangements: "To write the political history of sovereignty is to write a political history of the knowledges that makes sovereignty intelligible . . . a history of this referent and its formation in time" (46). This is neither a history of the evolution of the concept of sovereignty (conceptual history) nor a matter of ascribing stable definitions of sovereignty over time. Instead, it is a history of ruptures, or a reading of the discursive practice of sovereignty, which has mutated dramatically in consonance with changes in the organization of knowledge as well as its articulation with various knowledges (see Bartelson 1993: 39–78). Bartelson's point is not that new definitions or types of sovereignty emerged with changes in the epistemic order but that the intelligibility of sovereignty has been disrupted in keeping with clashes and contradictions within and between knowledges. He shows how the idea of the state as an abstract entity became a logical (and even ontological) possibility through a particular practice of the definition of sovereignty. While we cannot discern radical transformations in our own epistemological grounding or interpretations of being—and hence draw conclusions as to whether or not sovereignty is once again in crisis as far as its intelligibility is concerned—we can identify which political subjectivities are sustained or have emerged within long-standing and reconfigured logical spaces of political thought and action.

In the Chad Basin, while not necessarily undermining state power, regulators, acting on the basis of the military-commercial complex, and the regulated, who often assume their tactics of wealth creation and rights to extraction, are political subjectivities that arise out of novel configurations of power and wealth. In other words, dominion over persons and things may be surfacing out of ambiguous interdependencies (state/nonstate) while remaining consistent with the epistemological foundations of state power and the exigencies of the exercise of state power.

Appendix: Original French Letter

Transcription of a letter from a military soldier–coupeur de route to the prefect of the Logone and Chari Department, January 17, 1994

> *A. M.*
> *Elément de Soldat*   *La Brousse du 17-1ᵉʳ-94*
> *Militaire Tchadien dans le*
> *teritoire Camerounais*
> *dit Coupeur de Routes dans le*
> *departement de Logone et Chari*
>
>   *A Monsieur le Préfet du logone et chari*
>
> *C'est mois l'élément millitaire Tchadien qui vous est ecrit cette [illisible] Parce que on nous Paye chaque fin de mois 120 000 F Par mois. mais on ma Pas*

*Payer le mois de Decembre 93. don j'ai demissionner leur Bettisse la le 19 1er
mois 94. don je vous informe les Person qui nous soutins en Brousse. Sont: il ya
Alhadji XXX qui dit XXX.*[53] *Il ya Alhadji XXX il XXX Il ya Alhadji XXX
choucou choucou! Vendeur de Piece detacher à Kousseri. Il ya Alhadji XXX. Et
Puis christophe Pasteur qui nous delivre le vin « 33 » Export les Beaufort. Les
Castel. Et les Wiskis C'est le Proprietère de Bar XXX de Kousseri. Tous les
membre que je vous est siter là so. Son ceux qui nous Ravitaies avec tous chosse.
leur envoiyeur SePeciale. C'est aussi un mamabre qui rePon au nom de Kanto.
Il nous Son louer à 29.000 000 Fca Pourquoi Parce que le Secrait . . . d'état à la
défense XXX à amèner les militaire Pour tuè les arabe. Mais on a tuè les militaire camerounais 9 solda. maintenan il sont à la recherche du commisaire de
a Securutè Public Mr. XXX 2ème le commandant de comPagie 3ème le maire
de la ville. 4ème le Sous Préfet vous etait recherch . . . dans la ville de Kousseri
même à qu'elle Leur.*

*Je vous Remerci de mes informations. mais je vous quite. je Pars sur N'Dja-
mena je deman . . . de esquise de ma Pas de ce que fait au Cameroun.*

je vous envois mes Photos comme Souvenir.

Signé: A. M.

[53] All proper names have been replaced by "XXX."

Conclusion

THIS BOOK has spun many threads, all of which do not come together in a synthetic weave. In that manner, it is reflective of the object of my commentary. Not being neatly constructed through a linear history of stable representations, economic regulatory authority in the Chad Basin, and perhaps elsewhere, is produced out of an ensemble of historical traces that vacillate in their various powers to incite behavior, like paying tax, and institute material effects, like founding a public treasury. I have tried to elucidate these various threads in the history of regulatory authority in the Chad Basin, but I will not attempt to tie them up in order to summarize the story or coordinate the parts of a disjointed or discontinuous history. To close, I will simply review certain points, moving back through my narrative so as to highlight the genealogical aspect of this reading of the nature of economic regulatory authority in the Chad Basin and the ways in which it has become unsettled today.

The pluralization of regulatory authority in the Chad Basin is not, at least at present, indicative of the demise of state sovereignty or the emergence of alternative sovereigns to the state. What we can observe are transformations in representations of certain aspects of state power, which partly explains how regulatory authority has become a plural, or heterogeneous, field. Most important, over the last decade there have been changes in local people's perceptions of what economic transfers signify. There is not uniform change in these perceptions, of course. Instead, there is much debate, for instance, about what droits, or rights, signify: specifically, whether economic transfers found the right to access exchanges and wealth or, to the contrary, whether such transfers confirm acquiescence to an authority that guarantees the right to exchanges and wealth. These debates are inherently related to, or structured by, a larger field. While not having pretense to an exhaustive accounting of that field, I have indicated its contours by taking the incivisme fiscal, or Opération Villes Mortes, movement as "an event," or a productive moment that poses questions about the intelligibility of regulatory power and fiscal relations. The specific, historical institutionalization of regulatory authority in this region has been predicated on certain definitions of what constitutes wealth and on the delineation and definition of various economic categories—or the constitution of sectors of economic action and intervention. This has served to structure the various controversies we witness today, such that certain questions are now asked and others are not; certain concepts have come under scrutiny and are interrogated more than others.

One of them is the price-tax complex, or what I have referred to herein as impôt-taxer-prix. As a political technology, this conceptual whole exemplified the materialization of colonial power in its fiscal form and rendered local people consumers of French currency through nonrepressive techniques. It was at the heart of the translation of private wealth into public wealth, or the institutionalization of colonial wealth and colonial rights to a part of people's wealth. The delineation of tax as a particular, historical economic object transpired through the political objective of consumer protection, or price controls—making price, as well, a preeminent object of economic regulation. This abetted the private-public translation, since the subject of the consumer became the figure of the taxpayer, being both the political rationale for regulation (consumer protection) and the economic rationale for regulation (tax collection). Today, tax and price are still enunciated as an integral category; hence tax is still conceived of as a problem of price. In their questioning of the basis of the state's claim to a part of their wealth, many people have raised the matter of the means by which they are to procure money for tax. Until recently, the state has addressed that problem from within the paradigm of consumer protection, targeting "habits" that have been deemed illogical to the establishment of the "just" price. This has meant that economic regulatory authority has been conceptualized in terms of the constant disciplining of common practices such as rounding up, bargaining, and negotiating prices. Today, the regulation of such behavior is no longer taken for granted as part of consumer protection, or efforts to maintain "just prices" in the interest of the consumer-taxpayer. To the contrary, long-standing notions that rounding up, bargaining, and negotiation are the very means to account for social and economic differences are now being underscored. All of this points to the ambiguous status of the so-called intermediaries and the population flottante, who, historically located as the sources of price instability and tax evasion, are perceived more and more as critical agents in wealth creation. Of course, as I have reiterated throughout, they always have been essential to economically productive activity. This shift in representations of these categories as political and economic subjects is what is new in this region. It is one example of the productive nature of incivisme fiscal, as an event.

In tandem with this first problem, forms of debt creation are also being interrogated today. This includes debt produced out of macroeconomic relations, but it mostly involves the questioning of debt produced through local mechanisms of redistribution, such as pricing mechanisms (e.g., the tas and the kilo systems) and representations of the most just social hierarchy. In the local market, relations of dependency are factored into priced determinations, and so debt is almost inevitably at the heart of exchange. Challenging the nature of these relations of dependency—or inequalities—means asking questions about debt that has accrued under the jurisdiction of the prevailing sociopolitical hierarchy and, more important, representations of normal or just modes of redistribution and socioeconomic differences. Wealth produced through debt relations that recognize this jurisdiction is sanctioned, thus not being construed as a liability. But people are now asking about the normalcy of that situation. Hence debates about the nature of unsanctioned wealth—or wealth generated in exchanges taking place outside the confines of official regulatory relations—have come to the fore. Much of this latter form of wealth derives from activities transpiring on international borders and in frontier spaces, which have become realms of economic mobility that have subverted or upended the prevailing logics of redistribution and authority in the region. Those who question the dependencies and obligations that are normally associated with exchanges disagree about the idea that debt is an insolvable situation. They exercise these newly articulated claims to wealth through new forms of social mobility and often violent forms of appropriation, such as seizure. Claims to the right to wealth "regardless of means," as those engaged in so-called incivisme fiscal like to say, reflect mutations in the discursive field in which wealth itself is figured, making spoils a form of licit wealth in the Chad Basin today.

Representations of the ultimate foundations of wealth are also being scrutinized. Such perceptions have been transformed continually, especially under the impact of various colonizations and conquests. Nonetheless, I have refrained from setting out a list or series of representations of the foundations of wealth that have been replaced, over time, by novel or radically transformed ones. Throughout this inquiry into the production and transformation of economic regulatory authority in the Chad Basin, I have been struck by an overlapping set of notions of the foundations of wealth, which have more or less signifying power depending on the context. That is how I have presented them herein: as partaking in the temps multiséculaire. Thus we have come across the slave, the population flottante, the baaba sare, the consumer, the civil servant, and the citizen as pertinent referents in the construction of the sources and targets of wealth for economic regulatory authority. There have not been neat transformations from one to the other, but there have been moments when a specific category has emerged in the field of regulation. For example, while the slave remained an important representation of the foundation of wealth at the time of French colonization, the population flottante emerged as a target of regulation due to the way in which the intermediaries were theorized as both politically and economically problematic, being the source of both instability and productivity. Likewise, with the institutionalization of the tax-price complex, the consumer appeared as the source of both wealth and tax. The continuity of this representation has prevailed, because, despite recent economic liberalization reforms, consumer protection (or price controls) has been pursued most recently by regulation of "the failure to publicize prices." Generally speaking, though, claims to wealth have not been made in the name of the consumer today. Those who have engaged in Opération Villes Mortes in Cameroon have tended to emphasize their entitlements as citizens, and not their rights as consumers. These entitlements, or droits, have been construed for the most part as the right to access exchanges and sources of wealth regardless of means. In the face of this, state authorities have insisted less on consumer protection as the constitutive right of citizenship than on the idea that the citizen is at the heart of the fiscal relationship. That is, by enacting the transfer of wealth to the state, the subject can make claims to citizenship, tax payment becoming a founding economic transfer. Only then can the question of access to exchanges and sources of wealth be addressed.

The idea that the dramatization of citizenship should take place primarily through the fiscal relationship presupposes a stable representation of national affiliation. National wealth, as localized in the national treasury, rests upon national unity, which is construed as an objective reality. And yet the expansion and intensification of unregulated cross-border trade and road banditry, and the rise of nonstate figures of regulatory authority illustrate the ways in which national unity has become a challenge for the states that constitute the Chad Basin. Nonetheless, as the case of Cameroon shows, there has been a constant tension between "the nation" and "the bush": the latter has been variously constructed as the maquis, or the underground and the ground of war; the space of uncivilized practices, religious unbelievers, and slave reservoirs; the realm of unregulated economic life, and of social mobility or future sources of wealth. This dynamic has run throughout this book insofar as it has been manifested through the constant work of regulating what has been imagined as lying outside the bounds of the economy, society, and the nation-state. Evidently, that tension should not be read as an opposition, such as between civilized versus uncivilized space, since the bush has been perceived in varied and contradictory ways. And the very construction of national regulatory authority has depended fundamentally upon the limits between these two realms: on the brigand chief–tax collectors, "always on horseback on some frontier."[1]

In the Chad Basin today, the douaniers-combattants (always in the back of a Toyota pickup truck on some frontier) continue this work of domestication in equally ambiguous fashion. A primary example of the pluralization of economic regulatory authority in the region, these men emerged, nonetheless, from within the state apparatus. These soldiers, who have converted (partially and informally) to the customs service, often attained such status as recompense for their loyal service to the Chadian president, Idriss Déby, during the hard combat of the past two decades. Originating in the rebellion that Déby waged against former president Hissane Habré, they found themselves at the heart of state power and appropriated one of the most significant forms of accumulation in the region: control over economic activities taking place on the borders. This has been a source of financial autonomy for this category of people, who are implicated in military-commercial networks that prevail over unregulated commercial and financial exchanges in the region. In Cameroon, a similar logic now defines many municipal governments, which were granted financial autonomy from the local subprefectures in 1996. The municipalities, which had already lost significant revenues with the abolition of the *impôt forfaitaire* in 1995, turned to economic activities on the borders as an alternative source of rents (see Bennafla 2002: 329–31). For those lying in the rural areas and near the international frontier, this became a means to pay civil servants, who had recourse to payment of rights of entry to marketplaces and "illofficial" tariffs on contraband and contrabandiers. In that sense—or in a formal sense—both the douaniers-combattants and the municipalities compete, along with these networks, with state economic regulatory authority. But the state's failure to pay wages to civil servants, such as military personnel and customs officials, now takes place through the granting of these positions of economic accumulation, such that public transfers now transpire through private appropriations. In that way, the state is at the very heart of the proliferation of unregulated economic exchanges as well as the pluralization of regulatory authority. In turn, the fiscal crisis of the state is in some ways alleviated by its capacity to make claims on unregulated economic life, the transnational, the bush, and the realm of the illicit, which implies that the state is neither weak nor failed, as is often claimed (Kaplan 1994; Zartman 1995; Reno 1995).

[1] Note sur le banditisme dans le Nord-Cameroun (Logone et Chari), 11 July 1952, 2.

Similarly, the widespread assumption that unregulated economic activity, highly organized banditry and theft, and regional military-commercial networks are forms of "nonliberal" political complexes characterized by the fact that they "follow forms of economic logic that are usually antagonistic towards free-market prescriptions and formal regional integration" (Duffield 2001: 14) is unwarranted. While surely involving specific modes of protectionism and the fragmentation of national space, the regimes of exchange and non-state-based forms of economic regulatory authority that prevail in the Chad Basin are not averse to free-market principles and are often at the heart of regional economic integration. Regional military-commercial networks involved in unregulated economic life and their associated figures of regulatory authority escape binary categorizations, such as liberal versus nonliberal or formal versus informal. Although these figures of regulatory authority partake in the realm of the illicit and are bound up in the ethics of illegality described by those engaged in this realm, they are engaged in a war of values that does not fall neatly into the geographic boundaries of North versus South or ideological distinctions between liberal and nonliberal (cf. Duffield 2001: 12). The "new wars" are said to be, above all, wars of values. Evidently, the very idea of a homogeneous value system is problematic, as is the notion of self-contained, conflicting value systems. However, it is indeed pertinent to speak about values. For instance, in the Chad Basin, the ethics of illegality is a practice that traverses the state as well as the bush, being a mode of reasoning that makes sense of and formulates questions about the ambiguous and precarious situations that typify life in many parts of the world today.

In that sense, President Biya's choice between peace and wealth is *sans issue*. By claiming that wealth was dependent upon peace, questions about the intelligibility of certain forms of authority, such as fiscal authority, and particular practices, such as fiscal interventions, were to be quelled or circumvented. As he firmly reminded the electorate during the 1992 presidential election campaign, democracy is not a squaring of accounts: it is not "death," as in the "dead cities" (Opération Villes Mortes) campaign, but rather the choice of life. Peace was thus posited as prerequisite to wealth because the very integrity of society was at issue, the alternative being violence, civil war, and death. But the predicament of defining "the social"—like "the political" and "the national"—results in particular ways of defining "the economic." What constitutes wealth and how various forms of wealth are conceptualized—as public versus private, as debt versus assets, as a guarantee versus a liability—have great implications for the ways in which wealth is thought to be national or potentially nationalized through fiscal appropriations that make it part of the state treasury and national patrimony. Recent conflict over the intelligibility of regulatory authority and fiscal relations is then also a matter of struggle over the nature of the social, the political, and the national. What is at issue are the effects of truths about the relationships, concepts, and categories that regulation and regulatory authority presuppose. During the 1990s, those truths were challenged as fictions, the relationship between peace and wealth becoming so unsettled that, as Jean-Marc Ela, now in forced exile from Cameroon, said, "The contingent becomes a mode of organizing one's life."[2]

[2] Personal communication, Jean-Marc Ela, Yaounde, Cameroon, July 7, 1993. His statement was, "L'insignifiant devient une mode d'organisation de la vie." I have taken the liberty to emphasize the contingent aspect of *l'insignifiant* in light of his circumstances, hoping the presumption would cause him no offense. Read his *Le cri de l'homme africain* (1980). See also Rojtman 1991; Castoriadis 1996.

References

Abba Kaka, A. 1997. Cette fraude qui tue! *Le Temps* (N'Djamena), April 9–15, 8.

Abu-Lughod, J. 1987. The Islamic City: Historic Myth, Islamic Essence and Contemporary Relevance. *International Journal of Middle East Studies* 19: 155–76.

Abubakar, S. 1977. *The Emirate of Fombina, 1809–1903*. Zaria and London: Ahmadu Bello University Press and Oxford University Press.

Achu Gwan, E. 1992. The Nigeria-Cameroon Boundary and Nigerians in Cameroon. Paper submitted to the Nigeria-Cameroon Trans-border Cooperation Workshop. Yola, Nigeria, May 25–30.

Adama, H. 1999. Islam et relations inter-ethniques dans le Diamaré (Nord-Cameroun). *Histoire et anthropologie* 18–19:280–308.

Adeleye, R. 1985 [1971]. The Sokoto Caliphate in the Nineteenth Century. In Ajayi, J.F.A., and M. Crowder, eds. *History of West Africa*. Vol. 2. New York: Longman: 57–84.

Adler, A. 1981. Le Royaume Moundang de Lere au XIXe siècle. In Tardits, C., ed. *Contribution de la recherche ethnologique à l'histoire des civilisations du Cameroun*. Paris: CNRS: 101–19.

Africa Confidential. 1991a. Cameroon: Biya Besieged. July 26.

———. 1991b. Cameroon: Crisis or Compromise? October 25.

Agamben, G. 1997. The Camp as the *Nomos* of the Modern. In de Vries, H., and S. Weber, eds. *Violence, Identity, and Self-Determination*. Stanford, Calif.: Stanford University Press: 106–88.

———. 1998. *Homo Sacer: Sovereign Power and Bare Life*. Stanford, Calif.: Stanford University Press.

Aglietta, M., and A. Orléan, eds. 1998. *La Monnaie souveraine*. Paris: Odile Jacob.

Ahmad, A. 1994. *In Theory: Classes, Nations, Literatures*. London: Verso.

Ajayi, J.F.A., and M. Crowder, eds. 1985 [1971]. *History of West Africa*. Vols. 1 and 2. New York: Longman.

REFERENCES

Alexander, J., and P. Alexander. 1999. Setting Prices, Creating Money, Building Markets: Notes on the Politics of Value in Jaspara, Indonesia. Paper presented to the conference "Commodities and Identities: *The Social Life of Things* Revisited." Amsterdam, June 11–13.

Alkali, M. 1977. Factors in the Economic Development of Borno under the Seifawa Dynasty, 1500–1800 A.D. In Fadl Hasan, Y., and P. Doornbos, eds. *The Central Bilal Al-Sudan: Tradition and Adaptation.* Proceedings of the Third International Conference of the Institute of African and Asian Studies, University of Khartoum: 245–61.

Anderson, B. 1983. *Imagined Communities: Reflections on the Origin and Spread of Nationalism.* London: Verso.

———. 1996. Introduction. In Balakrisham, G. ed. *Mapping the Nation.* London: Verso: 1–16.

Appadurai, A. 1986a. Introduction: Commodities and the Politics of Value. In Appadurai, A., ed. *The Social Life of Things: Commodities in Cultural Perspective.* Cambridge: Cambridge University Press: 1–63.

———. 1990. Disjuncture and Difference in the Global Cultural Economy. *Public Culture* 2 (2): 1–24.

———. 1996. Number in the Colonial Imagination. In Appadurai, A. *Modernity at Large: Cultural Dimensions of Globalization.* Minneapolis: University of Minnesota Press: 114–35.

———, ed. 1986b. *The Social Life of Things: Commodities in Cultural Perspective.* Cambridge: Cambridge University Press.

Armstrong, D. 1998. Globalization and the Social State. *Review of International Studies* 24:461–78.

Ashforth, A. 2000. *Maduma: A Man Bewitched.* Chicago: University of Chicago Press.

Austen, R. 1979. The Trans-Saharan Slave Trade: A Tentative Census. In Gemery, H., and J. Hogendorn, eds. *The Uncommon Market: Essays in the Economic History of the Atlantic Slave Trade.* New York: Academic Press: 23–76.

———. 1990. Marginalization, Stagnation, and Growth: The Trans-Saharan Caravan Trade in the Era of European Expansion, 1500–1900. In Tracy, J. ed. *The Rise of Merchant Empires: Long-Distance Trade in the Early Modern World, 1350–1750.* Cambridge: Cambridge University Press: 311–50.

L'Autre Afrique. 1997. Un billet de banque, ça peut couter cher . . . August 13–19, 66–68.

Azarya, V. 1978. *Aristocrats Facing Change: The Fulbe in Guinea, Nigeria and Cameroon.* Chicago: University of Chicago Press.

Azevedo, M. 1998. Roots of Violence: A History of War in Chad. Amsterdam: Gordon and Breach Publishers.

Bach, D. 1998. *Régionalisation, mondialisation et fragmentation en Afrique subsaharienne.* Paris: Karthala.

Badie, B. 1999. *Un monde sans souveraineté: Les états entre ruse et responsabilité.* Paris: Fayard.

Bah, T. 1988. Le Facteur peul et les relations inter-ethniques dans l'Adamaoua au 19ᵉ siècle. In Boutrais, J. ed. *Du politique à l'économique: Études historiques dans le bassin du Lac Chad.* Actes du IVe colloque Méga-Tchad CNRS/ORSTOM. Paris, September 14–16.

Bah, T., and S. Issa. 1997. Relations inter-ethniques, problématique de l'intégration nationale et de la sécurité aux abords sud du Lac Tchad. In Nkwi, P., and F. Nyamnjoh, eds. *Regional Balance and National Integration in Cameroon.* Leiden: ASC/ICASSRT: 280–88.

Baier, S. 1980. *An Economic History of Central Niger.* Oxford: Oxford University Press.

Bakhtine, M. 1990. *The Dialogic Imagination.* Austin: University of Texas Press.

Balandier, G. 1985. *Sociologie des Brazzavilles noires.* Paris: Presses universitaires des sciences politiques.

Balibar, E. 2001. *Nous, citoyens d'Europe? Les frontières, l'état, le people.* Paris: La Découverte.

———. 2003. *L'Europe, l'Amérique et la guerre: Réflexions sur la mediation européenne.* Paris: La Découverte.

Balibar, E., and I. Wallerstein. 1991. *Race, Nation, Class.* London: Verso.

Banégas, R. 1998. De la guerre au maintien de la paix: Le Nouveau business mercenaire. *Critique internationale* 1:179–94.

Barber, K. 1995. Money, Self-Realization, and the Person in Yorùbá Texts. In Guyer, J., ed. *Money Matters.* Portsmouth, N.H.: Heinemann: 205–24.

Barkey, K. 1994. *Bandits and Bureaucrats: The Ottoman Route to State Centralization.* Ithaca, N.Y.: Cornell University Press.

Barkindo, B. 1985 [1971]. Early States of the Central Sudan: Kanem, Borno and Some of Their Neighbors to c. 1500 A.D. In Ajayi, J.F.A., and M. Crowder, eds. *History of West Africa.* Vol. 1. New York: Longman: 225–54.

Barry, A., T. Osborne, and N. Rose. 1996. *Foucault and Political Reason: Liberalism, Neo-liberalism and Rationalities of Government.* Chicago: University of Chicago Press.

Bartelson, J. 1993. *A Genealogy of Sovereignty.* Stockholm Studies in Politics 48. Stockholm: University of Stockholm.

Barthes, R. 1974. *S/Z.* New York: Hill and Wang.

Bataille, G. 1967. *La Part maudite, précédé de la notion de dépense.* Paris: Éditions de Minuit.

Baudrillard, J. 1975. *The Mirror of Production.* St. Louis: Telos Press.

———. 1981. *For a Critique of the Political Economy of the Sign.* St. Louis: Telos Press.

———. 1983. *Simulations.* New York: Semiotext(e).

Baumgardt, L. 1994. La Représentation de l'Autre: L'Exemple du répertoire d'une conteuse peule de Garoua (Cameroun). *Cahiers d'études africaines* 34, 133–35 (1–3): 295–313.

Bayart, J.-F. 1979. *L'État au Cameroun.* Paris: Presses de la Fondation nationale des sciences politiques.

———. 1986. La Société politique camerounaise (1982–1986). *Politique africaine* 22:5–35.

———. 1989. *L'État en Afrique.* Paris: Fayard.

———. 1994. L'Invention paradoxale de la modernité économique. In J.-F. Bayart, *La Réinvention du capitalisme.* Paris: Karthala: 9–43.

———. 1994. *La Réinvention du capitalisme.* Paris: Karthala.

———. 1996. *L'Illusion identitaire.* Paris: Fayard.

———. 1997. Le "Capital social" de l'état malfaiteur, ou les ruses de l'intelligence politique. In Bayart, J.-F., S. Ellis, and B. Hibou. *La Criminalisation de l'état en Afrique*. Brussels: Éditions Complexe.

Bayart, J.-F., S. Ellis, and B. Hibou. 1997. *La Criminalisation de l'état en Afrique*. Brussels: Éditions Complexe.

Beauvilain, A. 1989. Nord-Cameroun: Crises et peuplement. 2 vols. Ph.D. diss., University of Rouen.

Bennafla, K. 1996. Rapport sur les échanges transfrontaliers informels au Tchad. Unpublished manuscript. University of Paris X-Nanterre.

———. 1997. Entre Afrique noire et monde arabe: Nouvelles tendaces des échanges "informels" tchadiens. *Revue Tiers Monde* 38:879–96.

———. 1998. Mbaiboum: Un marché au carrefour de frontières multiples. *Autrepart* 6:53–72.

———. 2000. Tchad: L'Appel des sirènes arabo-islamiques. *Autrepart*, Éditions de l'Aube/IRD, 16:67–86.

———. 2001. *Le Commerce frontalier en Afrique centrale*. Paris: Karthala.

———. 2002. *Le Commerce frontalier en Afrique centrale: Acteurs, espaces, pratiques*. Paris: Karthala.

Bhabha, H., ed. 1991. *Nation and Narration*. London: Routledge.

Bloch, M. 1989. *La Société féodale*. Paris: Albin Michel.

Blok, A. 1972. The Peasant and the Brigand: Social Banditry Reconsidered. *Comparative Studies in Society and History* 14:195–504.

———. 1974. *The Mafia of a Sicilian Village: A Study of Violent Peasant Entrepreneurs 1860–1960*. Oxford: Oxford University Press.

Bocquené, H. 1981. Note sur le pulaaku. In *Itinérances en pays peul et ailleurs*. Vol. 2. Paris: Mémoires de la Société des africanistes: 229–46.

Bois, P. 1960. *Paysans de l'Ouest: Des stuctures économiques et sociales aux options politiques depuis l'époque révolutionnaire dans le Sarthe*. Paris: Éditions de l'EHESS.

Bonte, P. 1998. Fortunes commerciales à Shingitte (Adrâr mauritanien) au XIXe siècle. *Journal of African History* 39:1–13.

Botte, R., and J. Schmitz. 1994. Paradoxes identitaires. *Cahiers d'études africaines* 34 133–35 (1–3): 7–22.

Boulaga, E. 1993. *Les Conférences nationales en Afrique noire*. Paris: Karthala.

Bourdieu, P. 1977. *Outline of a Theory of Practice*. Cambridge: Cambridge University Press.

———. 1984. *Distinction*. Cambridge, Mass.: Harvard University Press.

Bourguinat, H. 1998. *L'Économie morale: Le Marché contre les acquis*. Paris: Arléa.

Boutrais, J. 1994a. Les Foulbé de l'Adamaoua et l'élevage: De l'idéologie pastorale à la pluri-activité. *Cahiers d'études africaines* 34, 133–35 (1–3): 175–96.

———. 1994b. Pour une nouvelle cartographie des peuls. *Cahiers d'études africaines* 34, 133–35 (1–3): 137–46.

Boutrais, J., et al. 1984. *Le Nord du Cameroun. Des hommes. Une région*. Paris: Éditions de l'ORSTOM.

Brantlinger, P., and D. Ulin. 1993. Policing Nomads: Discourse and Social Control in Early Victorian England. *Cultural Critique* fall: 33–63.

Bratton, M. 1989. Beyond the State: Civil Society and Associational Life in Africa. *World Politics* 41:407–30.

210

Braudel, F. 1972–73. *The Mediterranean and the Mediterranean World in the Age of Philip II.* Vol. 1. New York: Harper and Row.

———. 1979. *Civilisation matérielle, économie et capitalisme.* Vol. 2, *Les jeux de l'échange.* Paris: Armand Colin.

———. 1986. *L'Identité de la France: Espace et histoire.* Paris: Arthaud-Flammarion.

Brenner, L. 1974. *The Shehus of Kukawa.* Oxford: Oxford University Press.

Brown, S. 1995. *New Forces, Old Forces and the Future of World Politics.* New York: HarperCollins.

Buijtenhuis, R. 1987. *Le Frolinat et les guevies civiles au Tchad 1977–1984.* Paris: Karthala.

Burnham, P. 1972. Racial Classification and Identity in the Meiganga Region: North Cameroon. In Baxter, P., and B. Sansom, eds. *Race and Social Difference.* Harmondsworth, England: Penguin Books: 301–18.

———. 1975. "Regroupement" and Mobile Societies: Two Cameroonian Cases. *Journal of African History* 16:577–94.

———. 1980a. *Opportunity and Constraint in a Savannah Society: The Gbaya of Meiganga, Cameroon.* New York: Academic Press.

———. 1980b. Raiders and Traders in Adamawa: Slavery as a Regional System. In Watson, J., ed. *Asian and African Systems of Slavery.* Oxford: Basil Blackwell: 43–72.

Burnham, P., and M. Last. 1994. From Pastoralist to Politician: The Problem of a Fulbe "Aristocracy." *Cahiers d'études africaines* 34, 133–35 (1–3): 313–57.

Callaghy, T. 1994. Civil Society, Democracy, and Economic Change in Africa: A Dissenting Opinion about Resurgent Societies. In Harbeson, J., D. Rothchild, and N. Chazan, eds. *Civil Society and the State in Africa.* Boulder, Colo.: Lynne Rienner: 231–53.

———. 2001. Networks and governance in Africa: Innovation in the debt regime. In Callaghy, T., R. Kassimir, and R. Latham, eds. *Intervention and Transnationalism in Africa.* Cambridge: Cambridge University Press: 115–48.

Callaghy, T., R. Kassimir, and R. Latham, eds. 2001. *Intervention and Transnationalism in Africa: Global-Local Networks of Power.* Cambridge: Cambridge University Press.

Callaghy T., and J. Ravenhill, eds. 1993. *Hemmed In: Responses to Africa's Economic Decline.* New York: Columbia University Press.

Camilleri, J., and J. Falk, eds. 1992. *The End of Sovereignty?* London: Elgar.

Canguilhem, G. 1989. *The Normal and the Pathological.* New York: Zone Books.

Carter Center of Emory University. 1989. *Beyond Autocracy in Africa: Working Papers from the Inaugural Seminar of the Governance in Africa Program.* Atlanta: Carter Center of Emory University.

Castells, M. 1998. *End of Millennium.* London: Blackwell.

Castoriadis, C. 1996. *La Montée de l'insignifiant: Les carrefours du labyrinthe IV.* Paris: Seuil.

Champaud, J. 1991. Cameroun: Au bord de l'affrontement. *Politique africaine* 44:115–20.

Chapman, A. 1980. Barter as a Universal Mode of Exchange. *L'Homme* 20 (3): September: 33–83.

Cilliers, J., and P. Mason, eds. 1999. *Peace, Profit or Plunder? The Privatisation of Security in War-Torn Africa.* Pretoria: Institute for Security Studies.

REFERENCES

Clark, A., E. Friedman, and K. Hochstettler. 1998. The Sovereign Limits of Global Civil Society: A Comparison of NGO Participation in UN World Conferences on the Environment, Human Rights, and Women. *World Politics* 51:1–35.

Clastres, P. 1989. *Society against the State*. New York: Zone Books.

Clifford, J. 1988. *The Predicament of Culture: Twentieth-Century Ethnography, Literature, and Art*. Cambridge, Mass.: Harvard University Press.

Clifford J., and G. Marcus, eds. 1986. *Writing Culture*. Berkeley: University of California Press.

Cohen, R. 1966. Power, Authority and Personal Success in Islam and Bornu. In Swartz, M., V. Turner, and A. Tuden, eds. *Political Anthropology*. Chicago: Aldine: 129–39.

Cohen, R., and L. Brenner. 1985 [1971]. Bornu in the nineteenth century. In Ajayi, J.F.A., and M. Crowder, eds. *History of West Africa*. Vol. 2. New York: Longman: 93–128.

Cohn, B. 1987. *An Anthropologist among the Historians and Other Essays*. London: Oxford University Press.

Colvin, L. 1971. The Commerce of Hausaland, 1780–1833. In McCall, D., and N. Bennett, eds. *Aspects of West African Islam*. Boston: African Studies Center, Boston University Papers on Africa: 5:101–35.

Comaroff, J. 1980. *The Meaning of Marriage Payments*. New York: Academic Press.

Comaroff, J., and J. Comaroff. 2000. Millennial Capitalism: First Thoughts on a Second Coming. *Public Culture* 12:291–343.

———, eds. 1999. *Civil Society and the Political Imagination in Africa*. Chicago: University of Chicago Press.

Connah, G. 1981. *Three Thousand Years in Africa*. Cambridge: Cambridge University Press.

Connolly, W. 1996. Tocqueville, Territory, and Violence. In Shapiro, M., and H. Alker, eds. *Challenging Boundaries*. Minneapolis: University of Minnesota Press: 153–54.

Coquéry-Vidrovitch, C. 1972. *Le Congo au temps des compagnies concessionaires*. Paris: Mouton.

Cordell, D. 1983. The Savanna Belt of North-Central Africa. In Birmingham, D., and P. Martin, eds. *History of Central Africa*. Vol. 1. London: Longman: 30–74.

Coussy, J. 1994. Les Ruses de l'état minimum. In Bayart, J.-F., ed. *La Réinvention du capitalisme*. Paris: Karthala: 245–48.

Coussy, J., and J. Vallin, eds. 1996. *Crise et population en Afrique: Crises économiques, politiques d'ajustement et dynamiques démographiques*. Paris: CEPED.

Curtin, P. 1975. *Economic Change in Precolonial Africa: Senegambia in the Era of the Slave Trade*. Vol. 1. Madison: University of Wisconsin Press.

———. 1984. *Cross-Cultural Trade in World History*. Cambridge: Cambridge University Press.

Cutler, C. 1999. Locating "Authority" in the Global Political Economy. *International Studies Quarterly* 43:59–83.

Cutler, C., V. Haufler, and T. Porter, eds. 1999. *Private Authority and International Affairs*. Albany: State University of New York Press.

Czempiel, E.-O., and J. Rosenau, eds. 1989. *Global Changes and Theoretical Challenges*. Lanham, Md.: Lexington Books.

Daly, G. 1991. Discursive Constructions of Economic Space. *Economy and Society* 20, 79–102.

212

Das, V., and D. Poole, eds. 2004. *Anthropology in the Margins of the State*. Santa Fe, N.M.: School of American Research, forthcoming.

De Boeck, F. 1999. Domesticating Diamonds and Dollars: Identity, Expenditure and Sharing in Southwestern Zaire (1984–1997). In Geschiere, P., and B. Meyer, eds. *Globalization and Identity*. Oxford: Basil Blackwell: 177–209.

Dean, M. 1994. *Critical and Effective Histories: Foucault's Methods and Historical Sociology*. London: Routledge.

———. 1999. *Governmentality: Power and Rule in Modern Society*. London: Sage.

Delavignette, R. 1950. *Freedom and Authority in French West Africa*. London: Oxford University Press.

Deleuze, G., and F. Guattari. 1983. *Anti-Oedipus*. Minneapolis: University of Minnesota Press.

———. 1987. *A Thousand Plateaux*. Minneapolis: University of Minnesota Press.

Derrida, J. 1972. *Margins of Philosophy*. Chicago: University of Chicago Press.

———.1978. Structure, Sign, and Play in the Discourse of the Human Sciences. In *Writing and Difference*, by Jacques Derrida. Chicago: University of Chicago Press.

———. 1987. *The Postcard: From Socrates to Freud and Beyond*. Chicago: University of Chicago Press.

———. 1991. *Donner le temps*. Paris: Galilée.

———. 1992. Force of Law: The Mystical Foundations of Authority. Translated by M. Quaintance. In Cornell, D., M. Rosenfeld, and D. G. Carlson, eds. *Deconstruction and the Possibility of Justice*. New York: Routledge: 3–67.

Diallo, M. 1991. Qui Gouverne le Cameroun? *Jeune Afrique*, July 24–30, 18.

Difana, B. 1994. *La Nouvelle Expression*, March 22–28, 8.

Donzelot, J. 1994. *L'Invention du social: Essai sur le déclin des passions politiques*. Paris: Éditions du Seuil.

Dorce, F. 1996. Cameroun: Cette guerre qui cache son nom. *Jeune Afrique économie*, November 18, 54–56.

Duffield, M. 2001. *Global Governance and the New Wars*. London: Zed Books.

Dumas-Champion, F. 1983. *Les Masa du Tchad*. Paris: Maison des sciences de l'homme.

Dupire, M. 1962. *Peuls nomads: Étude descriptive des Wodaabe du Sahel Nigérien*. Paris: Institut d'Ethnologie.

———. 1994. Identité ethnique et processus d'incorporation tribale et étatique. *Cahiers d'études africaines* 34, 133–35 (1–3): 265–80.

Dupré, M.-C. 1995. Raphia Monies among the Teke: Their Origin and Control. In Guyer, J., ed. *Money Matters*. Portsmouth, N.H.: Heinemann: 39–52.

EDIAFRIC. 1984. *L'Economie camerounaise*. Paris: EDIAFRIC.

Eguchi, P. 1994a. *Fulfulde Tales of Northern Cameroon*. Vol. 4. Tokyo: University of Foreign Studies.

———. 1994b. Pastoralism in Fulbe Folktales. *Cahiers d'études africaines* 34, 133–35 (1–3): 461–71.

Ekejiuba, F. 1995. Currency Instability and Social Payments among the Ibo of Eastern Nigeria,1890–1990. In Guyer, J., ed. *Money Matters*. Portsmouth, N.H.: Heinemann: 133–61.

Ela, J.-M. 1980. *Le Cri de l'homme africain*. Paris: L'Harmattan.

———. N.d. Système lamidal et domination au nord du Cameroun. Unpublished manuscript.

213

Ellen, R. 1988. Fetishization. *Man* 23:213–35.

Elyachar, J. 2001. Finance internationale, micro-credit et religion de la société civile en Egypte. *Critique internationale* 13:139–52.

———. 2002. Empowerment Money: The World Bank, Non-Governmental Organizations, and the Value of Culture in Egypt. *Public Culture* 14:493–513.

———. 2003. Mappings of Power: The State, NGOs, and International Organizations in the Informal Economy of Cairo. *Comparative Studies in Society and History*.

Enoh, J. N.d. [drafted 1979]. *Recueil des textes sur la réglementation des prix et des poids et mesures au Cameroun*. Yaounde.

Evans, P. 1997. The Eclipse of the State? Reflections on Stateness in an Era of Globalization. *World Politics* 50:62–87.

Ewald, F. 1986. *L'État providence*. Paris: Grasset.

Fadl Hasan, Y. 1977. The Fur Sultanate and the Long-Distance Caravan Trade: 1650–1850. In Fadl Hasan, Y., and P. Doornbos, eds. *The Central Bilal Al-Sudan: Tradition and Adaptation*. Proceedings of the Third International Conference of the Institute of African and Asian Studies, University of Khartoum: 201–15.

———, ed. 1971. *Sudan in Africa*. Khartoum.

Faes, G. 1997. Le Dernier maquis. *L'Autre Afrique*, May 21–27, 64–69.

Fage, J. 1987. *A History of Africa*. London: Hutchinson.

Fanon, F. 1963. *The Wretched of the Earth*. London: Penguin.

———. 1986. *Black Skin, White Masks*. London: Pluto Press.

Fardon, R. 1988. *Raiders and Refugees: Trends in Chamba Political Development 1750 to 1950*. Washington, D.C.: Smithsonian Institute Press.

Fardon, R., F. Nyamnjoh, and J. Roitman. 2001. Autour d'un livre. *Politique africaine* 81:177–95.

Ferguson, J. 1985. The Bovine Mystique: Power, Property and Livestock in Rural Lesotho. *Man* 20:647–74.

———. 1999. *Expectations of Modernity: Myths and Meanings of Urban Life on the Zambian Copperbelt*. Berkeley: University of California Press.

Fisher, H. J. 1975. The Central Sahara and Sudan. In Gray, R., ed. *The Cambridge History of Africa*. Vol. 4. Cambridge: Cambridge University Press: 58–141.

———. 1977. The Eastern Maghrib and the Central Sudan. In Oliver, R., ed. *The Cambridge History of Africa*. Vol. 3. Cambridge: Cambridge University Press: 232–330.

———. 1986. Liminality, *Hijra* and the City. *Asian and African Studies* 20:153–77.

Fodouop, K. 1988. La Contrebande entre le Cameroun et le Nigéria. *Les cahiers d'Outre Mer* 161:5–26.

Foucault, M. 1966. *Les Mots et les choses: Une archéologie des sciences humaines*. Paris: Gallimard.

———. 1970. *The Order of Things: An Archaeology of the Human Sciences*. New York: Random House.

———. 1976. *The Archaeology of Knowledge*. New York: Harper and Row.

———. 1979a. *Discipline and Punish: The Birth of the Prison*. New York: Vintage Books.

———. 1979b. Governmentality. *Ideology and Consciousness* 6:5–21.

———. 1980. *Power/Knowledge: Selected Interviews and Other Writings 1972–1977*. Edited by C. Gordon. New York: Pantheon.

————. 1982. Why Study Power: The Question of the Subject. In Dreyfus, H., and P. Rabinow, *Michel Foucault: Beyond Structuralism and Hermeneutics*. Chicago: University of Chicago Press: 208–16.

————. 1984. *Histoire de la sexualité. Volume 2: L'usage des plaisirs*. Paris: Gallimard.

————. 1989. *Résumé des cours 1970–1982*. Paris: Juillard.

————. 1990 [1978]. *The History of Sexuality. Volume I: An Introduction*. New York: Vintage Books.

————. 1991. Governmentality. In Burchell, G., et al., eds. *The Foucault Effect: Studies in Governmentality*. Chicago: University of Chicago Press.

————. 1997. *"Il faut défendre la société": Cours au Collège de Frane. 1976*. Paris: Gallimard-Seuil.

————. 2001a. *Dits et écrits. I. 1954–1975*. Paris: Gallimard.

————. 2001b. *Dits et écrits. II. 1976–1988*. Paris: Gallimard.

La France militaire et L'Afrique. 1997. Brussels: Éditions Complexes-GRIP.

Frantz, C. 1977. Shifts in Power from Nomads to Sedentaries in the Central Sudanic Zone. In Fadl Hasan, Y., and P. Doornbos, eds. *The Central Bilal Al-Sudan: Tradition and Adaptation*. Proceedings of the Third International Conference of the Institute of African and Asian Studies, University of Khartoum: 171–91.

Fraser, N. 1991. Rethinking the Public Sphere: A Contribution to the Critique of Actually Existing Democracy. In Calhoun, C., ed. *Habermas and the Public Sphere*. Cambridge, Mass.: MIT Press: 109–41.

Friedman, M. 1993. Kalachnikov: Trente années de rafales. *Jeune Afrique,* no. 1701–02:98–101.

Garoua tradition: Historique d'une cité peule du Nord-Cameroun. 1980. Edited by Modibbo A. Bassoro and E. Mohammadou. Bordeaux: Centre national de la Recherche scientifique.

Gast, M., ed. 1987. *Hériter en pays musulman*. Paris: Éditions du CNRS.

Geschiere, P. 1994. Parenté et argent dans une société lignagère. In Bayart, J.-F., ed. *La Réinvention du capitalisme*. Paris: Karthala: 87–113.

————. 1995. *Sorcellerie et politique en afrique: La viande des autres*. Paris: Karthala.

Geschiere, P., and P. Konings, eds. 1993. *Itinéraires d'accumulation au Cameroun*. Paris: ASC-Karthala.

Giddens. A. 1987. *The Nation State and Violence*. Berkeley: University of California Press.

Godelier, M. 1996. *L'Énigme du don*. Paris: Fayard.

Goody, J. 1971. *Technology, Tradition and the State in Africa*. London: Oxford University Press.

————. 1980. Slavery in Time and Space. In Watson, J., ed., *Asian and African Systems of Slavery*. Oxford: Basil Blackwell: 16–42.

Gray, R., and D. Birmingham. 1970. *Pre-colonial African Trade: Essays on Trade in Central and Eastern Africa before 1900*. Oxford: Oxford University Press.

Grégoire, E. 1991. Accumulation marchande et propagation de l'Islam en milieu urbain: Le cas de Maradi (Niger). *Islam et sociétés au sud du Sahara* 5:43–55.

————. 1992. *The Alhazai of Maradi: Traditional Hausa Merchants in a Changing Sahelian City*. Boulder, Colo.: Lynne Rienner.

————. 1998. Sahara nigérien: Terre d'échanges. *Autrepart* 6:91–104.

Grey, T. 1980. The disintegration of property. *Nomos* 22. Special issue on property. Edited by J. Pennock and J. Chapman. New York: New York University Press.

Gubry, P. 1988. *Rétention de la population et développement en milieu rural: À l'écoute des paysans mafa des monts Mandara (Cameroun)*. Paris: 4e colloque Méga-Tchad.

Guivanda, R. 2002. Des coupeurs de route accusent. *L'Œil du Sahel*, February 21, 3.

Guyer, J. 1993. Wealth in People and Self-Realization in Equatorial Africa. *Man* 28:243–65.

———. 1995. Introduction: The Currency Interface and Its Dynamics. In Guyer, J., ed. *Money Matters*. Portsmouth, N.H.: Heinemann: 1–33.

Haas, P., ed. 1992. Knowledge, Power, and International Policy Coordination. *International Organization* 46:1.

Habermas, J. 1989 [1962]. *The Structural Transformation of the Public Sphere: An Inquiry into a Category of Bourgeois Society*. Cambridge, Mass.: MIT Press.

Hacking, I. 1975. *The Emergence of Probability: A Philosophical Study of Early Ideas about Probability, Induction and Statistical Inference*. Cambridge: Cambridge University Press.

———. 1983. *Representing and Intervening: Introductory Topics in the Philosophy of Natural Science*. Cambridge: Cambridge University Press.

Hall, S., D. Held, and T. McGrew, eds. 1992. *Modernity and Its Futures*. Cambridge, England: Polity Press.

Harding, J. 1996. The Mercenary Business. In Hindle, J., and A. Bennett, eds. *London Review of Books: An Anthology*. London: Verso: 3–9.

Hart, K. 1982. On Commoditization. In Goody, E., ed. *From Craft to Industry: The Ethnography of Proto-industrial Cloth Production*. Cambridge: Cambridge University Press.

Harvey, D. 1989. *The Condition of Postmodernity: An Enquiry into the Origins of Cultural Change*. Oxford: Basil Blackwood.

Hebdige, D. 1979. *Subculture: The Meaning of Style*. London: Methuen.

Held, D. 1995. *Democracy and the Global Order*. Cambridge: Polity Press.

Herbert, B. 1994. Les Vérités historiques sont claires. *La nouvelle Expression*, April 6 11, 9.

Herrera, J. 1995. Les Échanges transfrontaliers entre le Cameroun et le Nigeria: Rapport final de l'observatoire OCISCA. Paris: DIAL.

———. 1998. Du "fédéral" et des "Koweïtiens": La Fraude de l'essence nigériane au Cameroun. *Autrepart* 6:181–202.

Herrnstein-Smith, B. 1988. *Contingencies of Value*. Cambridge, Mass.: Harvard University Press.

Hibou, B. 1997. Le "Capital social" de l'état falsificateur, ou les ruses de l'intelligence économique. In Bayart, J.-F., S. Ellis, and B. Hibou. *La Criminalisation de l'état en Afrique*. Brussels: Éditions Complexe: 105–58.

———. 1998. Retrait ou redéploiement de l'état? *Critique internationale* 1:151–68.

———. 1999a. La "Décharge," nouvel interventionnisme. *Politique africaine* 73:6–15.

———. 2000. The Political Economy of the World Bank's discourse: From Economic Catechism to Missionary Deeds (and Misdeeds). *Les Études du CERI* 39.

———, ed. 1999b. *La Privatisation des états*. Paris: Karthala.

Hilaire, A. 1991. *Paysans montagnards du Nord Cameroun*. Paris: ORSTOM.

Hill, P. 1976. From Slavery to Freedom: The Case of Farm-Slavery in Nigerian Hausaland. *Comparative Studies in Society and History* 18:395–426.

———. 1985. Comparative West African Farm-Slavery Systems (South of the Sahel) with Special Reference to Muslim Kano Emirate (Nigeria). In Willis, J., ed. *Slaves and Slavery in Muslim Africa*. Vol. 2. London: Frank Cass: 33–50.

Hindess, B., and P. Hirst. 1975. *Pre-capitalist Modes of Production*. London: Routledge and Kegan Paul.

Hobsbawm, E. 2000 [1969]. *Bandits*. New York: New Press.

Hogendorn, J. 1977. The Economics of Slave Use on Two "Plantations" in the Zaria Emirate of the Sokoto Caliphate. *International Journal of African Historical Studies* 10:369–83.

Hogendorn, J., and M. Johnson. 1986. *The Shell Money of the Slave Trade*. Cambridge: Cambridge University Press.

Horowitz, M. 1967. A Reconsideration of the "Eastern Sudan." *Cahiers d'études africaines* 7, 27: 381–98.

Humphrey, C., and S. Hugh-Jones. 1992. *Barter, Exchange and Value: An Anthropological Approach*. Cambridge: Cambridge University Press.

Huntington, S. 1997. *The Clash of Civilizations and the Remaking of World Order*. New York: Simon and Schuster.

Hunwick, J. 1985 [1971]. Songhay, Borno and the Hausa States, 1450–1600. In Ajayi, J.F.A., and M. Crowder, eds. 1985 [1971]. *History of West Africa*. Vol. 1. New York: Longman: 323–70.

Hyden, G., and M. Bratton. 1992. *Governance and Politics in Africa*. Boulder, Colo.: Lynne Rienner.

Ikejiuba, F. 1995. Currency Instability and Social Payments among the Igbo of Eastern Nigeria, 1890–1990. In Guyer, J., ed. *Money Matters*. Portsmouth, N.H.: Heinemann: 133–61.

Issa, S. 1997. L'Impact de la crise tchadienne sur le Nord-Cameroun: 1979–1982. Mémoire de Maîtrise en Histoire, FALSH, Université de Yaoundé I.

———. 1998. *Laamiido* et Sécurité dans le Nord-Cameroun. *Annales de la FALSH* (Université de Ngaoundéré) 3:63–76.

———. 2001. *Sonngoobe*, Bandits Justiciers au Nord-Cameroun sous l'Administration Française. *Ngaoundéré Anthropos* (Université de Ngaoundéré) 6: 153–73.

Iyebi-Mandjek, O. 1993. Les Migrations saisonnières chez les mafas, montagnards du Nord Cameroun: Une solution au surpeuplement et un frien à l'émigration définitive. *Cahiers des sciences humaines* 29:419–41.

Jameson, F. 1984. Postmodernism, or the logic of late capitalism. *New Left Review* 141:53–92.

Jeune Afrique. 1992. November 19, 28–30.

Jeune Afrique économie. 2002. January 14–February 17.

Johnson, M. 1966. The Ounce in Eighteenth-Century West African Trade. *Journal of African History* 7:197–214.

———. 1970. The Cowrie Currencies of West Africa. *Journal of African History* 11:331–53.

———. 1976. Calico Caravans: The Tripoli-Kano Trade after 1880. *Journal of African History* 17:95–117.

REFERENCES

Joseph, R. 1977. *Radical Nationalism in Cameroon: Social Origins of the UPC Rebellion.* Oxford: Oxford University Press.

Kameni, T. 1995. "Derrière la sécurité, la politique et l'argent." *Le Messager,* March 27, 5.

Kant, I. 1965. *Critique of Pure Reason.* New York: St. Martin's Press.

Kaplan, R. 1994. The Coming Anarchy. *Atlantic Monthly,* February, 44–76.

Keck, M., and K. Sikkink. 1998. *Activists beyond Borders: Advocacy Networks in International Politics.* Ithaca, N.Y.: Cornell University Press.

Kintz, D. 1985. Archétypes politiques peuls. *Journal des africanistes* 55:93–104.

Kirk-Greene, A. 1960. The Major Currencies in Nigerian History. *Journal of the Historical Society of Nigeria* 2:122–42.

———. 1966. *The Emirates of Northern Nigeria.* London: Oxford University Press.

Klein, M., and P. Lovejoy. 1979. Slavery in West Africa. In Gemery, H., and J. Hogendorn. eds. *The Uncommon Market.* New York: Academic Press: 181–255.

Kom, A. 1993. Trahison d'une intelligentsia. *Jeune Afrique économique,* March, 122–23.

Kopytoff, I. 1986. The Cultural Biography of Things: Commoditization as Process. In Appadurai, A. ed. *The Social Life of Things: Commodities in Cultural Perspective.* Chicago: University of Chicago Press: 64–91.

Krasner, S. 1999. *Sovereignty: Organized Hypocrisy.* Princeton, N.J.: Princeton University Press.

Laclau, E., and C. Mouffe. 1987. Post-Marxism without Apologies. *New Left Review* 166:79–106.

Lacroix, P. 1952–53. Matériaux pour servir à l'histoire des peuls de l'Adamaoua. *Études Camerounaise,* Vols. 37–38, 39–40.

Lash, S., and J. Urry. 1987. *The End of Organized Capitalism.* Cambridge, England: Polity Press.

Last, M. 1956. An Aspect of the Caliph Mohammad Bello's Social Policy. *Kano Studies* 1:56–59.

———. 1967. *The Sokoto Caliphate.* London: Longman.

———. 1985a [1971]. The Early Kingdoms of the Nigerian Savanna. In Ajayi, J.F.A., and M. Crowder, eds. *History of West Africa.* Vol. 1. New York: Longman: 166–224.

———. 1985b [1971]. Reform in West Africa: The Jihad Movements of the Nineteenth Century. In Ajayi, J.F.A., and M. Crowder, eds. *History of West Africa.* Vol. 2. New York: Longman: 1–129.

Last, M., and M. Al-Hajj. 1965. Attempts at Defining a Muslim in Nineteenth-Century Hausaland and Bornu. *Journal of Historical Studies of Nigeria* 3:231–40.

Law, R. 1995. Cowries, Gold, and Dollars: Exchange Rate Instability and Domestic Price Inflation in Dahomey in the Eighteenth and Nineteenth Centuries. In Guyer, J., ed. *Money Matters.* Portsmouth, N.H.: Heinemann: 53–73.

Lebeuf, A.M.D. 1969. *Les Principautés kotoko: Èssai sur le caractère sacré de l'autorité.* Paris: Éditions du CNRS.

Lebeuf, J.-P., and A. Masson-Detourbet. 1950. *La civilisation du Tchad.* Paris: Payot.

Leiris, M. 1981. *L'Afrique fantôme.* Paris: Gallimard.

Lestringant, J. 1964. *Les Pays de Guider au Cameroun: Essai d'histoire régionale.* Published manuscript. Paris.

Levtzion, N. 1985. Slavery and Islamization in Africa: A Comparative Study. In Willis, J., ed. *Slaves and Slavery in Muslim Africa.* Vol. 2. London: Frank Cass: 182–98.

Lottin, J. 1994. Les Paris perdus de la relance. *La Nouvelle Expression* (Cameroon), April 6–11, 6.

Lovejoy, P. 1974. Interregional Monetary Flows in the Precolonial Trade of Nigeria. *Journal of African History* 15:563–85.

———. 1978a. The Borno Salt Industry. *International Journal of African History* 11:629–68.

———. 1978b. Plantations in the Economy of the Sokoto Caliphate. *Journal of African History* 29:341–68.

———. 1980. *Caravans of Kola: The Hausa Kola Trade, 1700–1900.* Zaria: Ahmadu Bello University Press.

———. 1985 [1971]. The Internal Trade of West Africa before 1800. In Ajayi, J.F.A., and M. Crowder, eds. *History of West Africa.* Vol. 1. New York: Longman: 648–90.

———. 1986. *Salt of the Desert Sun.* Cambridge: Cambridge University Press.

Lovejoy, P., and S. Baier. 1975. The Desert-Side Economy of the Central Sudan. *International Journal of African Historical Studies* 8:551–81.

Ludden, D. 1993. Orientalist Empiricism: Transformations of Colonial Knowledge. In Breckenridge, C., and P. van der Veer, eds. *Orientalism and the Postcolonial Predicament: Perspectives on South Asia.* Philadelphia: University of Pennsylvania Press.

Lyotard, J.-F., and J.-L. Thébaud. 1985. *Just Gaming.* Minneapolis: University of Minnesota Press.

Mahieu, R. 1989. Principes de l'économie africaine. *Revue Tiers-Monde* 30:725–53.

Manning, P. 1982. *Slavery, Colonialism and Economic Growth in Dahomey, 1640–1960.* Cambridge: Cambridge University Press.

Marchal, R. 1993. L'Invention d'un nouvel order régional. *Politique africaine* 50: 2–8.

———. 1997. Somalie: La Normalisation malgré tout? In Marchal, R., and C. Messiant. *Les Chemins de la guerre et de la paix.* Paris: Karthala: 209–56.

———. 1999. Des contresens possibles de la globalisation: Privatisation de l'état et bienfaisance au Soudan et en Somalie. *Politique africaine* 73:50–67.

Marchés tropicaux et méditerranéens. 1976. Cameroun: 1960–1980. October 29, 2812–956.

———. 1988. Cameroun, 1988. 2241, October 21, 2793–876.

Marcus, G., and M. Fischer. 1986. *Anthropology as Cultural Critique: An Experimental Moment in the Human Sciences.* Chicago: University of Chicago Press.

Martin, B. G. 1969. Kanem, Bornu, and the Fazzan: Notes on the Political History of a Trade Route. *Journal of African History* 10:15–27.

———. 1976. *Muslim Brotherhoods in Nineteenth-Century Africa.* Cambridge: Cambridge University Press.

Martinez, L. 1998. *La Guerre civile en Algérie.* Paris: Karthala-CERI.

Marx, K. 1977 [1976]. *Capital: A critique of political economy.* Vol. 1. New York: Vintage Books.

Masud, M. 1986. Shehu Usman dan Fodio's Restatement of the Doctrine of Hijrah. *Islamic Studies* 25 (2–3): 59–77.

———. 1990. The Obligation to Migrate: The Doctrine of Hijra in Islamic Law. In Eickelman, D., and J. Piscatori, eds. *Muslim Travelers: Pilgrimage, Migration, and the Religious Imagination.* Berkeley: University of California Press: 29–49.

219

Mauny, R. 1961. *Tableau géographique de l'ouest Africain au moyen âge.* Dakar.

Mauss, M. 1950. *Essai sur le don.* Paris: Presses Universitaires de France.

Mbembe, A. 1985. La Palabre de l'indépendence: Les Ordres du discours national-iste au Cameroun (1948–1958). *La Revue française de science politique* 35:459–86.

———. 1986. Pouvoir des morts et langage des vivants: Les errences de la mémoire nationaliste au Cameroun. *Politique africaine* 22:37–72.

———. 1989. Spectre et l'etat: Des dimensions politiques de l'imaginaire his-torique dans le Cameroun postcolonial. *Revue de la bibliothèque nationale,* 2–13.

———. 1990. Pouvoir, violence et accumulation. *Politique africaine* 39:7–24.

———. 1992. Provisional Notes on the Postcolony. *Africa* 62:3–37.

———. 1993. Epilogue: Crise de légimité, restauration autoritaire et déliquescence de l'état. In Geschiere, P., and P. Konings, eds. *Itinéraires d'accumulation au Cameroun.* Paris: ASC–Karthala: 345–74.

———. 1996. *La Naissance du maquis dans le Sud-Cameroun: Histoires d'indisci-plines.* Paris: Karthala.

Mbembe, A., and J. Roitman. 1995. Figures of the Subject in Times of Crisis. *Public Culture* 7:323–52.

McCall, D., and N. Bennett, eds. *Aspects of West African Islam.* Boston: African Stud-ies Center, Boston University Papers on Africa.

McClintock, A. 1995. *Imperial Leather: Race, Gender and Sexuality in the Colonial Contest.* New York: Routledge.

Méda, D. 1999. *Qu'est-ce que la richesse?* Paris: Aubier.

Meillassoux, C., ed. 1975. *L'Esclavage en Afrique précoloniale.* Paris:

Melone, M. 1996. *Le Messager,* February 25, 4.

Le Messager (Cameroon). 1993. Les Causes du naufrage économique du Cameroun. December 22.

———. 1994. Special edition. Extrême-Nord: Demain La Guerre? March 10, 5–13.

Meuret, D. 1988. Political Genealogy of Political Economy. *Economy and Society* 17: 225–50.

Miers, S., and I. Kopytoff, eds. 1977. *Slavery in Africa: Historical and Anthropological Perspectives.* Madison: University of Wisconsin Press.

Migdal, J. 1988. *Strong States and Weak States. State-Society Relations and State Ca-pabilities in the Third World.* Princeton, N.J.: Princeton University Press.

Millennium. 1994. Vol. 23. Special issue on global civil society.

Miller, P., and N. Rose. 1990. Governing Economic Life. *Economy and Society* 19:1–31.

Mills, G., and J. Stremlau, eds. 1999. *The Privatisation of Security in Africa.* Johan-nesburg: South African Institute of International Affairs.

Mitchell, T. 1998. Fixing the Economy. *Cultural Studies* 12:82–101.

———. 1999. Society, Economy, and the State Effect. In Steinmetz, G., ed. *State/Culture: State Formation after the Cultural Turn.* Ithaca, N.Y.: Cornell Uni-versity Press: 76–97.

Mohammadou, E. 1976. *L'Histoire des peuls férôbé du Diamaré: Maroua et Pétté.* Tokyo: ILCAA.

———. 1978. *Les Royaumes foulbé du plateau de l'Adamaoua.* Tokyo: ILCAA.

———. 1992. Le Soulèvement mahdiste de Goni Waday dans la Haute-Bénoué (juillet 1907). *SENRI Ethnological Studies* 31. Osaka: National Museum of Eth-nology: 423–64.

Monga, C. 1993. Les Dernières cartes de Paul Biya. *Jeune Afrique économique*, March, 116–23.

Mouvement anti-utilitariste dans les sciences sociales (MAUSS). 1993. *Ce que donner veut dire: Don et intérêt*. Paris: La Découverte.

Munn, N. 1986. *The Fame of Gawa: A Symbolic Study of Value Transformation in a Massim (Papua New Guinea) Society*. Cambridge: Cambridge University Press.

N'Djamena Hebdo. 1997. Lorsque démobilisation rime avec developpement. May 15, 6–7.

Newbury, C. W. 1966. North African and Western Sudan Trade in the Nineteenth Century: A Re-evaluation. *Journal of African History* 7:233–46.

Nicolas, G. 1986. *Don rituel et échange marchand dans une société sahélienne*. Paris: Institut d'ethnologie–Musée de l'Homme.

———. 1996. *Du don rituel au sacrifice suprême*. Paris: La Découverte/MAUSS.

Nietzsche, F. 1966 [1885]. *Beyond Good and Evil*. New York: Random House.

———. 1967 [1887]. *On the Genealogy of Morals: Ecce Homo*. New York: Random House.

———. 1974 [1882]. *The Gay Science*. New York: Random House.

Ngangue, E., and K. Salomon. 1995. Un secteur sans garde-fous. *Le Messager* (Cameroon), March 27, 5.

Ngarngoune, S. 1997. Alerte au Sud. *N'Djamena Hebdo*. May 8, 4.

Njeuma, M. 1973. The Foundations of Pre-European Administration in Adamawa: Historical Consideration. *Journal of the Historical Society of Nigeria* 7:3–15.

———. 1974. Uthman dan Fodio and the Origins of Fulani Jihad in Cameroon Hinterland, 1809–47. *Afrika Zamani, Revue d'histoire Africaine* 3 December: 51–68.

———. 1978. *Fulani Hegemony in Yola (Old Adamawa) 1809–1902*. Yaounde: PPCTR.

———. 1989. The Lamidates of Northern Cameroon, 1800–1894. In Njeuma, M. ed. *Introduction to the History of Cameroon*. New York: St. Martin's Press: 1–31.

Nkuété, J. 1980. *Monnaie et finances comme moteur de développement*. Yaounde: Éditions CLÉ.

Noble, K. 1991. Strike Aims to Bleed Cameroon's Economy to Force President's Fall. *New York Times*, August 5.

Nodjingué, J.-C. 1997. L'Insécurité dans le nord Cameroun. *N'Djamena Hebdo*, January.

Nord-Sud Export. 1989. Cameroun. June 5.

———. 1990. Dossier Cameroun. May 28.

———. 1991. Cameroun. February 11.

Nordstrom, C. 2001. Out of the shadows. In Callaghy, T., R. Kassimir, and R. Latham, eds. *Intervention and Transnationalism in Africa: Global Local Networks of Power*. Cambridge: Cambridge University Press: 216–39.

La Nouvelle Expression (V. Ndi Mbarga interview with the Club de la Presse). April 4, 4.

Observatoire Géopolitique des Drogues. 1995. *Géopolitique des drogues 1995: Rapport annuel de l'OGD*. Paris: La Découverte.

Offe, C. 1985. *Disorganized Capitalism*. Cambridge: Polity Press.

Ong, A. 1998. *Flexible Citizenship: The Cultural Logics of Transnationality*. Durham, N.C.: Duke University Press.

Ong, A., and D. Nonini, eds. 1997. *Ungrounded Empires: The Cultural Politics of Modern Chinese Transnationalism.* New York: Routledge.

Oumate, A. 2001–2. Un chef de village coupeur de route *L'œil du Shael,* December 27–January 10, 6.

Ousmane, D. 2001. Les Magistrats indexés. *L'œil duu Sahel,* December 21, 5.

Paba Salé, M. 1980. Maroua: Aspects de la croissance d'une ville du Nord-Cameroun (des années 50 à nos jours). PhD. diss., University of Bordeaux.

Parry, J., and M. Bloch, eds., 1989. *Money and the Morality of Exchange.* Cambridge: Cambridge University Press.

Peres, H. 1937. Relation entre Tafilalet et le Soudan à travers le Sahara, du XIIe au XIVe siècle. In Gautier, E. F., ed. *Mélanges de géographie et orientalisme.* Tours: 409–14.

Pideu, K. 1995. Une province abandonée aux coupeurs de route. *La Nouvelle Expression,* March 28, 6.

Pietz, W. 1993. Fetishism and Materialism: The Limits of Theory in Marx. In Apter, E., and W. Peitz, eds. *Fetishism as Cultural Discourse.* Ithaca, N.Y.: Cornell University Press: 119–51.

Polanyi, K., C. Arensberg, and H. Pearson, eds. 1957. *Trade and Market in the Early Empires.* Glencoe, Ill.: Free Press.

Polanyi, K., with A. Rotstein. 1966. *Dahomey and the Slave Trade: An Analysis of an Archaic Economy.* Seattle: University of Washington Press.

Pomian, K. 1984. *L'Ordre du temps.* Paris: Gallimard.

Poole, D. Forthcoming. Judicial Geographies on the Margins of the Peruvian State. In Das, V., and D. Poole, eds. *Anthropology in the Margins of the State.* Santa Fe, N.M.: School for American Research.

Pouillon, F. 1988. Cens et puissance, ou pourquoi les pasteurs nomades ne peuvent pas compter leur bétail. *Cahiers d'études africaines* 28, 110: 177–205.

Price, R. 1998. Reversing the Gun Sites: Transnational Civil Society Targets Land Mines. *International Organization* 52:613–44.

Le Progrès (N'djamena). 1997. Armée: Lumière sur la démobilisation et la réinsertion. May 13, 10–11.

Rabinow, P. 1986. Representations Are Social Facts. In Clifford, J., and G. Marcus, eds. *Writing Culture.* Berkeley: University of California Press: 234–61.

————, ed. 1997. *Ethics: Subjectivity and Truth,* by Michel Foucault. New York: New Press.

————. 2003. *Anthropos Today.* Princeton, N.J.: Princeton University Press.

Reddy, W. 1984. *The Rise of Market Culture.* Cambridge: Cambridge University Press.

Régis, A. 1986. *L'Histoire curieuse des Monnaies coloniales.* Paris: Éditions ACL.

Reisman, P. 1998. *Freedom in Fulani Social Life.* Chicago: University of Chicago Press.

Reno, W. 1995. *Corruption and State Politics in Sierra Leone.* Cambridge: Cambridge University Press.

————. 2001. How Sovereignty Matters: International Markets and the Political Economy of Local Politics in Weak States. In Callaghy, T., R. Kassimir, and R. Latham, eds. *Intervention and Transnationalism in Africa: Global Local Networks of Power.* Cambridge: Cambridge University Press: 197–215.

222

Rey, J.-M. 2002. *Le Temps du credit*. Paris: Desclée de Brouwer.

Reyna, S. 1990. *Wars without End: The Political Economy of a Precolonial African State*. Hanover, N.H.: University Press of New England.

Richards, P. 1996. *Fighting for the Rain Forest: War, Youth and Resources in Sierra Leone*. Portsmouth, N.H.: Heinemann.

Rivallain, J. 1986. *Les Collections monétaires: Paleo-monnaies africaines*. Paris: Administration des Monnaies et Médailles.

Roitman, J. 1990. The Politics of Informal Markets in Sub-Saharan Africa. *Journal of Modern African Studies* 28:671–96.

———. 1995. Queries on Cultural Capitalism. *Cahiers d'études africaines* 35, 138–39 (2–3): 629–645.

———. 1996. "Objects of the Economy and the Language of Politics in Northern Cameroon." Ph.D. diss., University of Pennsylvania.

———. 1998a. La Garnison-entrepôt. *Autrepart* 6:39–51.

———. 1998b. The Garrison-entrepôt. *Cahiers d'études africaines* 38, 150–52 (2–4): 297–329.

———. 1999. Le Pouvoir n'est pas souverain: Nouvelles autorités régulatrices et transformations des états dans le Bassin du Lac Tchad. In Hibou, B., ed. *La Privatisation des états*. Paris: Karthala-CERI: 163–96.

———. 2000. Économie morale, subjectivité et politique. *Critique internationale* 6:48–56.

———. 2001. New Sovereigns? Regulatory Authority in the Chad Basin. In Callaghy, T., R. Kassimir, and R. Latham, eds. *Intervention and Transnationalism in Africa: Global-Local Networks of Power*. Cambridge: Cambridge University Press: 240–63.

———. 2003. La Garnison-entrepôt: Une manière de gouverner dans le basin du lac Tchad. *Critique internationale* 19 (April): 93–115.

———. Forthcoming a. Modes of Governing: The Garrison Entrepot. In Ong, A., and S. Collier, eds. *Global Anthropology: Technology, Governmentality, Ethics*. Oxford: Blackwell.

———. Forthcoming b. Productivity in the Margins: The Reconstitution of State Power in the Chad Basin. In Das, V., and D. Poole, eds. *Anthropology in the Margins of the State*. Santa Fe, N.M.: School of American Research.

Rojtman, B. 1991. *Une grave distraction*. Paris: Ballard.

Rose, N., and P. Miller. 1992. Political Power beyond the State: Problematics of Government. *British Journal of Sociology* 43:173–205.

Rosenau, J. 1997. *Along the Domestic-Foreign Frontier: Exploring Governance in a Turbulent World*. Cambridge: Cambridge University Press.

Rothchild, D., and N. Chazan, eds. 1988. *The Precarious Balance: State and Society in Africa*. Boulder, Colo.: Westview Press.

Roupsard, M. 1987. "Nord Cameroun: Ouverture et développement." Ph.D. diss., University of Paris–Nanterre.

Rowlands, M., and J.-P. Warnier. 1988. Sorcery, Power and the Modern State in Cameroon. *Man* 23:118–32.

Sahlins, M. 1976. *Culture and Practical Reason*. Chicago: University of Chicago Press.

Salomon, N. 1997. Que le CDR se grouille, les déflatés s'impatientent! *Le Temps* (N'Djamena), October–4 November, 4.

223

Sarthou-Lajus, N. 1997. *L'Éthique de la dette.* Paris: Presses Universitaires de France.

Sassen, S. 1995. *Losing Control? Sovereignty in an Age of Globalization.* New York: Columbia University Press.

———. 1998. *Globalization and Its Discontents: Essays on the New Mobility of People and Money.* New York: New Press.

Schilders, K. 1994. *Self Esteem.* Leiden: African Studies Centre Research Series.

Schrift, A. 1995. *Nietzsche's French Legacy.* New York: Routledge.

Schultz, E. 1984. From Pagan to Pullo: Ethnic Identity Change in Northern Cameroon. *Africa* 54:46–63.

Seignobos, C., and O. Iyebi-Mandjek. 2000. *Atlas de la Province Extrême-Nord Cameroun.* Paris: IRD-MINREST.

Seignobos, C., and J. Weber. 2002. *Elements d'une stratégie de développement rural pour le Grand Nord du Cameroun.* Vol. 1, *Rapport principal.* Montpellier: CIRAD.

Seydou, C., ed. 1976. *La Geste de Ham-Bodedio, ou, Hama le rouge.* Paris: Armand Colin.

Shaw, M. 1998. The Historical Sociology of the Future. *Review of International Political Economy* 5:321–36.

Simmel, G. 1990. *The Philosophy of Money.* New York: Routledge.

Smaldone, J. 1977. *Warfare in the Sokoto Caliphate: Historical and Sociological Perspectives.* London: Cambridge University Press.

Smith, D., D. Solinger, and S. Topik, eds. 1999. *States and Sovereignty in the Global Economy.* London: Routledge.

Smith, J., C. Chatfield, and R. Pagnucco, eds. 1997. *Transnational Social Movements and Global Politics: Solidarity beyond the State.* Syracuse, N.Y.: Syracuse University Press.

Socpa, A. 1999. L'Hégémonie ethnique cyclique an Nord-Cameroun. *Afrique et développement* 24:57–81.

Soudan, F. 1996. La Guerre secrète. *Jeune Afrique,* November 12–15.

Spivak, G. 1993. *Outside in the Teaching Machine.* New York: Routledge.

———. 1999. *A Critique of Postcolonial Reason.* Cambridge, Mass.: Harvard University Press.

Stallybrass, P., and A. White. 1989. *The Politics and Poetics of Transgression.* Ithaca, N.Y.: Cornell University Press.

Steinmetz, G., ed. 1999. *State/Culture: State Formation after the Cultural Turn.* Ithaca, N.Y.: Cornell University Press.

Stenning, D. 1957. Transhumance, Migratory Drift, Migration: Patterns of Pastoral Fulani Nomadism. *Journal of the Royal Anthropological Institute* 87: 57–75.

———. 1959. *Savannah Nomads.* Oxford: Oxford University Press.

Strange, S. 1996. *The Retreat of the State: The Diffusion of Power in the World Economy.* Cambridge: Cambridge University Press.

Strathern, M. 1988. *The Gender of the Gift.* Berkeley: University of California Press.

Tabiu, M. 1989. Shari'ah in an Era of Transition: Some Judicial Practices in the Early Days of the Sokoto Caliphate. *Islamic Studies* 28:377–93.

Taguem Fah, G. 2003. Dynamique plurielle, regain de spiritualité et recompositin de l'espace islamique. Paper presented to the conference "The Chad Basin: Reconfigurations," Max Planck Institute for Social Anthropology, Halle, Germany, September 29–30.

Tardits, C. 1980. *Le Royaume Bamun.* Paris: Armand Colin.

———, ed. 1981. *Contribution de la recherche ethnologique à l'histoire des civilisations du Cameroun.* 2 vols. Paris: CNRS.

Taussig, M. 1987. *Shamanism, Colonialism, and the Wild Man.* Chicago: University of Chicago Press.

———. 1997. *The Magic of the State.* New York: Routledge.

Tchundjang Pouemi, J. 1980. *Monnaie, servitude et liberté: La répression monétaire en Afrique.* Paris: Éditions Jeune Afrique.

Teiga, M. B. 1997. Une armée, certes, mais combien de divisions . . . *L'Autre Afrique,* December 17–23, 14–15.

Terray, E. 1973. Technologie, état et tradition en Afrique. *Annales* 28:1331–38.

———. 1974. Long-Distance Trade and the Formation of the State. *Economy and Society* 3:315–45.

Théret, B. 1992. *Régimes économiques de l'ordre politique.* Paris: Presses Universitaires de France.

Thompson E. P. 1966. *The Making of the English Working Class.* New York: Vintage Press.

———. 1971. The Moral Economy of the English Crowd in the Eighteenth Century. *Past and Present* 50:76–136.

Tilly, C. 1985. War Making and State Making as Organized Crime. In Evans, P., and T. Skocpol, eds. *Bringing the State Back In.* New York: Cambridge University Press.

Tomlinson, J. 1983. Where Do Economic Policy Objectives Come From? The Case of Full Employment. *Economy and Society* 12:48–65.

Tribe, K. 1978. *Land, Labour and Economic Discourse.* London: Routledge.

Trimingham, J. 1959. *Islam in West Africa.* Oxford: Clarendon Press.

Trouillot, M.-R. 1995. *Silencing the Past: Power and the Production of History.* Boston: Beacon Press.

Um Nyobe, R. 1984. *Le Problème national camerounais.* Edited by A. Mbembe. Paris: Harmattan.

———. 1989. *Ecrits sous maquis.* Edited by A. Mbembe. Paris: Harmattan.

Usman, Y. 1981. *The Transformation of Katsina, 1400–1883.* Zaria: Ahmadu Bello University.

Vallée, O. 1989. *Le Prix de l'argent CFA: Heurs et malheurs de la zone franc.* Paris: Karthala.

———. 1999. La Dette privée est-elle publique? Traites, traitement, traite: Modes de la dette africaine. *Politique africaine* 73:50–67.

van Andel, A. 1992. Les Stratégies de subsistance de la population rurale du Nord Cameroun. Unpublished manuscript.

van de Walle, N. 1993. The Politics of Nonreform in Cameroon. In Callaghy, T., and J. Ravenhill, eds. *Hemmed In: Responses to Africa's Economic Decline.* New York: Columbia University Press: 367–97.

van Santen, J. 1993. Dot, commerce et contrebande: Stratégies d'accumulation chez les femmes "islamisées" de Mokolo. In Geschiere, P., and P. Konings, eds. *Itinéraires d'accumulation au Cameroun.* Paris: ASC-Karthala: 301–34.

Vereecke, C. 1994. The Slave Experience in Adamawa: Past and Present Perspectives from Yola (Nigeria). *Cahiers d'études africaines* 34, 133–35 (1–3): 23–53.

REFERENCES

Vidal, L. 1990. *Rituels de possession dans le sahel.* Paris: L'Harmattan.
Vincent, J.-F. 1991. *Princes montagnards du Nord-Cameroun.* 2 vols. Paris: L'Harmattan.
Walker, R.B.J., and S. H. Mendlovitz, eds. 1990. *Contending Sovereignties.* Boulder, Colo.: Lynne Rienner.
Wallerstein, I. 1999. States? Sovereignty? The Dilemma of Capitalists in an Age of Transition. In Smith, D., D. Solinger, and S. Topik, eds. *States and Sovereignty in the Global Economy.* New York: Routledge: 20–33.
Wapner, P. 1995. Politics beyond the State: Environmental Activism and World Civic Politics. *World Politics* 47:311–40.
Warnier, J.-P. 1985. *Échanges, développement et hiérarchies dans le Bamenda précolonial (Cameroun).* Stuttgart: Franz Steiner Verlag Wiesbaden.
Watson, J. 1980. Slavery as an Institution: Opened and Closed Systems. In Watson, J., ed. *Asian and African Systems of Slavery.* Oxford: Basil Blackwell: 1–15.
Watt, M. 1971. Hidjra. *The Encyclopaedia of Islam.* 2nd ed. Vol. 2. Leiden: Brill: 366–67.
Weiner, A. 1976. *Women of Value: Men of Renknown.* Austin: University of Texas Press.
———. 1992. *Inalienable Possessions: The Paradox of Keeping-While-Giving.* Berkeley: University of California Press.
White, H. 1987. *The Content of the Form: Narrative Discourse and Historical Representation.* Baltimore: Johns Hopkins University Press.
Williams, B. 1972. *Morality.* Cambridge: Cambridge University Press.
———. 1985. *Ethics and the Limits of Philosophy.* Cambridge, Mass.: Harvard University Press.
Willis, J. 1985. Jihad and the Ideology of Enslavement. In Willis, J., ed. *Slaves and Slavery in Muslim Africa.* Vol. 1. London: Frank Cass: 16–26.
World Bank. 1989a. *Adjustment Lending: An Evaluation of Ten Years of Experience.* Washington, D.C.: World Bank.
———. 1989b. *Sub-Saharan Africa: From Crisis to Sustainable Growth.* Washington, D.C.: World Bank.
Ymbert, Jacques-Gilbert. 1996 [1825]. *L'Art de faire des dettes.* Paris: Payot & Rivages.
Zartman, I., ed. 1995. *Collapsed States: The Disintegration and Restoration of Legitimate Authority.* Boulder, Colo.: Lynne Rienner.
Zinga, V. S. 1994a. Bamenda: Ultime étape avant la sécession? *Le Messager,* April 4, 4.
———. 1994b. Randez-vous manqués avec l'histoire. *Le Messager,* April 4, 4.
Zelizer, V. 1997. *The Social Meaning of Money.* Princeton, N.J.: Princeton University Press.
Zoua, Jean-Baptiste. 1997. Phénomène des coupeurs de route dans le nord-Cameroun: Une épine dans la plante des pieds des responsables du maintien de l'ordre. Unpubl. manuscript. Chef d'état-major de la région militaire No. 4 Garoua.

FORMATION *Series*